LIVERPOOL IN THE SIXTEENTH CENTURY

LIVERPOOL CASTLE.

RESTORED FROM AUTHENTIC PLANS AND MEASUREMENTS BY EDWARD W. COX.

Frontispiece: A reconstruction of Liverpool Castle by E.W. Cox, from *Transactions of the Hist*
Society of Lancashire and Cheshire, 42 (1892).

Liverpool in the Sixteenth Century

A small Tudor town

JANET E. HOLLINSHEAD

Town and city histories available from Carnegie:
Peter Aughton, *Liverpool: A People's History* (3rd edn, 2008);
Graham Davis and Penny Bonsall, *A History of Bath: Image and Reality* (2006)
Derek Beattie, *Blackburn* (2007);   David Hey, *A History of Sheffield* (new edn, 2005)
Alan Kidd, *Manchester*;   John K. Walton, *Blackpool*
Peter Aughton: *Bristol: A People's History*;   Andrew White (ed.), A *History of Lancaster*
John A. Hargreaves, *Halifax*

Forthcoming town and city histories:
Mark Freeman, *St Albans*;   Carl Chinn, *Birmingham*;   Andrew White, *Kendal*;
Trevor Rowley, *Oxford*;   Evelyn Lord, *Cambridge*;   John Doran, *Chester*;
Prof. W. Sheils, *York*;   Jeremy Black, *London*;   William Maguire, *Belfast*;
John A. Hargreaves, *Huddersfield*;   Fred Gray, *Brighton*;
Richard Rodger (ed.), *Leicester*;   Anthea Jones, *Cheltenham*;
Joan and Richard Allen, *Newcastle*;   David Hunt, *Preston*;   Andrew Walker, *Lincoln*

Of related interest:
Peter Kennerley, *The Building of Liverpool Cathedral* (3rd edn, 2008)
Mike Clarke, *The Leeds & Liverpool Canal: A History and Guide*
Adrian Jarvis (forthcoming), *A History of the Port of Liverpool*

Full details on www.carnegiepublishing.com

First published in 2007 by Carnegie Publishing Ltd
Carnegie House
Chatsworth Road,
Lancaster LA1 4SL
www.carnegiepublishing.com

Copyright © Janet E. Hollinshead, 2007

ISBN: 978-1-85936-149-8

British Library Cataloguing-in-Publication data
A catalogue record for this book is available from the British Library

Designed, typeset and originated by Carnegie Publishing
Printed and bound in the UK by Alden Press, Oxford

Contents

Notes

ORIGINAL SPELLING has been retained in quotations, apart from the rationalisation of the use of i and j, and u and v. Contractions have been expanded and capitalisation has been inserted. In the text the spelling of place-names has been modernised, as has the spelling of forenames. The spelling of surnames has been made uniform where clearly the same individual and/or family was intended.

Units of money are retained in their original form as pounds, shillings and pence: 12 pence (*d.*) to the shilling (*s.*) and 20 shillings to the pound (£).

Dates conform to the Old Style (Julian) calendar, except that the year has been taken to begin on 1 January.

References to counties are to the pre-1974 boundaries.

Abbreviations

APC	*Acts of the Privy Council of England*, J.R. Dasent (ed.), 32 vols (London 1890–1907)
BL	British Library, London
Econ HR	*Economic History Review*
HMC	Historical Manuscripts Commission
Lancs RO	Lancashire Record Office, Preston
Liv RO	Liverpool City Record Office
LTB I	*Liverpool Town Books*, J.A. Twemlow (ed.), vol. I, 1550–1571 (Liverpool, 1918)
LTB II	*Liverpool Town Books*, J.A. Twemlow (ed.), vol. II, 1571–1603 (Liverpool, 1935)
NA	The National Archives, Kew, London
RSLC	Record Society of Lancashire and Cheshire
TLCAS	*Transactions of the Lancashire and Cheshire Antiquarian Society*
THSLC	*Transactions of the Lancashire and Cheshire Historic Society*

Preface

L IVERPOOL during the Tudor period was a small place, its population probably never exceeding one thousand inhabitants. In the north-west of England the towns of Chester, Manchester and Preston were certainly all considerably larger and of greater consequence at this time. Nevertheless, Liverpool's size was on a par with many Tudor towns, and its urban experience must have been typical of many small communities. Tudor Liverpool shared the characteristics and concerns of other small towns and for that alone it deserves study.

Since its thirteenth-century creation Liverpool had been a port located beside a small natural anchorage near the mouth of the River Mersey. The distinctiveness and particular development of Liverpool lay in trade and the potential of the port. The consequences of its location and the prelude to future greatness as a port therefore deserve an explanation. Having said that, the context of Liverpool's hinterland also has great relevance in Tudor times. A small town, of necessity, retained an intimate relationship with its rural environs. Many years ago J. A. Twemlow observed in the introduction to the first volume of his transcription of the Liverpool town books that the study of any town becomes unreal when that place is treated as solitary, self-contained and self-sufficient. The hope is to overcome his anxiety by examining the small town of Liverpool within the wider circumstances of national demographic growth, new and sustained price inflation, economic diversification, religious change, and development in royal authority at central and local levels.

Much has been written of Liverpool's rise as a port from the seventeenth century onwards and of its activities during its maritime heyday in the eighteenth and nineteenth centuries. Much, indeed, was written at that time of greatness or soon after with the perspective of inexorable rise to prosperity: for instance, by Thomas Baines, Edward Baines, Ramsay Muir, James Picton, Ronald Stewart-Brown and James Touzeau. Material is now accessible in the National Archives, in the Cheshire and Lancashire county record offices and in the Liverpool city record office that was unavailable when they wrote. Most valuable of all are the transcriptions of the town books, the municipal records which survive from 1550. This immense labour was commenced by J. A. Twemlow, and resulted in the publication of two volumes (in 1918 and 1935) of Liverpool's Tudor records. Without his efforts this book would not exist, yet port books, probate records, family deeds and papers now add immeasurably to the picture.

Apart from the availability of many further archives, many historical perspectives have changed since the work of Liverpool's earlier historians. A great deal of study has been done on the Tudor economy and trade and, as well, on the development and nature of towns. The early modern urban experience and degrees of distinctiveness of towns both large and small has been much debated and considered by, among others, Jonathan Barry, Richard Britnell, John Chartres, Peter Clark, Alexander Cowan, Alan Dyer, Sybil Jack, Jennifer Kermode, David Palliser, Charles Phythian-Adams and Paul Slack. Social constraints of place and space, order and responsibility have been considered as well as economic opportunity and potential. In the light of all this new historical material and sources, it is now appropriate that the history of Tudor Liverpool should be re-visited afresh.

During the course of producing this volume I have incurred debts of both positive assistance and indefinable encouragement. For references, comment, ideas and hope I thank particularly Alan Crosby, Janet Gnosspelius, David Hey, Jenny Kermode, Terry Phillips, Fiona Pogson, the late Michael Power and Judy Smith.

About the author

Dr Janet Hollinshead originates from north Staffordshire, but has lived and worked in Liverpool since the early 1970s. Local studies and early modern periods of English and European history were all significant elements of her teaching career. Janet recently retired as head of history at Liverpool Hope University. For a number of years she has researched Liverpool's Tudor history using archives in Liverpool, Manchester, Lancashire, Cheshire and London. Recently she has contributed to *Liverpool 800: Culture, Character and History* (ed. J. Belchem), and has written a number of articles in various journals such as *Northern History*, *The Mariner's Mirror*, *Recusant History* and the *Transactions of the Historic Society of Lancashire and Cheshire*. Since coming to Liverpool Janet has been a member and has held almost all offices on the Council of the Historic Society and Lancashire and Cheshire.

CHAPTER ONE

The town and its population

L IVERPOOL IN THE SIXTEENTH CENTURY was a little place. Relatively few towns at this time were of any great size, and it has been the regional capitals and county towns – the large and the well documented – which have received the lion's share of attention and research. Yet there were about 650 market towns in England and Wales by Tudor times, the vast majority of which were small locations with populations of fewer than 2,000 inhabitants, and some even as small as 800–1,000 people. Indeed, many may have seemed scarcely like towns at all. To date little has been written of these smaller urban communities which nevertheless made up a large proportion of the early modern urban experience. These small towns had an intimate relationship with their surrounding countryside, serving as local marketing and administrative centres, and probably having no particular urban specialisation of commodity or distribution. The sphere of influence of a small Tudor town may have been only three to six miles.[1] Economic viability and stability must have been potentially precarious factors at this scale of operation. Competition with neighbours was fierce and not all towns prospered or responded to local challenges and opportunities.

Liverpool had arrived late on the English urban scene. In 1207 King John's letters patent had authorised the establishment of a new borough. with a Saturday market and an annual fair to be sited beside the natural anchorage on the north bank of the Mersey estuary. The king's interest lay in the possibilities for the transport of men and materials to Ireland. A new charter of 1229 defined more clearly the borough's administrative and financial position, but there was to be no rapid economic advance. Contact with Ireland remained limited and only modest urban development occurred. By the early fourteenth century there were just seven streets with a population of not more than 1,000. The fifteenth century saw stagnation and possible contraction. The local gentry acquired increasing interests and influence in the town; overseas trade failed to develop; the town remained commercially isolated with a restricted hinterland; and Chester took potential competition from a local rival seriously.[2] By the

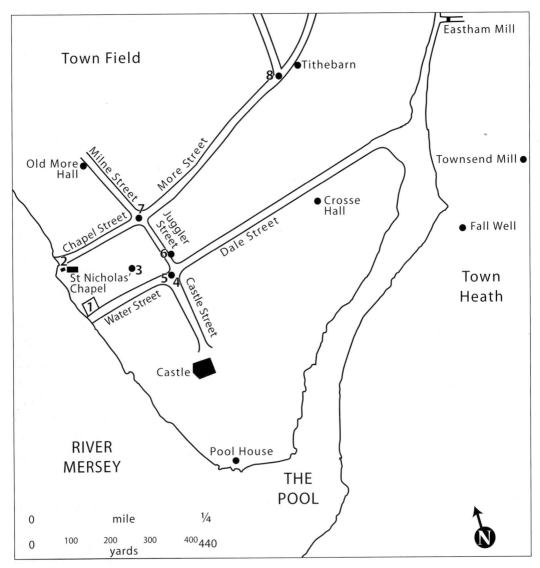

A reconstructed plan of Liverpool as it may have been for much of the Tudor period. The seven streets date to the thirteenth-century foundation of the town and little expansion had taken place by the sixteenth century.

1. The Tower, belonging to the earl of Derby
2. St Nicholas' chapel and chapel of St Mary del Quay
3. Granary
3. High Cross
5. Stocks
6. Common Hall
7. White Cross
8. St Patrick's Cross

commencement of the Tudor period Liverpool's economic prospects and potential for growth did not appear favourable.

Liverpool had a difficult location for economic success. It can be claimed that Tudor Lancashire was one of the poorest and remotest parts of England. Certainly many medieval market centres in Lancashire had failed to sustain their existence: an indication of the limited potential of the region.[3] The 1524–25 lay subsidy produced yields in the north and west of England that were low when compared with the south and east. The uniformly low returns for Lancashire may not, however, reflect the real wealth and population of the area. The poor return was due in part to the county's relative isolation from London and to the way the subsidy was imposed in a manner very different from that intended by the Exchequer.[4] Yet in the south-west of Lancashire, including around Liverpool, geography did impose a measure of isolation through the features of the coastline and the Mersey estuary and through the widespread distribution of marsh or moss land that hindered inland communication. Even by the end of the sixteenth century roads were used predominantly for local traffic and were insubstantial in poor weather.[5]

An indication of this isolation can be seen in the conservative development of surname practices in south Lancashire during the Tudor period. There was still a pronounced local character to surname usage with many locative surnames persisting and even patronymics appearing as late as the last quarter of the sixteenth century in the registers of Walton, Huyton, Childwall, Prescot, Farnworth and Hale churches.[6] John Nicholson of Liverpool and his brother Richard Nicholson (alias Thomason) were recorded as the sons of Nicholas Thomason in the 1550s, while their sons appear in the 1570s as Robert Johnson (alias Nicholson) and Nicholas Richardson respectively.[7] With the sea and Mersey estuary on two sides and moss and marsh inland, Liverpool was 'hemmed into the most isolated corner of an isolated county'.[8] Even the estuary did not lead to major navigable waterways. The hinterland in Lancashire was poor and thinly populated.

Sixteenth-century source material for the various localities of England presents a paradox; on the one hand records can be far more varied and numerous than for the preceding centuries, yet at the same time those sources can be fragmentary and insubstantial. In view of its size at this time Liverpool might have provided a relatively manageable unit of study with manageable records. To some extent this is true, but two factors militate against this happy circumstance: as a small town Liverpool did not generate the complexity and variety of records that some larger cities did and few parochial records, so valuable in the

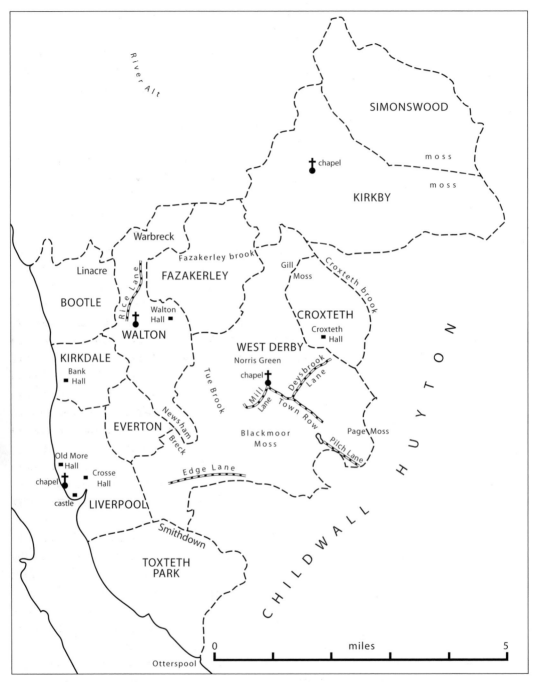

Lancashire was a county of relatively dispersed population in small towns, townships and hamlets. The county's parishes were notoriously large. This reconstructed map of the parish of Walton-on-the-Hill shows its various townships and locations which are known to have existed in the Tudor period. At this time the parish church was at Walton and there were dependent chapels at Kirkby, West Derby and Liverpool. The curates at these chapels were subservient to the rector and vicar at Walton – a loss of prestige for a small town.

sixteenth century, survive. Many small towns have not been studied because their Tudor archives are so variable in quantity and quality. In this context Paul Clark has drawn attention to the problematic state of parish data from both Cheshire and Lancashire.[9] Parish register survival from the sixteenth century is patchy, although some Lancashire registers do exist from the mid-century onwards, for instance for Childwall and Farnworth. Liverpool was situated within the parish of Walton-on-the-Hill where records do not appear particularly well kept and survive only from the 1580s. Worse is the total absence of any records at this time from three of Walton's chapelries: Kirkby, West Derby and Liverpool itself. St Nicholas' chapel in Liverpool was a major feature of the town but surviving ecclesiastically generated documentation is almost non-existent during the Tudor period.

Other sources provide varying assistance. Probate material provides invaluable personal detail, but in this area survives mainly from the 1580s onwards. Liverpool finds incidental reference in the records of the major local families such as the earls of Derby of Knowsley and Lathom and the gentry Molyneux family of Sefton and Croxteth, and also among the records of the lesser gentry, for instance Norris of Speke, Blundell of Crosby and More of Kirkdale.[10] Equally valuable are the records generated by the royal properties and jurisdiction of the Duchy of Lancaster in this area. From 1565 due to a measure of re-organization of customs collection, Liverpool began to maintain its own port books. Interpretation is not entirely straightforward because of the continuing relationship with the port of Chester, but at least discrete material survives for the town's shipping until the end of the century and beyond. Valuable as this assorted archival material is, the key to information about Liverpool in the sixteenth century is the survival of the town books. These run continuously from 1550 and take the form of a version of meeting-minutes with decisions on town policies together with their implementation and enforcement. The books provide crucial detail of the affairs of the town: its officials, the local bye-laws, economic activity, environmental concerns and administrative affairs.[11]

To create some idea of the population of Tudor Liverpool, one can link material from such sources as do survive; for instance, occupational evidence might appear in the town books, probate records, various leases and deeds, and in Duchy witness examinations and depositions. In the sixteenth century family and community reconstitutions are more or less impossible tasks in view of the limitations of the sources but in a small town such as Liverpool their outlines can be perceived and surprising detail recovered.[12] The great weakness is that it is the wealthy and the males who crowd the stage while some sections of society are

Liverpool's town books date from 1550 and their detail provides an invaluable source for the population, administration and some economic activity of the town in the later Tudor period. The material is divided not by calendar year but by mayoral year, and so runs from St Luke's Day, 18 October to 18 October the following year. Usually each year's entry commences with a list of the town's officials for that year. Latin phrases were still used in the books but substantially the material was recorded in English. Adam Pendleton was the recorder and clerk for these books from *c.*1550 until 1576 when his place was taken for thirty-five years by John Hewitt.

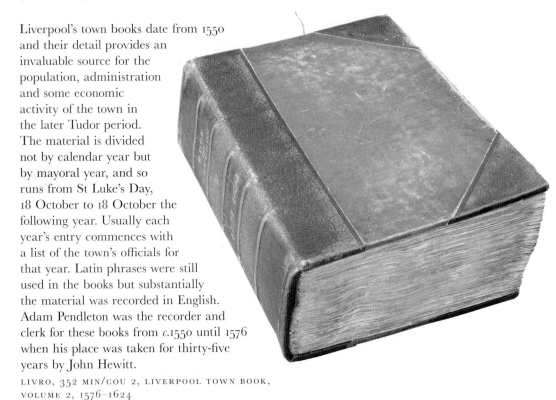

LIVRO, 352 MIN/COU 2, LIVERPOOL TOWN BOOK, VOLUME 2, 1576–1624

documented only sporadically, if at all; women, children, servants, the poor are all indifferently recorded.

The town (or township) was not identified separately in the 1524–25 subsidy return, since only Walton-on-the-Hill parish, which encompassed Liverpool and much more, was assessed. A 1548 survey produced as a result of the closure of the chantry foundations included some estimate of the numbers of 'houseling' (communicant) people within various parishes. Clearly there is debate now over exactly who was intended by this description; one north-west study claims the figure could represent 60 per cent of the total population. Based on this proportion, a population of about 550 can be postulated for Liverpool chapelry in 1548. Fortunately township and chapelry boundaries, albeit unmapped in the sixteenth century, appear at later dates to conform closely with each other and with the town at this time.[13]

A decade later the population in many parts of England was affected by seriously high mortality. It has been claimed that between 1555 and 1558 there were outbreaks of typhus, dysentery, influenza and plague in Lancashire.[14] The town books make it plain that Liverpool did not escape. 'Great sicknesse' was referred to from 1557 until 1559, and this was diagnosed as plague, with claims that it had been brought to the town from Manchester. The disease arrived in late 1557 and during the summer of 1558 'it encreysd daylye and dayle to a gret numbre that died'. In all the town officials estimated between 240 and 260 inhabitants died. The annual fair was cancelled in the autumn of 1558 and no weekly market was held until after Christmas that year.[15] The severity of this attack was such that up to one-third of the town's population may have died.

Not many years later another possible population indicator is the diocesan return made by the bishop of Chester to the Privy Council in 1563. He and his fellow clerics were asked to record the number of households in every parish in their dioceses. A suspiciously round figure of 100 households was returned for Liverpool chapelry, although numbers for other south Lancashire parishes were more specific.[16] Recent work on populations of small towns has suggested a multiplier of 4.25 persons per household in most circumstances during this period, but for the 1563 returns a multiplier of 5.05 may be more appropriate based on indications of under-estimation and on work using the Norwich listings.[17] The 1563 population estimate for Liverpool would then be 505 – not entirely out of line with the 1548 estimate, bearing in mind the population decline of the 1550s.

Certainly during the earlier part of the Tudor period Liverpool's population appeared to show little sign of increasing dramatically, and the contraction of the fifteenth century seems to have had long effect. However, by the second half of the sixteenth century parish register evidence from elsewhere in south Lancashire does appear to suggest a steady excess of baptisms over burials, notably from the 1560s onwards (other than for a few exceptional years of mortality such as 1587–88 and 1597–98).[18] Presumably this buoyancy of population locally was reflected in Liverpool. An assessment roll prepared in the town for contributions to the repairs of Walton church records 185 names in 1565. The names are apparently heads of households, listed by street of residence.[19] A not dissimilar levy for contributions to the schoolmaster's salary in 1566 records 162 individual contributors.[20] These listings from consecutive years highlight the obvious difficulty of ascertaining the completeness of any household list, but in a town so small deliberate evasion must have been well nigh impossible. In 1565 some forty-one contributors were assessed at a rate of only 1d. each, so intentional exemptions from contribution must have been evident at the time. These lists provide an estimate of a population in the region of 688–786 inhabitants, using a multiplier of 4.25; surely, an indication that growth in the population had reached Liverpool again.

It would appear that this increase in population was sustained through the later decades of the Tudor period. South-west Lancashire parish registers and Liverpool's town books do not testify to any dramatic setback, although some check to population growth would have been apparent from the general harvest difficulties of 1587–88 and during the 1590s. Two other local listings survive, both from 1581: one a list of subsidy contributors and the other for a levy to raise finance for the town to contest the claims of the Spanish Company.[21] Again names were carefully recorded by street, with a total of 203 for the subsidy and 214 for the levy. With the same multiplier of 4.25, on the basis that these are household assessments, population estimates of 863–910 are produced for the year 1581.

Table 1 *Liverpool households contributing to local rates*

	1565 for Walton church	*1566 for schoolmaster's salary*	*1581 subsidy contribution*	*1581 levy against the Spanish company*
Dale Street	56	53	60	68
Water Street	37	32	39	39
Castle Street	35	34	42	42
Milne Street	10	8	12	12
Chapel Street	17	7	16	19
Juggler Street	20	15	34	34
More Street	10	13		
Totals	**185**	**162**	**203**	**214**

Unfortunately no local assessment is available at the end of the century with contributions reaching as low as 1d. We might estimate a population for Liverpool of about 1,000 at the end of the Tudor period. During the sixteenth century the town's population had probably doubled, but it had recovered only to its early fourteenth-century size.[22] By 1600 the major Lancashire town was Manchester, with a population of around 5,000. Preston and Wigan mustered perhaps 2,000 each. Forming a third tier in the county came Lancaster, Blackburn, Rochdale, Bolton, Warrington and Liverpool: all with populations in the region of 1,000. Smaller still in the 500–1,000 range lay the smallest market centres with little more than aspirations to genuine urban status: places such as Bury, Chorley and Ormskirk.[23] Chester was the major urban centre in the north-west of England; in 1506 it was raised to the status of a county and by 1563 may have had a population of about 5,400. Chester had a sophisticated administration with significant jurisdiction, and it had over twenty craft gilds and could demonstrate clear signs of civic pride. All of these northern towns were, however, dwarfed by Tudor London. London was without rival in England as an urban centre by the opening years of the sixteenth century, and had consolidated its pre-eminence by the end of the century. Its population had more than doubled to around 200,000 by 1600.[24]

With its population of 1,000, Liverpool typified the Tudor urban experience for the majority of towns: 'small and unsophisticated'.[25] In view of its demographic pattern it is not surprising that there was little sign of development in the physical structure of the town: no new streets and little new housing. Seven streets were recorded in the later medieval period and they remained constant throughout the sixteenth century.[26] Some view of numbers of households in each of these streets may be derived from the local taxation lists. From these assessments it is clear that Chapel Street, More Street, Milne Street and Juggler Street had less substantial properties and/or residents, since assessment levels were often below the average. In Castle Street and Dale Street there were some contributors paying less than the average, but there were also some of the wealthier inhabitants. Water Street, however, appears to be the street with the more prosperous and higher-rated housing. In 1565 seven households here all paid one shilling or more towards the repairs at Walton church; only two households did so in Dale Street, two in Castle Street and one in Milne Street. This pattern changed little during the latter part of the century, for instance in the 1581 and 1594 subsidy assessments.[27] In 1594 three men paid more than one shilling in Juggler and Chapel Streets, four did so in Dale Street, yet fifteen were required to contribute at this level from Water Street. The attraction of Water Street for the wealthier inhabitants may be a reflection of the early town development near the castle and with good access to the anchorage.

Residential patterns in pre-industrial towns are the subject of continuing debate: whether the rich and powerful dominated the town centres or whether gild and occupational structures created their own patterns and zones. Certainly by the seventeenth century cities such as Newcastle and Exeter had peak residential areas. Changing patterns were also possible because of building activity as in Worcester, where construction was on a significant scale by the 1570s. In Winchester, however, there was no population pressure to increase housing demand and so building was undertaken individually by some of the wealthier inhabitants for owner-occupation.[28] In Tudor Liverpool something of this last characteristic predominated. No new streets or significantly lengthened streets appear, although individual rebuilding and property extension may have occurred. The king's rental of Liverpool property in 1533 makes reference to 'the stonehouse' as if the description needed no qualification since there was no other stone building, and also refers to vacant ground in Castle Street.[29]

John Leland (*c.*1540) did not have a great deal to say about 'Lyrpole' as he travelled in the north-west of England. He did, however, refer to it as a 'pavid towne'. William Camden (*c.*1586) added the comment that the town was 'neat and populous'.[30] Some explanation of these remarks may be found with the growing population of the last few decades of the sixteenth century, still contained within the seven medieval streets and with references to the town indeed having paved streets. In 1569, for instance, a paver from Warrington was employed to work on one half of Dale Street that year and the other half of the street the following year.[31] Evidently compact, the town may not, however, have been as neat and tidy as the published works suggest. Considerable individual responsibility and action were expected and encouraged by town assemblies in a small place where it must have been hard to escape the attentions of neighbours. Fouled water supplies were a persistent problem; citizens were constantly being urged to keep all wells covered, but still Thomas Fisher and his wife were fined for disposing of a dead pig and 'unlawful flesh' in a well. Ten years later, in 1568, Edmund Irlam and Ralph Roughley were typical of many offenders in being fined for washing fells, skins and wool in Fall Well.[32] Other noisome practices caused concern, such as glovers liming fells and skins in back yards and unfenced middens in front of the doors of houses. In 1560 so great was the obstruction in the town streets caused by middens, carts, wains, stones and piles of timber that the assembly tried to enforce the provision of a four-yard wide passageway along the town's streets.[33]

Enlargement and refurbishment of property would have required both money and motivation. Some merchants had opportunity for both; they could have known of the building work in London and other southern towns, and had a measure of wealth with which to emulate what they had seen. In Liverpool the signs of construction activity are sparse and suggest little concerted or substantial effort to alter the built environment. There is an isolated reference to Ralph Burscough undertaking the building of a 'new hall' for himself in Dale Street, but no other new work is mentioned.[34] A survey of probate inventories from Leicester during the Elizabethan period concluded that most houses were single-storey, of timber and plaster materials, with two or three rooms.[35] Presumably this type of housing predominated in Liverpool where perhaps more than half of the properties may more accurately have been described as cottages. The chantry commissioners' survey of 1548 had recorded 22 cottages with annual rents ranging from 1*s.* 4*d.* to 6*s.* 8*d.* At the same time burgage rents could reach 40*s.* a year.[36] Many

inheritance continued to dominate the urban fabric. The market, for instance, was held in the streets of the town without the benefit of a market hall or permanent structure. The harbour facilities were likewise rather primitive. King John's new borough had been sited to take advantage of a natural anchorage – the Pool – and little had yet been done to improve this feature. By Tudor times it still provided a usually sheltered but, nonetheless, quite open harbour. Ballast and rubbish were frequently, and illegally, deposited into the Pool or on to the bank that was uncovered at low tide. The 'great wynde and stormes' of November 1561 damaged this fragile facility sufficiently seriously for a town meeting to be summoned hastily to sanction repairs and some improvement. A small collection of money was immediately taken up, presumably for materials since the actual work was to be undertaken by a rota of labourers provided by each house in the town, one street at a time.[40]

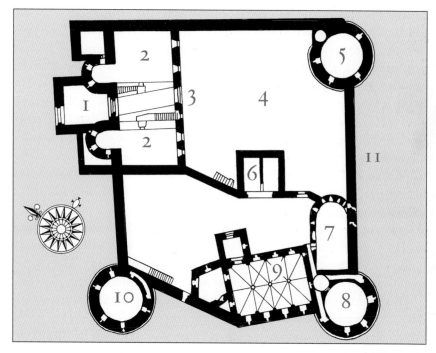

Plan of Liverpool castle, based on the work of Edward Cox (1882) who used archaeological and documentary data. By the reign of Queen Elizabeth I the castle had long since been un-garrisoned and was in a ruinous condition.

1.	Outer gate and barbican	7.	Chapel
2.	Gatehouse	8.	South-west tower
3.	Inner gate	9.	Great hall
4.	Outer ward or courtyard	10.	Great tower
5.	South-east tower	11.	Ditch
6.	Site of the well		

Little specialist labour or craftsmanship appears to have been considered necessary for this enterprise.

By the mid-thirteenth century a stone castle had been constructed in Liverpool, substantial but not very elaborate in design. It had curtain walls connecting four corner towers (three round and one square) enclosing a courtyard. A drawbridge allowed access over a ditch or moat that was possibly dry. During the fourteenth and fifteenth centuries some refurbishment and repairs were undertaken, but no substantial improvement was provided. Early in the reign of Queen Elizabeth I a royal survey reported the dilapidated state of the castle. The towers and gatehouse were unroofed and the walls themselves were in need of repair: attention that never came during the sixteenth century. The castle was supervised by an absentee constable and there was no permanent garrison.[41] The derelict state of the castle can have added little to the public image of the small town.

Nearby at the end of Water Street was the Tower. In the late fourteenth century Sir John Stanley had extended his family interests into the Lathom and Knowsley areas in south Lancashire and he had acquired land in Liverpool adjacent to the chapel. In 1406 he obtained permission to crenellate the structure he had built. The Tower was one of the few stone buildings in the town before the end of the Tudor period. It probably resembled a pele tower, but it seems to have had little more than a skeleton staff for most of the time. From 1485, with the Stanley elevation to the earldom of Derby, the Tower declined further down the list of favoured residences.[42] It remained a base for very occasional visits but, rather like the castle, it must have been an unproductive feature of the Tudor town.

The chapel of Our Lady and St Nicholas, on the waterfront, dated to the mid-fourteenth century, but had remained just a chapel-of-ease of the parish church at Walton-on-the-Hill, four miles away. The chapel had been consecrated with its graveyard in 1361. So near the shoreline was it that in a storm of 1565 a number of pinnacles and windows were damaged by wind and the walls by sea action.[43] Unfortunately no Tudor illustration or description of the chapel survives, although by the seventeenth century it was said to be 100 feet in length, some 23 feet wide and with a north aisle of the same width. There was a low tower at the west end.[44] From the beginning the advowson was controlled by the town, and the town retained a close relationship with its only church. By the time of the 1552 inventory of church goods, required of all churches and chapels in England, Liverpool chapel was better furnished than its mother church at Walton. St Nicholas' was equipped with eight sets of silk or satin vestments, four copes, various other items of clerical dress, two tabernacles, one chalice, one silver pax, and a great bell: not lavish, but decidedly better provided for than many south Lancashire churches.[45]

With so few suitable buildings available, Liverpool chapel (like other churches and chapels in Lancashire) served as a venue for public assembly as the occasion required. In 1560 gentlemen and freeholders of the area were instructed to meet the Queen's feodary there with proofs of their tenure. In 1573 the sheriff and justices of Lancashire, acting on instructions from the Privy Council, ordered butchers, alehouse and inn keepers to assemble in the chapel in an effort to enforce regulations concerning the eating of meat during Lent. The chapel was also a regular venue for the collection of the subsidy and for payment of local transactions; indeed, the subsidy collector John More esquire of Bank Hall gave notice in the chapel after morning service of his intention to make the collection.[46] One wonders what the impact on church attendance can have been.

In addition to St Nicholas' there was another small stone chapel in Liverpool, St Mary del Quay. This chapel pre-dated St Nicholas' by around a century, although both chapels were constructed on adjoining waterfront land. Donations to St Mary's and its three chantries continued during the following two centuries. In the early Tudor period John Crosse's bequest to the town allowed for the foundation of a school in this chapel to be taught by one of the chantry priests. Uncertainty surrounds the exact status of the chapel of St Mary del Quay: crucial at the time of chantry closure in the mid-sixteenth century. Not surprisingly, considerable interest was generated in Liverpool when a total of four quite well-endowed chantries were suppressed in the Tudor period. The endowments were in the form of burgages, tenements, cottages and land in the town field. They were leased immediately after suppression to a mid-Lancashire gentleman and to Sir Richard Molyneux of Croxteth, a very local landowner. About eighty households in the town were affected by this change of ownership.[47] The town was obliged to buy the building from the receivers of the Duchy of Lancaster, for 20s., in 1553 and for a while it continued to house the school. However, from 1572 the little chapel served the town as a common storehouse before reverting to a school by the end of the century.[48]

Liverpool possessed neither a monastery nor any friaries: surely indications of the limited medieval development of the town. This did mean that during the Tudor period the physical impact of the Reformation, in particular the dissolution of religious orders, was of little consequence to the town, unlike many other urban centres. Since the fourteenth century there had been a granary in Water Street belonging to the monks of Birkenhead Priory and this was purchased after the dissolution by the More family who were already significant owners of town property.[49] The ferry facility across the River Mersey had also been a perquisite of the Birkenhead monks since the thirteenth century. The facility continued after the priory closed, but in private hands.[50]

The 1515 benefactor of Liverpool's school, John Crosse, also bequeathed to the town a 'new' house (a thatched building) in Juggler Street for use as a meeting and court house by the town's burgesses.[51] For much of the sixteenth century the 'common hall' was the usual description of the building. The lower floor was used as a common warehouse with access controlled by one of the town's officials. The upper floor, reached by a flight of outside stone steps, served as a court room and assembly location. This upper room also did duty as a community facility for the town's residents: it could be hired for banquets and wedding celebrations, although by 1571 such was the state of repair that the floor was in danger of collapse. By this decade the upper floor did have glass windows, and the ground floor was serving as the town's gaol. There was discussion at an assembly about the possible provision of an alternative gaol, but instead a privy was provided for the ground-floor facility.[52]

During the Tudor period Liverpool was thus a small town with limited facilities and amenities. Liverpool was a town of just seven streets, a decaying castle, one chapel and one common hall. It is perhaps telling that during the winter months at 8.00 p.m. a curfew bell was rung in the town.[53] The one bell (with clock) at St Nicholas' chapel sufficed for all one thousand people to hear.

CHAPTER TWO

Merchants and traders

S OMETHING TO SELL was a prerequisite of urban development, and in any town the range of different craftsmen provided a clear indication of the diversity and scale of the market. Tudor Liverpool, with fewer than 1,000 inhabitants, offered somewhat limited economic opportunity to both craftsmen and merchants. Nonetheless, complexity was present in the trading activities of a small port and in the provision of services to sustain both an urban population and its rural hinterland. In such a small-scale environment many individuals earned their living from more than one activity and distinctions of manufacturer, retail trader and service provider must have been uncertain, if at all discernible to contemporaries. Merchants and traders, in some capacity, formed the distinctive occupational element of a town. As in all Tudor towns, the merchants formed a significant minority of the population: perhaps about twenty merchants being active in Liverpool in any one year of the sixteenth century.[1] Not all were equally successful or prominent, but most were connected with the port in some way: as ship owners, part-owners of vessels, or as ships' masters. Mainly they were involved in whatever trading opportunities were available: specialisation was rare and terms such as draper, mercer or vintner are inappropriate.

A few merchant families had long connections with the town: the More family since the thirteenth century, the Walker and Secum families from the fourteenth century and the Ives family since the fifteenth.[2] During the sixteenth century several families sustained three genera-tions of trading activity in the town, for instance, the Abraham, Bailey, Bannester, Bolton, Chambers, Johnson, Mather, Rainford, Sekerston and Winstanley families.[3] Most common, however, was trading by just two generations of the same family. The majority of even quite successful merchants failed to sustain family continuity, such as Thomas Bastwell, Thomas Bavand, John Bird and Alexander Garnet during the reign of Queen Elizabeth I. Mercantile operations of father and son were, therefore, a possibility throughout the Tudor period but, more common, was joint activity by brothers, as in the Bannester and Bird families.

The map of Lancashire known as Lord Burghley's map was used by Queen Elizabeth I's chief minister. Lord Burghley (formerly Sir William Cecil) had served the queen since she came to the throne in 1558 and he had amassed considerable knowledge of all areas of England, especially of the landowners and influential local officials in all counties. It used to be thought that Lord Burghley annotated the map with small crosses to indicate Catholic, and therefore potentially suspect, gentry. However, recent work suggests that not all Catholic landowners are so identified. 'Leverpoole chappel' is identified, although it almost certainly never had a spire; this is the stylised symbol used by the mapmaker.

Since south-west Lancashire was scarcely an area of major economic opportunity at this time, and in view of the modest size of Liverpool, migration into the town from beyond the immediate hinterland was not on a significant scale. A few merchants did move to Liverpool to trade and in a number of cases there is the suggestion that Liverpool was the preferred choice to Chester even though this would have been a nearer and larger commercial centre for some of the migrants. William Crook and Robert Wytter were both from Frodsham, Miles Fells was from Bidston in Wirral, Peter Starkey from Great Budworth and John Mainwaring was probably a member of one of the leading families in Nantwich: all from parts of Cheshire. Richard Hitchmough moved from Widnes and Thomas Bastwell from Upholland, both in south Lancashire.[4] Ralph Burscough appeared in Liverpool in 1559 and remained until 1588. He was the illegitimate brother of Gilbert Burscough of Lathom, a gentleman who died in 1558. Could Ralph have acquired his capital, however modest, from his family to begin trading operations in Liverpool? Gilbert Burscough appears to have had no surviving children to provide for in 1558, only a widow, three sisters and another brother who was a priest.[5] Thomas Bavand was the son of one prominent Chester merchant and the brother of Richard who was mayor of Chester in 1581. John Bird's father and grandfather had both been mayors of Chester. Their option of migration, like that of Richard Hodgson who was described as a 'northern merchant' on his settlement in the town in the 1570s, suggests that there was some attraction for adult males with modest capital and the means to commence trading to choose Liverpool. Thomas Bastwell who moved into the town in 1545 from Upholland was able to lease a burgage immediately.[6]

Apprenticeship does not seem to have been a major mechanism for significant migration into Liverpool in the Tudor period, not least because of the small number of apprenticeships that were available. It became more frequent by the end of the period as the town's population recovered its vitality: Giles Brooke (later mayor) served his apprenticeship with George Rainford.[7] Another reason for migration by a few individuals was presented by the opportunity of official appointments. Richard Andleser became customs' searcher in 1563 and then traded in the town until 1597. Thomas Wickstead became deputy customer based in Liverpool from 1573; he traded from Liverpool, by 1581 was part-owner of a ship, and also became factor for several merchants. He did not leave the town until 1592.[8] A more likely explanation for the slow but steady migration of merchants into Liverpool throughout the sixteenth century may well be found in what were perceived as less onerous trading restrictions and tolls, compared with those of Chester, as well as with the steady development of contact between Liverpool and Ireland.[9] John Crosse, described in 1562 as 'esquire' of Chorley, bought land in Liverpool, as well as in Fazakerley and Walton nearby, and apparently chose to move to Liverpool to become seriously involved in commercial activity. His attitude perhaps typifies others; John Crosse just had greater resources than most.[10]

By the late medieval period in England urban inter-marriage and re-marriage links and connections could be very complex and of considerable significance. It has been found that in the sixteenth century most London merchants married into like families providing extensive networks of connection.[11] In Tudor Liverpool there was a measure of this inter-marriage within the merchant community, but probably in a small town merchants looked elsewhere as well. Marriage negotiations were of great concern to individuals, families, kin and the wider community. Unfortunately surviving records are poor in this respect, particularly as no chapelry register is available at this time; only fragmentary details remain from other sources. Among some of the élite merchants of Liverpool there was also the desire to marry into local gentry families: perhaps where they aspired to be, as well as an indication of how they regarded their own status. Roger Walker, merchant and gentleman who died in 1558, had married Alice the sister of Thomas Eccleston esquire of Prescot parish. Ralph, the son of merchant Thomas Secum, married in 1578 Catherine the daughter of John Poley gentleman of Melling. As his second wife, however, Ralph Secum married in 1602 Anne, the widow of Richard Catton a substantial Halewood yeoman. The Crosse family, as landed gentry and also merchants, was in something of an anomalous situation among the Liverpool merchant community, but in their marriage arrangements the family demonstrated where true interests lay. John Crosse esquire (died 1575) married three times: firstly Alice the daughter of Roger Ashall gentleman of Heath Charnock, secondly Alice the daughter of Ralph Ashton esquire of Great Lever, and thirdly Anne the daughter of Robert Langton esquire of Hindley. His son and heir, John Crosse, married closer to home: Alice the daughter of John More esquire of Bank Hall.[12] Other merchants married within the Liverpool merchant community: Alice, the daughter of merchant Alexander Garnet, married Robert Wytter a merchant, and Cecily, the daughter of merchant Ralph Sekerston, married merchant Thomas Bavand. There were also marriage links between Liverpool merchants and similar families from nearby Ormskirk and Prescot; Margaret, the daughter of George Rainford a Liverpool merchant, married Thomas Potter a prominent Prescot merchant.[13] The surviving evidence may be fragmentary but there is sufficient to highlight the interrelated nature of the merchant community in Liverpool, particularly when more than one generation is considered.

By the Tudor period the subsidy rolls provide only a dubious guide to a person's wealth, but they can be used for their indications of those in a position to pay at all and for comparative purposes. At Norwich the pyramidal social structure of a major provincial town is demonstrated by the 1524–25 subsidy assessments; twenty-nine men were individually assessed at more than £100, fifty-two men were assessed between £40 and £99. Probably about six per cent of Norwich's population owed sixty per cent of the town's wealth. The total number of those paying the subsidy could run to several hundred individuals in many of the larger towns.[14] During this early part of the Tudor period the subsidy returns for towns in the north-west of England are not comparable with those for the majority of the country. By the second half of the sixteenth century, however, several Liverpool subsidy returns highlight the small scale and general impoverishment of the town. Just five men were assessed in 1563, eight in 1581 and six in 1599. Throughout the period the Crosse family headed the Liverpool assessments, although the distinction between their landed and mercantile interests is unclear. At times members of this family were involved heavily in trading ventures. The only other

Table 2 Liverpool subsidy assessments

1563	1572	1581	1581	1593	1599
John Crosse L* £3	John Crosse L £4	John Crosse L £4	John Crosse L £4	John Crosse L £4	John Crosse L £4
Thomas Secum L £2	Thomas Secum L £2	Thomas Secum L £2	Ralph Secum L £2	Ralph Secum L £2	Ralph Secum L £2
Robert Corbet G† £7	Robert Corbet G £6	William Secum G £6	William Secum G £6	Robert More G £4	Robert More G £4
Alexander Garnet G £7	Ralph Sekerston G £6	Ralph Burscough G £5	Ralph Burscough G £5	John Bird G £5	John Bird G £5
Ralph Sekerston G £8	William Secum G £8	John Mainwaring G £3	John Mainwaring G £5	Richard Hodgson G £5	William Dixon G £6
	Ralph Burscough G £5	Robert More G £4	Robert More G £4	William Golborne G £5	Giles Brooke G £5
			John Bird G £5		
			Thomas Wickstead G £4		

* L = land   † G = goods

NA, E179/131/211, 234, 272; BL, Additional Charters 53074; *LTB* II, pp. 815–17.

freeholder family in the town, the Secums, definitely obtained their wealth from commerce. All Liverpool merchants were assessed at very low levels: no more than £8 and usually £5. At Norwich, in comparison, five men were assessed in 1576 at over £30 each and no fewer than 975 men at over £3 each.[15] The relative poverty of the Liverpool merchants is again evident in 1588, when those able to loan money to Queen Elizabeth I were listed: only one, John Crosse, was recorded.[16]

Poor as they may have been by national standards, the dominant financial position of this small group of subsidy contributors within Liverpool is, nonetheless, revealed by local taxation lists which survive and allow comparison to be made with the less wealthy merchants of the town. Local leys (or rates) were collected infrequently; usually they were sanctioned for some particular purpose, such as to augment the schoolmaster's salary, to make an exceptional contribution for repairs at the parish church at Walton, or to fund the defence of the town against the claims of the Spanish Company. Presumably when local taxation was imposed in a town as small as Tudor Liverpool evasion of responsibility was rather unlikely. The range and scale of inclusion in these leys had relevance for contemporaries and rank-order had significance, even if the total collection raised was variable. Not surprisingly, in the main, the subsidy contributors headed the local taxation lists but little differentiated the wealth of the majority of the merchant group after the leading six or seven men.

On a national scale, all of the Liverpool merchants were relatively poor. There were no merchants to compare with those in York, probably the sixth largest city in England, where a Company of Merchant Adventurers controlled all imported goods and where some merchants belonged to national trading companies, such as the Muscovy or the Eastland. There were no attempts such as in Chester to form a new merchant company of 'mere' merchants to monopolise continental trade.[17] The nature of Liverpool's trade was such that it scarcely

RIGHT

A detail of a painting of Liverpool in c.1680 by an unknown artist. The circumstances of the production of this view are not known but this is the earliest representation we have of Liverpool. Some details may not relate to the Tudor period, for instance the general impression of stone housing and the 1670s Town Hall to the rear and centre of the view. However, Water Street did lead right down to the River Mersey and the Tower, the fortified stone house of the earls of Derby, had existed to one side of Water Street since the early fifteenth century. The shipping in the river may contain some artistic licence, yet the preponderance of two- or one-masted vessels, as well as quite small rowing and sailing boats, may well reflect the Tudor period.

BY KIND PERMISSION OF MERSEYSIDE MARITIME MUSEUM, NATIONAL MUSEUMS LIVERPOOL

Map of Burtonhead in Prescot parish produced in c.1580. The map contains sufficient information for orientation: Wigan church to the north, Newton, Leigh and Winwick to the east, Warrington church and stone bridge to the south-east. The detail, however, concerns Burtonhead hall with its stone roof and red brick chimney and the land and thatched cottages around it. Most importantly, five coal pits are identified to the rear of the hall (*detail, left*) – Pemb[er]ton's coal mine. This was just one of the locations in Prescot parish from which coal was carted into Liverpool for sale to the town's population and for transport to Ireland. This must be one of the earliest representations of a coalmine. The map also shows some of the surrounding hedges and strip farming, as well as the gated lane to the hall and Peasley Cross.

LRO, SCARISBRICK OF SCARISBRICK PAPERS, DDSC 32/1

Edward, third earl of Derby, by a follower of Hans Holbein (c.1640s), oil on panel, 10¼ × 8 ins.

Knowsley Hall, the principal seat of the Stanley family may have been some miles outside Liverpool but the earls of Derby, nonetheless, exercised considerable influence over the small town. The earls were treated with deference and care by the mayor and officers of Liverpool. Edward Stanley, 3rd earl of Derby (1509–72) was a leading nobleman throughout the reigns of Henry VIII and Edward VI. He was particularly prominent as a royal councillor in Mary Tudor's reign and served on Elizabeth I's privy council. His sons were given the honorific role as mayor of Liverpool – Thomas in 1568/69 and Henry in 1569/70.

Ralph Edgecer's probate inventory represents the poorer level of craftsmen in Tudor Liverpool. His work tools as a joiner form a small part of his possessions. He has a few pigs, some barley and oat malt and a mixed supply of fuel (turf, gorse and coal) – bearing in mind that the inventory was compiled in January. His household goods are basic and minimal. The only small touch of luxury appears to be his six silver spoons. During the Tudor period the new year commenced on 25 March so the dating of this document as January 1577 would be recorded as 1578 in modern style. This document is transcribed, with the original spelling, on the page opposite

[LRO, WCW RALPH EDGECAR, LIVERPOOL, 1577/8]

Inventarie of all and singular goods and chattels
moveable and immoveable belonging
Radulphi Edgeker de Levepole in county
of Lancaster on the day he died. Appraised and valued
by four honest neighbours
that is Richard Eccleston
Thomas Bannister, Richard Haydocke,
and John Smith, 21 Januarii 1577/8.

First ii sowes & iiii piggs	xvi s.
Item: his joyners work tooles	x s.
Item: in salte	iii s. iiii d.
Item: one litle table	iii s. iiii d.
Item: an olde heare	ii s.
Item: in turffe, cole & gorse	xx s.
Item: one leade	vi s. viii d.
Item: in irone vessels	vi s. viii d.
Item: in barlie malte	£iii
Item: in oten malte	vi s. viii d.
Item: in beddinge	£iii
Item: in bedstedds	xiii s. iiii d.
Item: iii square tables & i round table	xiii s. iiii d.
Item: forms, chairs and stoles	xiii s. iiii d.
Item: in pewter	x s.
Item: in brasse	x s.
Item: his bodies apparell	xxvi s. viii d.
Item: in iron ware	xiii s. iiii d.
Item: napperie ware	vi s. viii d.
Item: chandlers	iii s.
Item: an old cupborde	v s.
Item: sixe sylver spones	xiii s. iii
Item: an old copper	ii s.
Lastlie, ii old carpetts &	
iiii old quisshins	iiii s.

Summa totalis	£xvi viii s. viii d.

Table 3 *Liverpool local taxation assessments*

	1565			1581			1594	
s/m	John Crosse	2s. 0d.	s/m	John Crosse	2s. 8d.	s/m	John Crosse	4s. 8d.
s/m	Robert Corbet	2s. 0d.	m	Thomas Bavand	2s. 0d.	s/m	John Bird	4s. 8d.
s/m	Alexander Garnet	1s. 8d.	s/m	William Secum	2s. 0d.	s/m	Ralph Secum	3s. 4d.
s/m	Thomas Secum	1s. 8d.	s/m	Ralph Burscough	1s. 8d.	s/m	Robert More	3s. 0d.
s/m	Ralph Sekerston	1s. 8d.	s/m	Robert More	1s. 8d.	m	Giles Brooke	2s. 8d.
	Henry Bedford	1s. 4d.		Ms. Anne More	1s. 8d.		Edmund Rose	2s. 8d.
	Ms. Fairclough	1s. 4d.	s/m	John Bird	1s. 4d.	s/m	Richard Hodgson	2s. 8d.
m	Richard Andleser	1s. 4d.	s/m	John Mainwaring	1s. 4d.		Robert Berry	2s. 6d.
m	Thomas Bavand	1s. 0d.	m	Edward Nicholson	1s. 4d.		William Dixon	2s. 0d.
m	Thomas Rowe	1s. 0d.	s/m	Thomas Wickstead	1s. 0d.	s/m	William Golborne	1s. 8d.
m	William Secum	1s 0d.	m	Thomas Bolton	10d.	m	William Secum	1s. 6d.
m	Thomas More	1s 0d.	m	Thomas Walker	10d.	m	Richard Bird	1s. 6d.
	Ralph Jamison	10d.					Thomas Gardener	1s. 6d.
m	Ralph Burscough	10d.				m	Gilbert Formby	1s. 4d.
	Humphrey Webster	10d.		and others taxed at smaller amounts			John Gifford	1s. 4d.
	Thomas Inglefield	10d.					Thomas Rose	1s. 4d.
	Thomas Uttyn	10d.					widow R. Bailey	1s. 2d.
							Margery Smith widow	1s. 2d.
							Roger Rose	1s. 0d.
	and others taxed at smaller amounts					m	Cuthbert Lawrence	1s. 0d.
						m	Thomas Bolton	1s. 0d.
							Evan Richardson	1s. 0d.
							John Sandford	1s. 0d.
						m	Edward Nicholson	1s. 0d.
						m	Thomas Tarlton	1s. 0d.
							Robert Ball	10d.
						m	Henry Moneley	10d.
						m	Robert Blundell	10d.
						m	William Towers	10d.
						m	Thomas Bannester	10d.
							widow T. Knype	10d.
							and others taxed at smaller amounts	

LTB I, pp. 436–440 s: subsidy contributor; *LTB* II, pp. 817–819, 823–826 m: known to be a merchant.

provided opportunity for the acquisition of considerable wealth. The average merchant estates in both Exeter and Bristol were more than £1,900. Many of the aldermanic class in Norwich during this period were wealthy enough to invest in land within a few miles of the city where they purchased tenements, pastures and mills. In 1585 a York draper died leaving debts of £17,000 to four London merchant tailors, and even a Nantwich mercer left lands and leases worth over £18,000 and shop goods of £300 in 1594.[18] In Exeter the merchants lived 'in considerable ease, relieved by frequent touches of extravagance', and by the end of the sixteenth century had plaster ceilings, wainscotted walls, some tapestries and a few pictures.[19] This level of wealth tended to be found only in larger towns and in particular economic circumstances. In Tudor Manchester only the Mosley family used their wealth to acquire landed estates and only one clothier had a probate inventory valuation of over £1,000.[20]

It is unlikely that any Liverpool merchant in the Tudor period had a level of wealth to approach the living standards of London and the larger towns. In Liverpool evidence is limited to just seven merchant inventories. From this restricted evidence there is indication of only one three-storey house: that of Giles Brooke in Water Street (died 1614). His inventory mentions a parlour, Mr Brooke's chamber, a kitchen, a brewhouse, a larder and a stable (perhaps all on the ground floor); then a chamber over the kitchen, a chamber over the parlour, a chamber over the entry (making a second storey); and then a turret which seems to have constituted a small third storey. In all, this scarcely amounts to spacious living. The total valuations of the Liverpool merchant inventories do not suggest luxury, although some afforded a measure of comfort. Thomas Bavand's inventory of 1588 listed all the wainscot and glass in the parlour and other chambers in the house, but only at the modest value of £8, while Thomas Bolton's 1597 inventory recorded thirty-eight feet of glass throughout the house at a value of 15s. Richard Hitchmough, however, had only laths of wood in the windows of his house, worth just 8d. in 1574.

Inside their houses few Liverpool merchants had items of individual value: William Secum had playing tables, two pictures and a looking glass: scarcely luxury. John Bird had two carpets in his parlour, six framed pictures, playing tables, twelve Spanish earthenware dishes and books to the value of 10s. Thomas Bavand did have twenty-seven beds included in his inventory as well as nineteen banqueting dishes, twenty silver spoons, five gilt bowls, two double-gilt drinking bowls, one double-gilt drinking cup and one double-gilt salt. John Bird had silver and gilt plate of all kinds to the value of £47 14s. 0d. In comparison, the other merchants had no where near this quantity of possessions and had only small items of plate; William Secum had silver worth £9, Thomas Bolton had twelve ounces of silver worth £3, Richard Hitchmough had just seven silver spoons valued at 23s. 4d., while Richard Bird had just three gold and two silver rings.

Robert More (merchant, but younger son of a gentry family) did have clothes to the value of £26 13s. 4d. in an inventory (1608) which totalled £418 10s. 8d. Unfortunately the garments are not itemised, although his will did mention his best doublet of Lyons rash fabric. The inventory of Robert's younger brother (1619) provides the only indication of what a Liverpool merchant's wardrobe might have comprised by the late Tudor/ early Stuart period. The clothing was valued at £15 and comprised a stuff gown, four pairs of breeches, two doublets, two jerkins, a cloak, a horseman's coat, a pair of silk stockings, two pairs of linen stockings, three shirts, two hats, a coarse waistcoat, two pairs of boots, a pair of shoes, a pair of garters, and a sword with a girdle and hangers.

For all Liverpool merchants farm goods were of little importance; none had any agricultural equipment, although they did have a few animals. Richard Hitchmough had pigs and geese, Richard Bird had poultry, Robert Wolfall had an old horse, Thomas Bolton had one horse and two cows, while Thomas Bavand had four horses, an ox, three cows, pigs and hens. The sample of Liverpool merchant inventories is too small and idiosyncratic to be of decisive value, but it would seem that predominantly their wealth lay with their trade goods. Thomas Bavand had been one of the town's leading merchants; his household goods indicate his lifestyle, although his trade goods cannot be representative of his true commercial activity. Richard Bird's inventory is more typical

Table 4 *Probate valuations of Tudor Liverpool merchants*

	Household goods	Farm goods	Trade goods	Money	Total valuation	Debts owed to the testator	Debts owed by the testator
Richard Hitchmough, 1574	34%	2%	64%		£8 0s. 0d.	£63 8s. 10d.	
Robert Wolfall, 1578	94%	6%			£7 16s. 11d.	£2 19s. 2d.	16s. 3d.
Thomas Bavand, 1588	72%	11%	17%		£40 0s. 0d.	£146 17s. 7d.	
William Secum, 1593	26%	18%	55%	1%	Incomplete	£105 7s. 7d.	
Richard Bird, 1595	36%		36%	28%	Incomplete	£53 8s. 0d.	
Thomas Bolton, 1597	71%	15%	14%		£149 7s. 0d.	£31 19s. 1d.	
John Bird, 1603	43%	28%	29%		Incomplete	£442 4s. 2d. and £450 14s. 1d. at Chester	

of the scale of many Liverpool merchants; however, he traded with his older surviving brother and so the possessions identified as his alone may be deceptive. Thomas Bolton testifies to the modest nature of some mercantile activity, but the large debt owing to him distorts the overall picture. Richard Hitchmough did possess a quantity of trade goods; his inventory, unfortunately, records them only as 'wares in his shop'. Robert Wolfall's inventory is too limited to be useful.

Only two of the Tudor probate inventories, those of William Secum and John Bird, provide a convincing view of the nature and scale of trade by two of the more prominent of Liverpool's merchants.

William Secum had been active in trade with his father and then with his brother for at least twenty years by the time of his death. He had lived in Castle Street until moving to his father's house in Water Street where there are modest indications of comfort. His goods 'in the shop' bear witness to the nature of his trade: mostly small quantities of various fabrics and clothing, measured to the quarter of a yard. He had felt, frieze, cotton, Penistone, broadcloth, flannel, Kentish cloth, bays, kersey, holmes, velour, Milan fustian, tufted taffeta, grograine, buffen, worsted, canvas, buckram, sackcloth, silk rash, silk, lace, thread, buttons, girdles, garters, gloves, four pairs of spectacles, six pounds of pepper and six ounces of cloves. The most expensive item was eleven yards of Kentish cloth at £4 8s. 0d. The most expensive cloth was the tufted taffeta at 6s. 8d. per yard. In a similar manner the stock in John Bird's shop was itemised, but he appears to have dealt with a greater diversity of commodities. There was plenty of cloth: Bolton bay, Bolton frieze, Bolton fustian, London cotton, black buffen, Yorkshire cloth, Penistone green, tufted canvas, sackcloth, velvet, coloured silk, cambric, calico cloth, taffeta, and Levant taffeta. There was also haberdashery: silk hose, worsted stockings, silk points, lace, fringing, silk and gold buttons, steel buttons and buckles, thread points, gloves, hats, hat bands, starch and three boxes of combs. John Bird was also a stationer; he had paper, parchment, sealing wax, pens, inkhorns and books of all sorts. Dyes, spices and exotic foodstuffs had also found their way to this Water Street emporium: madder, verdigris, ochre, chalk, saffron, turmeric, wormseed, pepper, cloves, mace, almonds, sugar, ginger, rice, currants, sugar candy and comfits. Among the miscellaneous items were quicksilver, alum, brimstone, lead, Spanish iron, a cross-bow and Castile soap. Presumably many of these goods could have been valued using the small balance and weights or the beam and scales found in the premises.

This listing of mixed merchandise in small quantities appears typical of the trading habits of the major Liverpool merchants. Specialisation of economic activity and large-scale operations were rare, as the local demand was insufficient to support them. From 117 individuals identified as merchants during the second half of the sixteenth century just six are mentioned as 'draper': Richard Aspinwall, for instance, in the 1550s, Alexander Garnet during the 1550s and 1560s, Ralph Sekerston from the 1550s to the 1570s. A further five men are identified as 'mercer', such as Richard Hitchmough in the 1560s and 1570s.[21] Although indicating a degree of specialisation, even these terms may be misleading. They may reflect a wish for status on the part of the individual in question since the terms are rarely used with any consistency. Two more traders are mentioned as merchant/tailors, one as a merchant/blacksmith, one as a merchant/dyer, one as a merchant/tallow chandler and four as merchant/yeomen. Giles Brooke, who died in 1614, had a cellar at his Water Street house in which his inventory listed three butts and a remnant of red wine, three empty butts, two hogsheads, three kilderkins, three barrels and two firkins: possibly supplies for his own consumption but, more likely, an indication of some specialism as a vintner.

Despite a number of Liverpool merchants operating with a degree of specialisation, it is doubtful if in a small town the trading opportunities could support entirely specialist operations. For many merchants the most likely combination of activities was trade with the practice of master mariner. In twenty-three instances this was specifically recorded, usually in the town books or the port books; for example, Thomas Uttyn and William Walker both operated in this way for more than twenty years during the mid sixteenth century.[22] Small town potential meant many merchants began and finished their careers in this way.

A small number of merchants are known to have worked at the chapman/pedlar level of business. John Corbet (probably the son of a merchant) maintained a livelihood as a pedlar from 1573 until 1600. Likewise William Dalton was recorded consistently as a chapman during the late 1580s and 1590s. In 1587 he became a freeman of the town as a 'petty chapman'.[23] At much the same time William Scarisbrick appears as both mercer and chapman, These appellations suggest an itinerant nature to their trading activity on a regular basis. What the subtle distinctions were in the minds of Tudor scribes is now elusive. Perhaps scale and volume of operation or diversity of commodity influenced the choice of attribution.

Small towns such as Liverpool were not necessarily isolationist and introverted. The merchants could and did travel and trade in northern England, in the Midlands, in London and abroad, but local economic potential and international relations did not encourage significant growth in the volume of the town's trade nor the size of the merchant community. Those merchants who did operate from Liverpool showed concern to improve their environment, protect their financial interests and ensure their social survival. They did form a distinctive occupational group well able to dominate the modest civic affairs of the town; they were not, however, so wealthy that they could escape the pervading influence of the local gentry and the earl of Derby.

CHAPTER THREE

Making a living

M ANY FEATURES of Tudor towns were ubiquitous: the activities of craftsmen and service providers were part of the structural characteristics of pre-industrial society. The numbers of men involved in various crafts can provide a valuable indication of local economic specialisms, such as the dominant role played by the cloth industry and its associated processes in Tudor Worcester and the importance of the preparation and manufacture of leather goods in Elizabethan Chester.[1] With sufficiently detailed evidence changes over time can be identified. Unfortunately for Tudor Liverpool, the identification of male occupations is restricted by the surviving sources. The town books from 1550 make reference incidentally to a number of inhabitants and their employment, and this material can be combined with evidence from probate records and other miscellaneous documents. Sadly, the accumulated data represents only poorly the first part of the Tudor period and is not comprehensive enough for statistical analysis; during the second part of the sixteenth century there is sufficient material to detail some urban livelihoods. Liverpool was a small town; its crafts and services were primarily those that were essential in supporting the immediate population and that were viable within the limited scope of the town's market. Diversity and specialism were severely restricted.

Craftsmen

Leather workers, of various types, were among the most traditional of craftsmen in a predominantly rural area. In south-west Lancashire, because of the mixed pattern of farming and because of trading opportunities with Ireland, leather workers were important in the local economy. The two branches of the craft, the preparing and the processing of the leather as well as the manufacture of finished articles, provided employment for a significant number of people. The butchers of south Lancashire generated a supply of hides, and imported raw materials from Ireland augmented this. Next to fish, hides and skins were Ireland's most important export, and Liverpool was a prime port of entry. By the 1590s considerable quantities of sheepskins were reaching the town, mainly to be used locally, although some were transported on to Chester. To a lesser extent sheep fells and hides reached Liverpool also from the Isle of Man.[2]

The tanner was the backbone of this craft. Horse hides, cattle hides and calf skins were cleaned and soaked in pits or vats with an oak-bark solution over a period of six months to two years. After drying the tanned leather could be finished with tallow or train (whale) oil.[3] Because of this lengthy process tanners required an amount of capital for tools and equipment, a site with an adequate water supply, space for pits and sheds and, most especially, funds to cover the stock in hand during the tanning process. Throughout south Lancashire in the Tudor period there was a scattering of tanners in various parishes and Liverpool attracted a small concentration. There were probably about six tanners operating in the town at any one time.[4] The value of their materials is indicated by the complaint of a tanner from Cuerdley (fifteen miles away) who claimed his consignment of leather had been hijacked and stolen while *en route* to the River Mersey for transport to Liverpool.[5]

Most tanned leather went to shoemakers, saddlers and harness makers, since glovers required finer skins obtained from sheep, goats or calves. This lighter leather was not normally tanned; rather it was dressed with train oil or alum in a shorter process requiring some weeks.[6] In Liverpool there were a few skinners and whitawers engaged in this craft although, from their numbers, they were not supplying anything like the quantity of leather that was produced by the tanners.[7] The train oil and alum were both readily available through imports into Liverpool.

The leather workers themselves may have required relatively small amounts of finished leather to work with, a small outlay in necessary tools and only a small work space. Most leather workers had a work-shop. John Smith, a Liverpool glover (1591) had tools to the value of 3s. 0d., 150 English calfskins, 150 English and Irish sheepskins, lambskins and undressed oxenskins to the value of £9 5s. 4d., as well as £28 9s. 4d. worth of finished goods. Shoemakers easily predominated among the different types of leather workers; by the reign of Elizabeth about seven or eight worked in Liverpool at any one time. A few glovers operated; one purser is recorded; and one pointmaker.[8] This limited diversity among the leather craftsmen provides an indication of the restricted local market available to them.

A further sign of this restriction is provided by evidence of dual occupation. The pointmaker, Edmund Irlam, was also a skinner; the purser, William Hughson, kept an alehouse. A few of the shoemakers had alternative or supplementary means of livelihood. Most leather workers were making low-value items in an area with a limited and predictable market. Many leather workers were among the poorer craftsmen. Even in a larger-sized town such as Worcester the leather craftsmen came low on the economic scale.[9] John Smith, the Liverpool glover, appears more comfortably off than usual with a probate inventory valuation of £65 15s. 8d. (1591) but this is perhaps explained by his diversity of interests as a skinner, whitawer and glove-maker.

Table 5 *Liverpool craftsmen during the 1590s* [10]

Leather craftsmen: tanner, shoemaker, glover, purser, pointmaker	28%
Wood craftsmen: carpenter, joiner, cooper, ship's carpenter	25%
Textile craftsmen: weaver, dyer, tailor, hatmaker, ropemaker	25%
Metal craftsmen: blacksmith, cutler, goldsmith	13%
Building craftsmen: mason, slater, plasterer, glazier	9%

Leatherwork was a significant but not dominant occupation. In the town the tanning processes must have provided some intermittent and casual employment for labourers in addition to the recognised craftsmen. However, a greater impact for the majority of the population may well have been the environmental unpleasantness caused by the activities of leather workers; the smell from tanning leather cannot have been attractive and tanners were in trouble frequently for polluting water supplies.[11] For at least ten years John Smith carried on a protracted dispute with his neighbour in Castle Street, Thomas Bavand. In 1571 John Smith was reprimanded for the state of the lime pits at the rear of his house, and he promised not to keep fells and skins in these pits 'next adjoyning to mayster maiors [Thomas Bavand's] bed chambers and dynying chamber'. The matter did not rest. In 1574 Thomas Bavand was presented to the assembly for allowing his servants to empty chamber pots on to John Smith's property, while in 1577 John Smith was accused of diverting watercourses to soak his skins and building a dunghill against Thomas Bavand's wall. The last heard of the neighbourly affair was in 1581.[12]

Another traditional craft supporting and supported by a predominantly rural economy was that of the blacksmith. His skills were necessary for a range of metal work used about the house and farm.

Virtually all townships in south Lancashire had at least one blacksmith, whereas Liverpool had a small concentration: perhaps five or six at one time during the sixteenth century.[13] A smithy and specialist tools were essential for this craft, and this may have generated an element of family continuity in this occupation. Thomas Bannester, for instance, divided his equipment between his two sons in Liverpool (1598). Most blacksmiths had one or more stiddies, bellows, files and grindstones amounting to a few pounds in value. Reginald Melling had just eight per cent of his total inventory valuation (1572) tied up in his tools, the one stiddy, bellows, files, pitch, a pair of balances and 612 pounds weight of iron. Probate inventories provide also an indication of the type of work undertaken by blacksmiths: the shoeing of horses; the making of coopers' metal bands, hinges and latches for all kinds of doors, nails of all sizes; and the construction of the metal components of many farm tools. Blacksmiths could also make security features: locks, keys and door-plates, window bars and chains. Reginald Melling had ten dozen hinges, coopers' bands, horse rails and cupboard hinges in his stock, amounting to £2 in total. Repair work, however, eluded the inventory appraisers. Most blacksmiths served the needs of the domestic and agricultural markets. Sometimes they did have an interest in farming, such as the oxen, horses, three cows and quantity of barley that Reginald Melling had. The two sources of income could have provided a reliable and complementary livelihood. During the Tudor period only Reginald Melling was referred to as an ironmonger, suggesting perhaps a greater scale of operation with a variety of goods that were possibly not all made by him.

An intriguing aspect of this metal work is where the iron came from, since south Lancashire did not provide an immediate source. Chester and Liverpool's coasting trade meant that cargoes could be trans-shipped from other English ports, although it appears that distance to English supplies and considerations of quality made it worthwhile to import Spanish iron directly. Until the very late sixteenth century when Liverpool's continental trade was severely curtailed, supplies of iron had been readily available. One or two ships a year made the voyage to the north Spanish coast with four, five or six Liverpool merchants sharing the cargo; iron was usually the main commodity they imported with small quantities of soap, pitch or train oil. Occasionally a French ship brought iron into Liverpool. Despite the international difficulties of the late sixteenth century some supplies of Spanish iron were still available in the 1590s.[14]

Specialist metal workers needed a wider marketing area and, hence, were not numerous in a small town. No nailers are known in Liverpool, although William Green of Prescot did trade through Liverpool.[15] Three cutlers operated from Liverpool during the second half of the sixteenth century; perhaps taking advantage of the growing contacts with Ireland. Pewter work was not well developed, possibly because the Wigan area had a reputation in this field and supplies were adequate.[16] One brazier/panmaker is known to have worked in Liverpool, but not until the 1590s.[17] Goldsmiths certainly needed a luxury market for their products; Chester, for instance, had a small gild of goldsmiths by the Tudor period. Liverpool had just the beginnings of development in this craft; late in the sixteenth century two goldsmiths appeared in the town. George Charlton operated as a freeman from 1592 to 1596, and Edward Holme was made a freeman in 1598.[18] Both testify to a modest initiative taking place in the town's craft structure, but they were probably short-lived phenomena at this time.

At the time of Domesday Book in the late eleventh century south Lancashire had been an area of considerable woodland; medieval clearance had much reduced this by the Tudor period. It is difficult to assess the availability of timber for wood workers; their products were in demand and presumably they used local supplies when available. Brief details from Childwall and Prescot churchwardens' accounts suggest that supplies from the parks of local gentry and from royal woodland in West Derby were of considerable importance.[19] Some specialist wood workers are known and others may have existed, subsumed in the records under more general terms. Joiners were concentrated in Liverpool, perhaps six at a time. Mostly they made furniture and interior fittings. One Liverpool joiner, Ralph Edgecar, panelled the walls of the common hall and made a new table for it in 1561.[20] The probate inventory of Peter Ireland (1580) records a small amount of partially completed work: three dozen panel-boards, six short sawed-boards and two dozen mountings.

The coopers were another specialist group that had a small concentration in the town; three of them worked there. With the prevalence of home brewing and the requirements of a port town there must have been steady demand for their wares. One wheelwright, Miles Kirkdale, is recorded during the sixteenth century, although the supply and repair of wheels for various types of cart may not have been of great significance in an area where the roads were not well suited to this type of transport. Few carts are recorded in probate inventories. During the later part of the Tudor period one bowyer, Richard Whitfield, worked in Liverpool but he surely represented a declining craft at this time.[21]

Six ships' carpenters are recorded in the town during the second half of the sixteenth century, yet what exactly they did is an intriguing question. They are referred to as 'ships' carpenters', never as shipwrights or boatwrights. Possibly they made small vessels such as the river craft used by Liverpool's ferrymen or small coastal and fishing vessels. It seems unlikely that they made ocean-going ships. No details of local transactions survive, so that the scale of this activity is obscure. Most likely they could have fulfilled a small, but steady, demand to repair and refit ships. A tantalising detail in the town books of 1576 refers to the existing prohibition on the construction of boats in the streets of the town.[22] Until the capacity of the port expanded considerably the work available to ships' carpenters must have remained fairly static.

The majority of wood workers had no known specialism; they operated simply as general carpenters. Their work may have involved house construction, modification or repair, and work about barns, sheds, stables, gates and fences. In view of the predominantly timber-framed housing in Liverpool, many of the population would have required the services of a carpenter, at least intermittently. Many carpenters must have existed for most of the time with a variety of small commissions. The probate inventories of two Liverpool joiners suggest they were among the poorer craftsmen. Ralph Edgecar's tools were valued at 10s. (1578) and Peter Ireland's at £1 2s. 6d. (1580). In 1589 four carpenters were paid 8d. per day for work at Childwall church.[23]

Parts of south-west Lancashire did provide some supplies of stone and helped to support other construction workers. The one mason recorded in Tudor Liverpool, and the slaters, obtained stone from quarries on the heath outside the town. Supply of stone was controlled and the slaters were ordered in 1583 not to sell slate to 'foreigners' without licence from the mayor. In 1573 two of Liverpool's slaters were fined in West Derby for taking flagstones and slates without permission.[24] In view of the predominance of timber buildings the slaters presumably found more work than the masons. This may explain why a mason and his apprentice had to be hired from Cheshire to repair the chapel in 1565.[25] Rather surprisingly, no thatchers are mentioned in this area, although it can be supposed some buildings required their services. One roughcaster, Alan Gogney, had his own lime kiln in Juggler Street. His job may have been somewhat similar to that of Gilbert Whitstones, the plasterer in Liverpool, with perhaps a degree of sophistication in the case of the plasterer. His job, however, cannot have been in great demand since for a number of years he was hayward of the town and referred to as a labourer.[26]

Glaziers were recorded in the Chester freemen rolls from 1571 onwards. When exactly this craft became available in Liverpool on a regular basis is not entirely apparent. During the 1570s and 1580s the Ormskirk glazier, William Brown, was used at Liverpool chapel, while

John Gower's probate inventory is also from the poorer level of craftsmen in Tudor Liverpool but the men who listed and valued his possessions went to some trouble to record and detail his weaver's equipment (looms, reeds and shuttles) as well as to indicate that he wove with both flax and wool. The coffer 'in the shop' implies that Gower had a workshop as part of his premises. Luxury appears confined to just two silver spoons. For some unknown reason John Gower the weaver had three swords, two black bills and one spear for a footman in his possession. Money values at this time were recorded using Roman numerals and in pounds, shillings and pence. The document is transcribed below and opposite.

LRO, WCW, JOHN GOWER, LIVERPOOL, 1594

A trewe inventory of all the goods and cattels of John Gower of Liverpoole, decessed. Praissed by Thomas Rose, Rychard Mather, Raffe Gower and William Stanisbrooke, the xviith day of June anno dom 1594.

Imprimis: one cobbord praissed to	iii s. iiii d.
Item: one board with a fframe	iiii s.
Item: one other board with forms & benches in the house	ii s.
Item: iii peare of loomes praissed to	xxvi s. 8d.
Item: viii flaxen riedes	iiii s.
Item: viii canvas & ii hempe rieds	iii s. iiii d.
Item: one doble twille ried	viii d.
Item: viii reedes which ar broken	xii d.
Item: ix wollen riedes	v s.
Item: one troughe and while	ii s.
Item: ii littill pales to mack starche in	iiii s.
Item: i coffer in the shope	vi d.

Item: shuttiles & temples	vi d.
Item: ii peare of bedstockes in the chamber without	ii s.
Item: one peare of bedstockes	xii s.
Item: ii cofferes in the chamber without	ii s. vi d.
Item: i turnell	xvi d.
Item: one ladder	viii d.
Item: ine brewing pane	vi s. viii d.
Item one brewing combe with all the brewinge vesseles	iiii s.
Item ii hogesheads and one pype	ii s.
Item ine iron great	v s.
Item: one spyt, golbart with tongs and pothoockes	iii s.
Item: iii old cheres & iii stoles	ii s. vi d.
Item ii spyning whyles	xx d.
Item: vii wyndeles of barly malt	xvi s. iiii d.
Item: iii olde brasse pottes	x s.
Item: for Spanishe rieds	ii s.
Item: ii littill panes & a brassen ladell	ii s. vi d.
Item: one fleche of bacon	iiii s.
Item: one soww	v s.
Item: in pewtar	x s.
Item: vii candellstickes of brasse	iii s. iiii d.
Item: iii bere potes	ix d.
[continued]	
Item: in the chamber where he ley ii pere of bedstockes	iiii s.
Item: ii ffethar bedes	xiii s. iiii d.
Item: iii bolsters & iiii pellowes	vi s. viii d.
Item: v covarlets & ii blanckets	xxviii s.
Item: one board	ii s.
Item: iiii cofferes	vi s.
Item: iii swords & ii blacke biles	v s.
Item: ii gownes & one cloake with all his other apparell	xl s.
Item: vi peare of shytes	xviii s.
Item: iiii pelowe beres & ii toweles	iii s.
Item: in tryne weare	xii d.
Item ii littill silvar spones	vi s.
Item: one speare for a foote man	viii d.

Sume is £xiiii xiii d.

in the 1590s Richard Brown undertook glazing commissions in both
Liverpool and Prescot. A glass furnace is known to have existed near
Ormskirk at this time.[27] A degree of expertise may have been necessary
for ecclesiastical work, but the inference remains that not until the very
end of the Tudor period did the town have a resident glazier. William
Corker then settled in the town and practised his trade throughout the
south-west Lancashire area. Glass windows were undoubtedly available
in some houses in the town before this; the limitation of Liverpool's
potential for new craftsmen is evident in the late arrival of a permanent
glazier.[28]

The traditional and growing manufacturing craft of many Tudor
towns was that of textiles. The major centre in Lancashire was in the
Manchester area, while the south-west of the county retained production
mainly for domestic consumption.[29] Weavers were to be found in all
of the parishes around Liverpool and the town contained a further
concentration of this activity. The type of cloth produced is difficult
to identify precisely. A variety of woollens such as rugs, friezes, kerseys
and cottons were all narrow fabrics woven on a loom operated by one
person. In 1582 William More of Kirkdale, adjacent to Liverpool, paid
three local weavers for wool, kersey and buffet as well as for weaving
flax.[30] The Liverpool weaver, John Gower, had wool, flax and canvas
reeds among his possessions (in 1594). Probably woollen weaving was
quite limited, and many weavers were accustomed to dealing with both
woollen and linen cloth. There is little evidence of the crafts associated
with widespread woollen production; just one shearman and three dyers
are mentioned in the town.[31]

There is much more reference to the use of hemp and flax for
various fabrics. Some weavers were identified as linen specialists and
from probate evidence this would seem to be the case in additional
instances.[32] They used some local supplies of hemp and flax as well
as imported Irish flax and yarn; by the 1590s these imports were at
record levels.[33] Considerable preparation was necessary with both flax
and hemp before they could be woven. After pulling, it was soaked for
up to twelve days, creating a foul smell, while the stems of the plant
rotted. The fibre was then dried over a fire and, when dry, beaten
(or gigged) to separate the fibres before carding. In the town this flax
preparation was both noisome and a fire hazard. A Liverpool bye-law
of 1540 punished with a fine the drying of flax in houses and in 1556,
since the hazardous activity continued, the fine was increased to 6s. 8d.
Even so the practice continued, as did gigging flax in houses. The water
supplies of the town were also used for soaking flax and for washing
yarn.[34] It is evident from the individuals presented for these offences

that a considerable assortment of people in the town was involved in flax preparation in some way. In addition to this preparatory work, probably four or five individuals were necessary to undertake sufficient carding and spinning to keep one weaver supplied with yarn. Spinning wheels are quite common in probate inventories throughout the area and among all groups of people. Yarn production must have been a significant bye-employment.

Much of the fabric that was manufactured was probably disposed of by independent weavers; there is no sign of complex organisation or the activities of clothiers that characterised other parts of England. In 1572 permission was obtained for just four weavers to establish a gild in Liverpool. Compared with the substantial gilds of many Tudor towns this level of activity is minimal.[35] Only a few drapers operated from Liverpool. Some cloth was exported to Ireland but much of it originated from east Lancashire, Yorkshire and beyond.[36] The products of Liverpool's weavers were probably intended mainly for local domestic consumption and contributed to the supplies of fabric for the tailors working in the town. Up to ten tailors operated at any one time, with enough of them to form a gild in 1559.[37] The only specialist clothing manufacturers that are known are Thomas Bolton, father and son, hat makers, although two felt makers may have practised similar skills.[38]

Hemp, in addition to its use for coarse cloth, could have been used for the manufacture of rope and nets. Domestically a great variety of twine, cord, and braid must have been produced in many households. If the fibre was plaited and twisted then rope could be made, but it is a reflection of Liverpool's modest shipping fleet that only two specialist rope makers are known. Like the drying of flax and hemp, the tarring of rope and cables was regarded as a fire hazard. John Sandiford used his own house in the town for this purpose. No sail makers are recorded in the town, although it was felt necessary for the assembly in 1582 to condemn the practice of sail making in the chapel – a practical use of one of the few available large buildings in Tudor Liverpool.[39]

It is clear from the probate inventories that no fortunes were to be made from the manufacture of textiles in Liverpool. A few specialist weavers did produce a diversity of cloth, such as John Gower, but even he had modestly valued equipment and a low total inventory valuation. Many weavers were probably among the poorer craftsmen, and tailors may have been even worse off since they required next to nothing by way of tools or equipment; their skill was their marketable commodity and in Tudor Liverpool it was unlikely to have been well paid. The majority of craftsmen were typical of a small town surrounded by an area with a mixed agrarian economy; they processed and supplied goods for a local

Table 6 *Probate valuations of Tudor Liverpool craftsmen*

	Household goods	Craft equipment	Farm goods	Total valuation	Debts owed to the testator	Debts owed by the testator
Reginald Melling, blacksmith, 1572	32%	25%	43%	£60 13s. 3d.	£12 9s. 3d.	£18 18s. 11d.
Ralph Edgecar, joiner, 1578	72%	3%	25%	£16 8s. 8d.		£15 6s. 8d.
Peter Ireland, joiner, 1591	56%	44%		£3 12s. 10d.		£ 4 13s. 0d.
John Smith, glover, 1591	20%	43%	37%	£65 15s. 8d.		
John Gower, weaver, 1594	75%	18%	7%	£14 1s. 1d.	£14 1s. 8d.	5s. 0d.
James Melling, shoemaker, 1603	82%		18%	£14 0s. 6d.	£2 17s. 4d.	£2 2s. 6d.

market and were virtually dependent on that market. Specialisation and sophistication were severely limited. Details of the crafts and the craftsmen are not abundant, but sufficient material survives to indicate the nature and scale of activities. The south-west Lancashire economy did not generate the demand for goldsmiths, pewterers, lace makers and embroiderers found in some towns. London had around one hundred gilds, the ultimate in Tudor specialisation.[40] Craft products in Liverpool were made and used locally, and the scope for development was slow. Potential for individual craftsmen remained restricted and, in consequence, their links with the agricultural environment strong.

Service providers

Service providers are necessary in any community; a small town was bound to have its share. Some services were those of a marketing location: the provision of food and drink by the butcher, the miller and the alehouse keeper. Some were the services found in any concentration of population: the clergyman, the school teacher and the barber-surgeon. Others still provided the services of a coastal community: the ferryman and the sailors. The claim has been made that between one quarter and one third of a town's population in the pre-industrial period was involved in service provision.[41] In Tudor Liverpool limitations of scale created by the small population both encouraged dual-employment and restricted service opportunities. The size of the service sector is, therefore, obscured by these factors and the problems of categorisation occasioned by sailors. Many seafarers had temporary and/or dual employment. It also seems likely that in a small port at this time sailing expertise was regarded only as a form of labouring.

South-west Lancashire was an area of both watermills and windmills (and even horsemills, presumably because of the unreliability and restrictive practices affecting other forms of milling). There had been a watermill on the stream draining into the Pool at Liverpool, but by the Tudor period it had been replaced by the use of two windmills, Eastham and Town End mills. Both were let as part of the fee-farm of the town. During the early part of the sixteenth century control was acquired by the Molyneux family of Croxteth, and then both mills were sub-let to the town authorities for £10 *per annum*. The lease was renewed at the existing rent during the Tudor period.[42]

In addition, individuals were taking matters into their own hands. A dispute in the town illustrates the contention that the use of horsemills could cause. One such mill had been functioning since at least 1554, but in 1588 William More esquire took his right to operate this mill to the Duchy of Lancaster courts. He claimed that he had the permission of the lessee of the windmills, Sir Richard Molyneux, to operate his horsemill, although by this time several of the town's leading merchants, such as Giles Brooke, John Bird and Richard Shaw, had also established horsemills. Part of their defence was that William More was pursuing the case out of 'private malice' and to protect his own profits. Milling was clearly a potentially profitable activity, at least when troops *en route* for Ireland were delayed in the town by adverse weather and the level of demand could not be met by traditional mills at times of calm weather.[43]

Whatever the exact profits, all of these mills needed millers to operate them. At any one time, therefore, there must have been at least two millers working in the town, although little is known of them. Probably their work was seasonal and most were part-time farmers. Leases to the millers were often fairly short-term: the Town End mill was let in 1557 to Thomas Bank for sixteen years at £4 a year.[44] With such leases it must have been difficult to establish family continuity, but Thomas Bank did hand over Town End mill to his son Ralph.[45] How profitable this occupation was for the millers is not easy to assess. Their activities were essential even if practised only intermittently in an area of mixed agriculture. Perhaps in some respects millers were regarded as employees or labourers, albeit with a specialism, working for the mill lessees.

Because of the nature of farming practice in this part of south-west Lancashire, butchers were an essential adjunct of the agricultural system.

Livestock were an important source of food, and leather products were a lucrative aspect of the economy. Predictably, butchers were concentrated in Liverpool where they could serve the largest market in the area and where, increasingly during the reign of Queen Elizabeth I, they were able to benefit from levies of men passing through the port to Ireland. Six butchers, at least, operated regularly in Liverpool, with a number of other butchers also using the trade of the town.[46] Towards the end of the century these numbers increased, although perhaps on a part-time basis.

In Liverpool the butchers had to use the market in the town to distribute their meat. The town books make plain the necessity to appoint annually two 'setters of fleshboards' to superintend the butchers' stalls on market days. Usually this task fell to two butchers, but for some periods of time their widows continued in the office, for instance John Taylor's widow from 1562 to 1573 and Hugh Brodhead's widow from 1573 to 1587.[47] Because of the numbers of butchers who were using the market at the same time there seems to have been intermittent attempts by them to 'fix' or corner the trade to their mutual advantage; in 1590 five butchers were accused of operating as partners, and in 1596 the same charge was levied against four of them.[48] Aspects of the butchery trade which must have long existed were the salting of meat for its better preservation, and the use of tallow from animals for various purposes, particularly candles. No salter is known by name in Liverpool, although Cheshire salt was readily available via the River Mersey. Candles and tapers were essential items, possibly made domestically by many people from their own supplies of tallow, while the two known tallow chandlers presumably supplied the market with better quality products.[49]

Another service providing a valuable foodstuff in this locality was, of course, fishing. The River Mersey itself was an important source of fish and along its shoreline fishing rights were important manorial perquisites. The lords of manors exploited their resources for their household consumption, and also sub-let fishing rights. Only one Liverpool merchant, however, had some old nets recorded in his probate inventory.[50] This evidence is slight, but it may indicate that most Mersey fishing was undertaken as a part-time activity or supplementary form of employment by the farmers and craftsmen of the coastal area. The low level of fishing activity recorded in probate evidence may be misleading. In 1576 it was necessary for the earl of Derby to convene an Admiralty Court in Liverpool in an attempt to prevent the use of herring boats in the Mersey and in an attempt to regulate the constriction caused by fishyards along the river; he ordered an eight-yard open channel to be maintained in the river.[51]

From Liverpool sea fishing was an obvious possibility; the principal catch seems to have been herring. This fishing began during the week after Michaelmas along the north Wales coast and continued until about St Andrew's Day at the end of November. In 1562 George Ashton had a small ship, a pickard called the *Falcon*, which sailed with a master and three crewmen. They sold their herring in Bristol and returned to Liverpool with a cargo of wheat. Hugh Kettle died in 1572 while on a fishing trip 'in the northe'.[52] Presumably a number of vessels were involved in this intermittent, small-scale activity; fishing boats had to pay only 2d. *per annum* to the town. There were attempts to control the rubbish that fishermen left about the town and to restrict the smoking of herring in houses in Liverpool. From 1574 at least, fishing on Sundays was subjected to a 20s. fine and from 1578 fishermen were ordered not to mend their nets and carry fish on Sundays until after evening prayer.[53] Although dealing in herring was by the barrel, on several occasions the water bailiffs were required to see that some fish was sold in smaller quantities: just 1d. or 2d. worth. In 1595 six herring cost 1d.[54] Not all of the fish sold in the town came, however, from local boats. During Lent it was usual for two or three pickards from Scotland, Ireland or 'the North' to arrive in Liverpool to sell barrels of herring and small quantities of white fish or salmon. In 1573 eighty barrels of salted herring were sold by Dublin men at 16s. 8d. a barrel.[55] At some times of the year fish must have been quite readily available in the town, but fishing remained an intermittent and, perhaps subsidiary, activity. William Ainsdale of Kirkdale, the adjacent township to Liverpool, had nets worth 6s 8d. and an old boat valued at nearly £7; he had also a yoke of oxen, cattle, a horse, pigs and barley recorded in his 1578 probate inventory.

It seems most unlikely that any individual in Liverpool depended solely on fishing as a means of livelihood. During the herring season greater numbers of men were involved, but during most of the year the crews of the fishing vessels must have found employment as sailors on trading vessels or in a non-maritime occupation. In the second half of the Tudor period over seventy men from the town are known to have been sailors, although little is known of their activities.[56] Some are recorded for only a short length of time, while others clearly found their principal living over much of their lives from working at sea. All mariners were probably hired for the duration of each voyage unless, of course, they were working in family concerns. Because of the nature of Liverpool's trade many of their voyages were coastal or to Ireland; a few did get to France and Spain. John Lambert returned to England in 1586 after twelve months and twenty days of captivity in Bilbao in northern Spain.[57]

Some families in Liverpool had an enduring interest in the sea (or could find little alternative employment): the Ainsdale, the Kettle, the Lawrence, the Rimmer and the Walker families all had three members at sea during the second half of the sixteenth century. Several more families had two relatives who were sailors.[58] These mariners were to be found in residence throughout the town; the town was so small that there does not appear to have been any maritime residential segregation. Several of the mariners are known to have had subsidiary and/or part-time employment, and in view of the uncertain nature of seafaring, it would seem likely that many more had a dual type of occupation. Sailors, were not, however, without some education; some did make their mark on indentures and various documents but the majority were able, at least, to sign their names.

The most direct maritime service provided in Liverpool was the ferry across the River Mersey. The operation of this ferry had belonged to the monks of Birkenhead Priory before passing to the Crown in the earlier part of the sixteenth century. The actual ferry had long been sub-let, and by the second half of the century had been leased by Sir Richard Molyneux who, needless to say, sub-let it again. In 1529 it was claimed that three boats operated the service, whereas in the later century the service had dual operators, for instance Peter Gregory and Ralph Oliver in 1565. On occasions the service could be maintained by their widows.[59] Most ferrymen worked the boat for only a few years, perhaps on a part-time basis. Some families, however, sustained an intermittent interest over several generations, such as the Corbet and Jumpe families.[60] Sometimes the ferrymen were referred to as labourers, providing an indication of contemporary opinion of their status. Two of the ferrymen came from among the migrants to Liverpool and were perhaps glad of the even temporary employment: John Gregory came from Dublin and Thomas Lorimer (alias Scot) from Scotland.[61]

A variety of restrictions governed the operation of the ferry and clearly a smooth service was not always provided. The vessel must have been usually sail-powered since, when adverse weather or the tide disrupted the crossing, rowers had to be hired. However, the ferrymen were not always available when their passengers were and quite frequently various ferrymen were reported at town assemblies for charging tolls from the freemen of the town. The one-way fare was 4½d. in 1572. Freemen and their families were entitled to travel freely, although charges could be made for their horses and goods. The ferrymen were, not unexpectedly, reluctant to undertake the crossing without remuneration. Another disruption to the regular service was caused by the ferrymen taking the boat elsewhere, presumably for a worthwhile fee or about their own business, such as to Chester or Warrington.[62]

The most prevalent service occupation in Tudor Liverpool was the provision of food and drink. National legislation governed the licensing and operation of alehouses and was enforced by the local magistracy with the assistance of town officials.[63] It is evident from surviving documentation that it was not easy to distinguish between permanent alehouses properly licensed and operating regularly and the more temporary phenomena. Temporary might mean that the operation of the alehouse was short-lived because the proprietor was seeking a short-term, supplementary means of livelihood, for instance a widow or a labourer. Temporary might also mean that the alehouse was a regular facility but operated only at worthwhile times such as market and fair days. It seems likely that many temporary operations were unlicensed. During the 1580s Lancashire justices were seeking to regulate prices and unlicensed activity.[64]

Alehouses operated in many hamlets in south Lancashire but, understandably, Liverpool had a greater concentration, even if some were temporary features of market day. The town assembly in 1579 pronounced there to be too many ale and tippling houses, yet just three years later agreed that Catherine Diall, a widow, could bake and brew for maintenance of herself and her poor family.[65] The uncertain existence of unlicensed alehouses obscures the more substantial operations. It seems unlikely, however, that many alehouses in Liverpool provided their proprietors with their sole means of income. The competition from other alehouses was too great and the local market too restricted to provide a flourishing sole occupation. Alehouse-keeping was a significant service in terms of numbers of people associated with it and the opportunity it afforded for female participation, yet in this location it was largely a bye-employment.[66]

In a small town there were few providers of professional services. Thanks to the impact of the Reformation and the disappearance of the chantry chapels, the numbers of clergymen in Liverpool declined. By the second half of the sixteenth century there was St Nicholas' chapel with just the one clergyman, whereas in the first half of the century there had probably been four or five clergy. The survey of 1548 had recorded four chantry priests, at least one of whom had been in the town since 1512.[67] From 1557 to 1563 Evan Thomasson alias Nicholson, the younger son of a local burgess, served as curate at St Nicholas', seemingly to the satisfaction of the congregation. In 1559 the town books recorded he 'hath well and diligentlie served as minister'.[68] Yet replacement may not have been easy; not until 1572 is John Milner known of, and then he was dead by 1574. In October of that year James Seddon was licensed. Again he was a local man who continued in post until his death during the winter of 1588–89, despite inferences that he had been unfit for duty in 1584.[69] Hugh Janion ministered in the town from 1590 until 1596, also with references to his unsuitability for the job. Ralph Bentley was recognised as his successor but by only 1598 he was called upon to explain 'whether he be mynded to continewe in his place'.[70] Clearly the chapel in Liverpool was not a desirable living that could be easily filled by a well-qualified clergyman. Changing religious opinion and considerations of the town council may have played their parts, but a stipend of £12 5s. 7d. was scarcely attractive. The town collected £8 by ley, and £4 17s. 5d. was provided by the Duchy of Lancaster from the proceeds of the dissolved chantries. The sum had to be collected at Halton Castle (Runcorn) with 11s. 10d. deducted for fees, portage, the clerk and transport.[71] By the end of the Tudor period this lowly stipend must have been declining still further in real terms. A telling testimony to a small town must have been this provision of just one, possibly inferior, clergyman.

One of the chantry priests had from 1515 fulfilled the role of schoolmaster. By the 1540s at the time of the dissolution of the chantries this had been Humphrey Crosse.[72] The town had eventually recovered control of the endowment for the school and was able to continue with the appointment of one schoolteacher.[73] Early in 1565 Ralph Higginson of Everton was the schoolmaster, but he had left by the end of the year to go to Oxford University where he obtained his BA in 1569. Presumably he had been teaching temporarily in an unqualified state. He was replaced early in 1566 when four of the town's aldermen hired John Ore BA in London, although he probably never appeared in Liverpool.[74] In March 1568 John Ryle was licensed by the bishop of Chester, settled in the town, married and took up residence in Dale Street. His salary continued at the rate established in 1565, £10 per annum. He was replaced in 1583 by Richard Welling, an ex-pupil of Farnworth School near to Widnes, who had gone to Oxford in 1578. Richard Welling taught for ten years until illness forced his retirement just prior to his death in 1594. His successor Robert Baker had just graduated, but clearly chose to move on rapidly from Liverpool and by 1598 a replacement proved difficult to find.[75] The town's clergyman, Thomas Wainwright, agreed to run the school 'untill God sende us some sufficient learned man', suggesting that there was not great demand for this poorly paid teaching post in a small town in the north-west of England. By 1600 a ley collected for the schoolmaster's salary indicates that the post had been filled and by 1602 Hamlet Webster was the holder of the office, remaining until 1616 when he moved back to his former school in Farnworth.[76]

A map or 'plot' that was drawn in the early 1560s to show the boundary between the queen's manor of Wavertree and Richard Lathom's manor of Allerton. Some landmarks appear on the map such as Childwall church (*centre, top*) but the whole is rather crudely executed, suggesting that the map was produced by someone who was inexperienced in the new Tudor skill of map-making. Liverpool at this time was surrounded by rural areas such as these and the town operated as an important centre for local marketing.

NATIONAL ARCHIVES, DUCHY OF LANCASTER MAP AND PLAN COLLECTION, DL31/73, WAVERTREE AND ALLERTON *c.*1564

In the Tudor period Childwall parish was one of the typically large south Lancashire parishes. A priest was recorded there in Domesday Book. The church building (*left*) appears to date from a fourteenth-century rebuilding and the Norris family from Speke funded a chantry chapel here. Quite probably the finely engraved brasses of Henry Norris and his wife Clemence dating to the early sixteenth century were originally located in this chapel. With the dissolution of chantry chapels as part of Reformation policy in the mid-Tudor period the brasses were relocated.

BY KIND PERMISSION OF THE VICAR, ALL SAINTS CHILDWALL

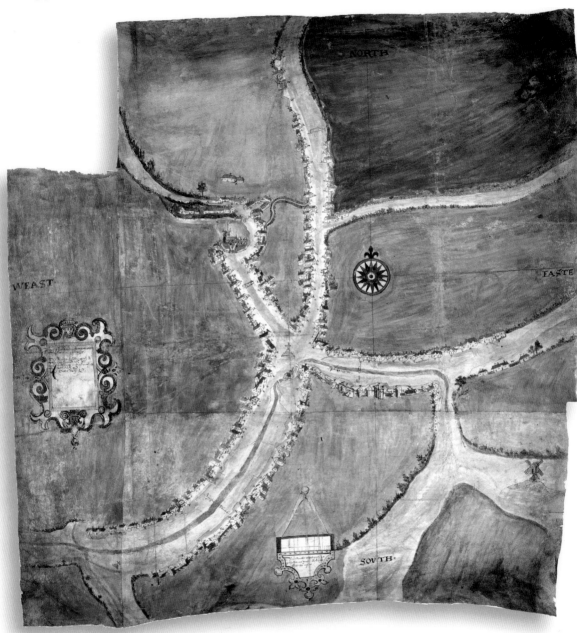

This lovely map of Ormskirk in 1609 provides detail of a small Lancashire market town with a simple plan. Houses line the streets in all directions from the crossroads but there is no sign of development behind the street frontages. As in Liverpool, the market took place in the streets themselves, with temporary stalls. Although having a smaller population than Liverpool at this time, Ormskirk was, nonetheless, a serious rival for local trade.

NATIONAL ARCHIVES, DUCHY OF LANCASTER MAP AND PLAN COLLECTION, DL31/105, ORMSKIRK 1609

The disappearance of the chantry priests had also perhaps created the opportunity for the town's scribe/clerk and recorder of the town books, Adam Pendleton. He did all sorts of public and private writing and collected a variety of fees for his services, such as 6d. for a bond of recognisance by an alehousekeeper or 6d. from each new freeman. He also enrolled apprenticeship indentures and undertook all sorts of miscellaneous clerical commissions. By the later sixteenth century the schoolmaster did duty as the chapel clerk, with wages of £1 15s. 0d. Both scribes were able to command a certain amount of private work such as the writing of wills.[77]

Many schoolteachers and clergymen in south-west Lancashire were local products, particularly of Farnworth school. Elsewhere in the country the quality of these professional people could have been improving during the Tudor period, but in this area there is evidence of only a BA degree by way of qualification, and not always that.[78] The salaries available were insufficient to attract the better qualified and interest to 'outsiders' was minimal: the penalty of a small town environment. This characteristic in itself says something about the service occupations available in Liverpool during the sixteenth century. Millers, butchers and fishermen were all providing their own type of processing and service in a small town. To some extent they were specialists and their specialisms were very traditional and necessary in a locally based economy. Services of a less essential, or even luxury, nature were almost non-existent. During this period, for example, Chester had several barbers, barber-surgeons and apothecaries; in Liverpool just one barber is known, Richard Lyle who lived in a house in the chapelyard (possibly formerly a chantry priest's house) from 1590.[79] Likewise only two surgeons are recorded, although probably only one spent a brief period of time in Liverpool. William Dorter had his freeman's fine remitted in 1576 providing he took up residence in the town, but there is no evidence that the inducement was effective. John Ulster alias Derby settled briefly, from 1592 to 1598.[80] For a proportion of Liverpool's population service occupations bolstered their income and livelihood, but in a small town the market potential for services remained too restricted to provide a full-time form of employment for many.

Servants and labourers

The appellations 'servant' and/or 'labourer' are terms not easy to interpret with precision. During the Tudor period these words can sometimes be used in an almost interchangeable manner with very generalised meanings or, at other times, in quite specific ways. Some individuals thus identified may have been at a transitory stage in their employment pattern; others may have found it impossible to escape from their situation. Whatever their exact circumstances all servants and most labourers were performing some form of service for those that could afford to employ them.

Numbers of servants are difficult to calculate. Most of the merchants in Liverpool must have had a few household servants and used some casual labour at least from time to time. Anne More chose to refer in her 1589 will to five domestic servants, but whether she employed more is impossible to know. Board and lodgings were provided usually for servants, with varying degrees of comfort, but cash wages may have been difficult to find and pay regularly. The only substantial indication of the range of wages available in this area is provided in the 1587 rental of William More esquire of Bank Hall, adjacent to Liverpool. His servants were paid quarterly, in addition to receiving board and lodging. One male servant received £8 *per annum*, but the rates for other men were lower, £5 6s. 8d. and £4 a year. The highest paid female servant had £3 12s. 0d., while the majority of both male and female servants got from £1 12s. 0d. to £2 16s. 0d. a year.[81]

Labourers may not have had accommodation provided with their employment, but their status did have a level of recognition that distinguished them from itinerant and more casual labour. From 1576 onwards the town books record some labourers securing their freedom in the town: four men in 1576 and 1582, two in 1588, one in 1590 and 1594, three in 1596 and one more in 1600.[82] This recording may have been some response to the dictates of the 1572 Poor Law and demonstrate a wish to identify formally the labourers that were known locally, yet freemen-labourers are also a testimony to the unsophisticated state of the economy in a small town. Accommodation in Liverpool in shared tenements and cottages built at the rear of burgages must have been available and accessible.[83] In 1593 the town did fix the wages for agricultural labourers at not more than 3d. per day. By 1599, however, two labourers were presented at the town's assembly for receiving wages in excess of this rate: surely not an act of generosity on the part of the employer but a reflection of the demand for at least some labourers.[84] Even so, existence for a family at this level of pay and without food, fuel and accommodation being provided must have been very marginal.

The tantalising difficulty with these labourers and servants is to distinguish them from each other and, separately or together, estimate what proportion of the population they represented. Estimates suggest they could form between a fifth and a third of a rural community.[85] In Liverpool it seems unlikely that many families employed servants in large numbers, and that craftsmen and tradesmen had need of more than very small numbers of labourers, if any. Perhaps a quarter to one third of the population would be a reasonable estimate for servants and labourers, with the recognition that many labourers must have been employed only casually. Five servants of one of the wealthier merchants, Thomas Bavand, are identifiable during the 1580s: Thomas Anderton, Ellen Dawbie, Alice Lufton, Anne Shepherd and Anne Woodward. Interestingly all of the surnames are unusual in Liverpool at this time, and Dawbie, Lufton and Shepherd are unusual throughout south-west Lancashire.[86] There is the suggestion here that for the migrant in this area employment as a servant was one of the few options available.

Agricultural interests

One of the great uncertainties about a small town is the extent to which the economy and occupational structure were identifiable from those of the rural hinterland. Many of Liverpool's population in the Tudor period were probably always involved in dual forms of employment and, for many, agricultural activities were a part of this diverse occupational existence. The lowland area of south Lancashire lent itself to pasture land and meadow, while the climate allowed the cultivation of wheat and barley on suitable soils.[87]

The surviving town field and heath adjacent to Liverpool had a strong influence on the urban economy. There was unrestricted transfer and division of strips in the field, that was not enclosed until the eighteenth century; the land was used for both arable and pasture activities. The heath to the east of the Pool was controlled by the town and used for supplies of gorse, turf, marl and clay as well as for pasture.[88] During the Tudor period the town appointed annually a series of agricultural officials: burleymen to supervise the use of the town field, a hayward, and moss reeves to supervise the exploitation of the heath. Intermittent attention to the pinfold, regulations governing access to the town field, and bye-laws to ensure all swine and sheep were driven from the town in the morning and not returned until 4.00 p.m. testify to ever-present agricultural concerns.[89]

What is uncertain is the extent to which these agricultural interests were subsidiary to other economic activities and forms of employment or, for some of the population, dominant. For the merchants of the town farm goods were of little importance; they had virtually no agricultural equipment and only a few animals. Richard Hitchmough (1574) had pigs and geese, Richard Bird (1595) had just poultry, Robert Wolfall (1578) had an old horse, and Thomas Bolton (1597) had an old horse and two cows. For these men agricultural interests ensured a household supply of some food and perhaps a horse for transport. For some craftsmen, such as the joiner Ralph Edgecar (1578) and the glover John Smith (1591) this same balance of interest obtained.

For others in a small town agriculture could be of dominant importance. Some Liverpool men, even by the end of the sixteenth century, were identified by their contemporaries as 'yeomen', such as Thomas Hitchmough (1591) and Gilbert Formby (1596). Even into the 1590s husbandmen could be admitted as freemen of the town.[90] The probate inventory of husbandman Richard Denton (1580) shows no differences from those of neighbouring rural farmers; he had a pair of wheels, two corn wains, a turf wain, a muck wain, three ploughs, two pairs of plough irons, two harrows, three yokes, a hammer, a little axe, two forks, one spade, a worthing hook, one horse, two oxen, one bullock, one cow, six ewes and six lambs, a sow and five pigs, four ducks, three geese, barley, oats, vetches and hay. Some individuals in Liverpool throughout the Tudor period were virtually dependent on agricultural activities for their livelihood and local circumstances at the end of the period enhanced rather than diminished this characteristic.

Additional land became available for exploitation adjacent to Liverpool in Toxteth Park. The area had been afforested in the thirteenth century and by the fourteenth century was probably paled. The earl of Derby had acquired control of the former royal park and by the mid-sixteenth century was appointing a keeper to supervise it from the new lodge at Otterspool. In 1590, however, the sixth earl petitioned the Queen to dispark the area. Local interest was such that by the time official permission was granted a year later Liverpool's assembly had discussed the plans.[91] By the mid-1590s William, the sixth earl, claimed that much of the park had been 'improved' and let to tenants. Prior to disparking the inhabitants of Liverpool and surrounding manors had, on payment, pastured cattle in the park and presumably were well aware of the opportunities the park offered. The earl ultimately sold the park and by 1604 it was in the hands of Sir Richard Molyneux. By this time much of the area of the park was enclosed and converted to arable and pasture land, while two watermills and over twenty houses had been erected.[92]

Individuals from Liverpool clearly played a major part in this exploitation. About twenty households were resident in the park by the early seventeenth century and a further eleven people rented land there.[93] Those able to take advantage of this opportunity were those with the resources for additional entry fines and rents. Many Liverpool merchants discovered new agricultural interests. By 1603 John Bird's inventory recorded his house in the park with £40 of corn (in February) and oxen valued at £25. His widow kept 'the Parke house' with its modest furniture and agricultural equipment (1611). Robert More had a park barn in addition to his barn in Liverpool (1608), as did Giles Brooke (1614). Ellen, the widow of the merchant Richard Hodgson, had the profits of her husband's investment in Toxteth Park until her death in 1609: land, barns, edifices, buildings and one of the new watermills.

Far from declining, the farming interests of many in Liverpool had been strengthened by the 'development' of Toxteth Park. Those that benefited directly were those with the resources for investment: the merchants of the town. In addition, the development must have created new opportunities for servants, labourers, some craftsmen and some providers of services. In a small town expansion of opportunity for all forms of employment was usually quite restricted. Ironically for an urban community, Toxteth Park and its agricultural exploitation provided a welcome possibility for development and exploitation.

CHAPTER FOUR

Domestic trade

T HE PRIME FUNCTION of even the smallest town was to provide
a local marketing venue. The merchants, the craftsmen and the
service providers had to have an outlet through which to operate; the
rural hinterland had to have a location through which to distribute
surplus produce. Since its thirteenth-century foundation Liverpool's
Saturday market and annual fair days had provided the town with this
trading focus, but not all medieval markets flourished or even sustained
themselves. South Lancashire was a thinly populated area with an
agrarian economy based on some pastoral activity for cattle, horses and
sheep and some cultivation of food and fodder crops. Much farming
activity at this time was at near subsistence level; not promising material
for a thriving market. A measure of the small-scale nature of Liverpool's
trade is to be found in the continuing use throughout the Tudor period of
a 'common' warehouse in the town. As late as 1572 the town's assembly
took the decision to rent the former chapel of St Mary del Quay as their
'new warehouse', rather than persisting with the use of the lower part of
the common hall for this purpose. A confirmation of the modest level of
trade is found in the possibility of town 'bargains' being negotiated for
certain commodities on behalf of all freemen in the town.[1]

The market

In view of this limited volume of trading activity there was little
physical provision for the weekly market, although there were plenty
of regulations about its conduct. Streets were designated for the sale of
particular produce. Butter and eggs were sold beside the High Cross,
with perennial attempts to prevent forestalling of these easily portable
commodities. The grain market was in Castle and Dale Streets, with
Lancashire dealers restricted to the east side and Cheshire dealers to
the west side of the streets. There was an attempt to confine the cattle
and livestock market to the area near the castle, but it did not prove
easy to restrict the animals from access to the other streets in the town.

Local interest was protected through the regulation that 'foreigners' (non-Liverpudlians) could not buy until one hour after the market bell had been rung to commence trading activities. In Liverpool market stalls, or booths, were used by some traders in the absence of any covered market facility. It was customary throughout the Tudor period to appoint annually a 'setter of fleshboards' to superintend the placement and the clearance of butchers' stalls and their refuse. From 1589 two general officials for 'booths' were appointed by the town; perhaps a small indication of growing market activity.[2]

The existence of shops as retail outlets is the subject of some conjecture in the sixteenth century. Some kinds of shop may have been operated by craftsmen who simply had an accumulation of stock. More genuine shopkeepers would have depended primarily on their retail trade of goods that they themselves did not produce.[3] In Tudor Liverpool there is no substantial indication that the former of these possibilities obtained, but there is some suggestion that a few merchants may have had a version of a retail shop. Alexander Garnet had a draper's shop

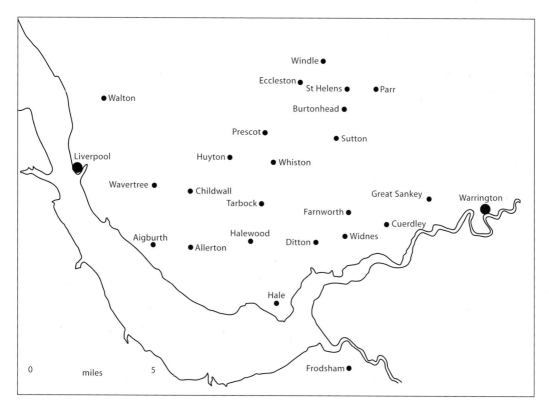

Locations from which traders came to Liverpool's market during the sixteenth century. Places such as Ormskirk, Prescot and Warrington provided some competition for a small town.

by 1564, while James Berry was in trouble with the town's assembly in 1567 for 'openyng his shoppe and retaylyng his wares' when he was not a freeman. Robert Hitchmough had certainly been operating a mercer's shop for some years before his death in 1584.[4] It seems likely that during the later Tudor period a small number of these shops had come into existence. An intriguing comment in the town books of 1589 alludes to Jane Aspendine, a spinster, who was keeping a shop when not a freeman; this represents the only indication of female involvement in retailing.[5]

Considerable interest was shown in regulating trading activities, perhaps a realistic possibility in such a small town. As in many towns, intermittent attempts were made to enforce standard weights and measures. In 1560 the town's assembly specified that wool, flax, hemp and tallow were to be sold at a weight of eighteen pounds to the stone, and that the town would provide certain standard measures: a banded barrel, a banded windle, a brass yard, and a beam and scales. Whether these provisions assisted smoother transactions is not known; certainly only a few years later there were market disputes over corn sales. During the later 1560s three attempts were made to enforce the use of a standard windle of fifty-six quarts or fourteen gallons; it had to be fastened with a lock to a bench in the common hall.[6] Interest in weights and measures continued and the leavelooker officials were required to check the weights of brass, iron, lead and stone to ascertain that they registered sixteen ounces to the pound and that all yards, ells and sticks were tested for length against the town's iron standard. This activity did not, however, prevent William Pendleton buying with a 'greate' measure and selling by a 'smale' measure in 1579. Disputes over websters' weights continued into the 1580s. Even water could cause problems, and in 1590 a half-windle measure was provided for water that was to be taken on board ships.[7] Provision of standard weights and measures was clearly a desirable, but not easily enforceable, market practice.

The mainstay of Liverpool's weekly market was the exchange of local produce: fish, cattle, wool, grain, butter, cheese, eggs, poultry, vegetables, fruit; and the distribution of goods produced by the town's craftsmen: harness, shoes, boots, gloves, clothing, nails, hinges and joinery. From Liverpool's immediate hinterland the only significant commodity was coal that was available from several locations in Prescot parish.[8] By the second half of the sixteenth century some of this coal was being regularly distributed in Liverpool. It was conveyed on horseback and by cart with such regularity that it was blamed for damage to the paving of the town's streets, and from 1574 those carrying coal in carts into the town were obliged to pay 2d. a cart towards repair of the streets. Some of this coal was for export and some was sold in the town. Four

Liverpool and two Everton probate inventories record supplies of coal, and Miles Kirkdale was required to remove his stack of turf and coal from beside his neighbour's house.[9]

The annual fairs were an opportunity for Tudor Liverpool to widen the activities and potential of the weekly market. A number of other locations in south Lancashire had acquired grants in the thirteenth or fourteenth centuries to establish fair days: Ormskirk, Wigan, Newton, Warrington, Farnworth, Prescot, Roby, Tarbock and Hale, in addition to Liverpool.[10] Few survived into the Tudor period; the local economy was too restricted. The two fair days in Liverpool were the feast of St James (25 July) and Martinmas (11 November). During the sixteenth century the two fairs did operate, but little evidence survives to provide detail of the range and volume of trading activity. Chester goldsmiths attended, and during the 1570s horse sales involved Shrewsbury, Gloucester, Caernarfon, Lincolnshire and Berwick.[11] At least one of these transactions involved a soldier *en route* to or from Ireland, so it is possible that rather unusual trading patterns prevailed at certain times. Probably Liverpool's fairs during the Tudor period had mainly local agricultural significance, particularly for livestock, and their impact was confined mostly to south-west Lancashire.

The paucity of material relating to Liverpool's fairs is typical of much domestic trade in England during the Tudor period. Since this trade was largely untaxed it generated few systematic records. Relatively little is known about roads and land transport. This means that the trading activities of markets, fairs, pedlars, shops and craftsmen are impossible to discern fully. The extent of influence of a market depended much on the nature of its agricultural hinterland, on the industrial possibilities of an area, on the local terrain and transport facilities, and on external trading opportunities.[12] Research on the market town of Preston in Lancashire has considered distance to next available markets, the homes of stall-holders, and the lists of out-burgesses to conclude that the area dominated by the market lay within a seven-miles radius. Up to twelve miles away Preston's market still had a considerable influence. Manchester's market in the later Tudor period had an inner zone of influence of seven to twelve miles and an outer zone of up to twenty miles.[13]

In all likelihood the extent of the influence of Liverpool's market was somewhat similar to that of Preston. Insufficient probate debt lists and inadequate market records provide only disconnected indications of market activity. The town books refer to individuals from Everton, Kirkdale, Crosby, Formby, Woolton, Huyton and Prescot trading with some regularity at Liverpool's market: a not unexpected catchment area of about eight miles in radius.[14] Money lending, goods on credit and payment by instalment were all commonplace forms of transaction in the Tudor period. The probate records of some Liverpool craftsmen indicate some scale of indebtedness. Many debtors and creditors lived within the immediate locality and common names in the town were carefully distinguished by occupation and use of 'junior' and 'senior'. Beyond the town individuals were identified by place of residence. Two Liverpool joiners owed money at distances up to ten miles away, in Knowsley, Halebank and Tarbock. A glover owed money in Bolton and had a debtor from Wirral. A weaver was owed money from Farnworth, Prescot, Manchester and the Isle of Man, and a shoemaker was anticipating money from Knutsford in Cheshire and Drogheda in Ireland.[15] Debt lists from other south-west Lancashire parishes substantiate this local connection with Liverpool, for example in several probate records from Huyton.[16] On its side of the River Mersey Liverpool's market area probably extended beyond these eight miles, for instance to Ormskirk. It was worthwhile for John Lee to sell the shoes he had made in Liverpool.[17] Trade beyond about eight miles was certainly possible in the Tudor period, but remained intermittent and limited. Ormskirk to the north-east and Prescot to the east probably provided the usual extent of the regular use of Liverpool's market, as well as the saturation of opportunity for a small town.

The local market in Liverpool was typical in many respects of those in many small towns. It did, however, have the additional attraction of its coastal location and of the merchants who were able to trade overseas. Their contacts brought some goods to the domestic market even if they were destined principally for export. Attempts were made at the market to protect local interest from activity by 'foreigners' such as the Bolton and Blackburn men selling iron and timber in 1564 or the Bolton, Wigan and Manchester merchants bringing hops, tallow and soap into the town in 1582. During the 1580s and 1590s a number of Wigan merchants attempted to deal regularly in the town.[18] The Shuttleworth family from Gawthorpe near Burnley obtained Spanish iron from Liverpool in 1593, while the accounts of Lord Mounteagle from Hornby in north Lancashire indicate that on occasions a servant travelled to the town for purchases of wine.[19] Most of these contacts were quite infrequent. The most regular Liverpool trading connection lay with the Manchester area and its supply of textiles. During the early 1560s Adam Byrom of Salford had sufficient business to use John Hewitt as his factor in Liverpool and to lease premises in Juggler Street.[20] In 1564 Alexander Garnet's shop in the town was stocked with Manchester cloth, and several Liverpool merchants exported cloth and imported other goods through the port in conjunction with Manchester merchants. The usual commodities were Manchester narrow cloths: cottons, kerseys, rugs and friezes. More variety was, however, possible; over a thirty-years period Richard Fox of Manchester sent hops, soap, alum, aniseed and nails to Dublin and Drogheda in Liverpool ships, while importing linen yarn and wool. Several other merchants from Manchester, Salford and Ashton-under-Lyne operated in this manner during the reign of Queen Elizabeth I.[21]

Land and water transport was needed to support this trade. Pickards and other small boats were used for travel via the River Mersey to Frodsham and Warrington; the owner of Liverpool's largest vessel in 1565, the 40-ton *Eagle*, had also a very small boat for local work.[22] The Mersey provided the connection to the Manchester area and also to north Cheshire and via Frodsham to the central Cheshire salt area. At the time of the disastrous fire in Nantwich in 1583 we know that several Liverpool merchants had interests there.[23] A few Kendal merchants from Cumberland used Liverpool for the export of their textiles, a Yorkshire butcher was in Liverpool in 1567, and a rich stock of goods belonging to a Yorkshire clothier was lost from a Liverpool ship in 1574. During the 1560s Liverpool's own merchants frequented Barnsley fair, dealt with Coventry merchants and arranged for the export to Ireland of Hallamshire (Sheffield) knives.[24] More distant, but not surprisingly, Liverpool had direct links with London. The capital dominated trade during the Tudor period as a national market emerged. Some London merchants had interests in the north-west of England; they are mentioned, for example, in the 1550s and 1560s. A London grocer supplied Adam Pendleton in Liverpool with calico cloth, pepper, saffron, raisins, dates and sugar.[25] Despite a distance of some two hundred miles, transport between Liverpool and London could be quite prompt. Many of the town's merchants were familiar with the capital. In 1555 the mayor and several merchants spent some weeks in London. Usually there was some specific reason to make the long journey, in particular legal activities, such as the evidence provided for the Admiralty Court in Southwark about a grounded Dublin vessel in 1566. While in London it was usual to transact a variety of business on their own, as well as on the town's and friends' accounts.[26] Travel to the capital, although possible, was expensive. Robert Wytter allowed 50s. for himself and 13s. 4d. for horse hire to reach London in 1574. The previous year a deputation from Liverpool to the Privy Council had breakfasted at the mayor's house on 20 April and reached London seven days later. They had transacted their business by 8 May and so left on the 9th; they reached Liverpool again on the 16th.[27] Transport from Liverpool to all parts of England and Wales was feasible in the Tudor period; frequently the expense and time did not warrant it. Without significant growth in the town's population the domestic market was of finite proportions. Quite extensive geographical contacts brought a variety of goods to Liverpool's market and fairs but routine and regular trade remained confined to an eight-mile radius.

The port

King John can have had little interest in the foundation of a borough in the north-west of England other than for its value as an alternative port for the embarkation of troops and supplies to Ireland. By the Tudor period that potential had been realised: the natural anchorage – the Pool – on the northern shore of the Mersey estuary had become the focus for Liverpool's shipping activities. The development, however, was only modest and a small Tudor town the result. During the sixteenth century there were never a great many ships in the port, and many of the small fleet were vessels of only moderate size. Nonetheless, this shipping provided the town with one of its distinctive characteristics: seaborne trade.

During the Tudor period it is hard to produce precise statistics for any one year, but 1558 was an exception. In that year the mayor of Liverpool reported that there were just thirteen ships sailing from the town. When a national certificate of shipping was produced two years later it was claimed Liverpool had no vessel over 100 tons, and 61 mariners. At this same time Chester had two vessels over 100 tons and 74 mariners, while London had twenty-two such ships and 703 mariners. Not long afterwards a little more detail emerges when commissioners listed twelve vessels in Liverpool of 6 tons or more and 74 mariners. By 1582 the town was reported to have ten ships, all of them less than 80 tons, ten ships' masters and 46 mariners. During the next two decades no further listings appear, although in 1597 all new ships constructed since 1581 with a £25 royal allowance were recorded; there were forty-six in total and just one from Liverpool. By 1601 Liverpool's mayor had occasion to complain about the excessive requisitioning of his town's ships for transport to Ireland; he alluded to twenty vessels.[28]

Clearly it is hard to know which vessels exactly were being counted and how accurately any list was made. In all likelihood, Liverpool never had more than about fifteen ocean-going ships at any one time during the Tudor period. In addition there may well have been some smaller fishing and coastal vessels of 6–8 tons. What is clear is that even the ocean-going vessels were never large. Some official listings may well have exaggerated the tonnage that was available, such as that recorded in 1582 when the *Hope* was listed as 60 tons and the *Lantern* as 36 tons; the port books for this period record these ships consistently at 30 and 26 tons respectively. Many of Liverpool's ships were of less than 20 tons and the larger components of the small fleet were only 30–36 tons.[29]

Using Liverpool's port books, after they become available from 1565, an indication can be gleaned of the number of vessels at sea.[30] Using the searcher's and the customer's accounts from Michaelmas 1565 to Michaelmas 1566 a total of thirteen vessels were recorded with Liverpool as their home port. Tonnage figures may vary slightly from one entry to another and, occasionally, there is uncertainty about the home port of Wirral-based vessels. The two largest ships were the *Eagle* and *George* at 30 tons each, and then there were four ships at 24–26 tons each: the *Michael*, the *Saviour*, the *Henry* and the *William*. Four of these larger, but not large, ships made voyages to Spain and France. The remainder of Liverpool's modest fleet comprised vessels of 14–16 tons: the *Peter*, the *Falcon*, the *Mary George*, the *Bartholomew*, the *Sunday*, the *Elizabeth* and the *Michael*. The larger ships carried crew of 8–12 men while the smaller vessels required 5–8 mariners, although the exact crewing of vessels was likely to have been a rather fluid practice.[31] In addition to this fleet there was a number of smaller coastal and estuary boats (not recorded in the 1565–66 port books), such as the *Swallow* of 8 tons and the *Good Luck* of 6 tons: both requiring just three men to crew them.[32]

By 1582–83 this Liverpool fleet had probably increased in size slightly; sixteen vessels were recorded and the tonnage had grown a little. The *Michael* was listed as 40 tons and the *Hope* at 36 tons. Five other vessels were more than 20 tons and seven were in the 12–18 tons category. The port books recorded also the *Ellen* of 10 tons and the *Bee* of just 6 tons. Probably there were other small boats such as these. By the end of the sixteenth century, however, the loss of Franco-Iberian trade and the impact of persistent transport demands for Ireland had had their effect. From Michaelmas 1597 to Michaelmas 1598 only ten Liverpool vessels were recorded in the main port books and five more mentioned just once each among the coastal trade entries. The size of the shipping had fallen as well. The largest vessels in the fleet were five at 26 tons: the *Phoenix*, the *Steven*, the *George*, the *Hope* and the *Valentine*. Otherwise vessels were of 10–12 tons.[33]

Unfortunately the entries in the port books are rarely consistent enough during the Tudor period to provide abundant information about the length of voyages that were undertaken by these vessels. During the second half of the sixteenth century many ships appear to have made only two or three return trips in a twelve-month period. A few vessels were busier than the majority of the fleet. The *Michael*, for instance, made at least six voyages during 1565–66: five to Ireland and one to La Rochelle in France. The fastest return trip to Ireland from Liverpool was fourteen days in total, while the French journey took forty-eight days. During the 1582–83 period the *Michael* (probably a different ship with the same name) was again apparently busier than the rest of the fleet. This 16-ton ship, with John Williamson as the usual master, spent all year making return trips to Ireland; twelve were recorded throughout all months of the year. Thirteen days was the swiftest journey. Some men served as master on more than one vessel during any year. During 1597–98, for instance, Robert Kettle and William Rice shared the mastership of both the *Ellen* and the *Phoenix*. The voyages made to the northern coast of Spain lasted a few days more or less than sixty days. The Iberian journeys seem to have been undertaken by just a few of Liverpool's masters, although the limited frequency of these voyages must have made it difficult for mariners to gain this experience.

Identification of particular ships at this time is somewhat uncertain, since some names were quite popular and re-used and some ships evidently had their names changed.[34] This clearly happened in the case of the *Gift of God* that was re-named the *Marigold* in 1585. Conceivably the same happened to the *Valentine* of 1598; she may well have become the *Strange*, since the same two masters continued to operate a vessel of similar tonnage.[35] Notwithstanding a degree of imprecision of identification, Liverpool's fleet was small enough and the port books detailed enough after 1565 to allow some comment on ownership to be made. Most of the vessels were owned either independently or jointly owned. Thomas Uttyn was the sole owner from 1558 until 1582 of the 35-ton *Saviour*; Thomas Bastwell was the sole owner of the 8-ton *Swallow*; the 14-ton *Sunday* was jointly owned by William Walker and Thomas Mason; and the 26-ton *Michael* by Edward Nicholson and John Williamson. Many of these shipowners sailed as master of their own vessel, as did Thomas Uttyn and Thomas Mason, although not necessarily on every voyage. During any one year it was possible for two or three men to captain the ship on different voyages. Arrangements seem to have been reasonably fluid, but limited by the number of experienced masters available in a small town. The rotation of masters is perhaps an indication of the part-time nature of their employment and their commitment to another form of livelihood.[36] As master and/or shipowner and/or merchant these men must have had a very real and immediate interest in the success of their voyages. The frequency of the voyages must, in turn, have had a big influence on the viability of other marketing operations within Liverpool.

Although ships' carpenters operated in Tudor Liverpool, as well as the manufacturers of ropes and sails, little is known of the specifications and cost of these vessels. Aside from the smaller coastal craft, two sizes of bark predominate (the word 'ship' was rarely used): those of 12–14 tons and those of 30–40 tons. Probably all may be described as a form of pinnace with usually two masts. The hull form of a bark made it well suited for dealing with small cargoes between locations with limited port facilities. In confined waters they were quite manoeuvrable and, with almost flat hulls, they could be grounded without undue danger or difficulty.[37] The tidal Pool at Liverpool provided a sheltered anchorage and some cargoes were probably discharged straight on to the foreshore. In addition there was probably a quay of timber piles and horizontal boards at the end of Water Street near to the Tower and chapel.[38] The probate inventory of Giles Brooke (1614) valued his bark, the *Steven*, with all its loft tackle, ground tackle and other equipment, at £70. The 26-ton vessel was recorded in the port books from 1597, and so was at least seventeen years old by the time of the valuation. Sylvester Starkey's bark, the *Valentine*, was also of 26 tons. It is known since at least 1598 and was valued seventeen years later with its ground and loft tackle and cock-boat at £45. Perhaps condition as well as age was a significant factor. John Bird's vessel, the *Phoenix*, with all its furniture was assessed at £120 in 1603. Again she was of 26 tons but was only six years old. Wirral vessels of 15–30 tons were valued in the £50–£150 range, depending on size, age and condition.[39] The bark belonging to Robert Johnson of Ince Blundell, a few miles from Liverpool, was worth just £28 in 1593. As he had animals, crops, ploughs and other farm equipment recorded in his inventory, possibly his ship represents a valuation for a small coastal vessel. Certainly he had three barrels of salt, maybe from Cheshire. The vessel was important enough, however, to be bequeathed jointly to his son-in-law and step-son.

For those who owned and sailed Liverpool's ships, trade in the sixteenth century could be uncertain and success precarious. A number of Irish ports were familiar to the mariners, yet shipwreck around the coasts of the Irish Sea was not uncommon.[40] The international political situation could result in imprisonment in Spain or service in Spanish galleys. In 1586 Richard Mather persistently tried to claim compensation for his new ship laden with goods which had been seized in Bilbao. He may have inflated the losses but, nonetheless, claimed £500. Thomas Knype's *Ellen* for some reason met disaster in August 1594 while in the Mersey estuary and presumably within sight of very familiar land.[41] For merchants and shipowners from a small town, investment, without insurance, at this level was a real and ever-present risk.

The depredations of piracy were yet another routine hazard to be faced by Liverpool's ships. The level of international piracy fluctuated in seriousness in line with the vagaries of foreign policy, but it was never absent during the Tudor period. In 1562 the earl of Derby complained to the Privy Council of losses when pirates took his ship. More precise was the claim of Robert Wytter to Queen Elizabeth I's councillor, Sir Francis Walsingham, in 1581; Wytter wrote that while trading to Spain he had several times been 'spoiled' by Frenchmen and had lost £300. In consequence, Wytter went on to claim, he had only a small boat, the *Michael* of 8 tons, with which to make a poor living trading to Ireland. In foul weather, this vessel had then been driven ashore off the coast of Scotland where it and its £100 cargo had been seized by a local lord. After imprisonment Wytter and his crew had escaped to Ireland and returned to Liverpool. Robert Wytter had failed to recover his losses from King James VI of Scotland and, as far as is known, had no more success with the English government.[42]

International activity on distant seas was one aspect of this problem, but piracy could also strike close to home. During the 1580s pirates were intercepting Irish, Chester and Liverpool shipping off the north Wales coast and even off Wirral, only a few miles from home.[43] Throughout the sixteenth century all Liverpool seamen had to contend with some risk of piracy. The small town had personal testimony of the local and international perils. Nothing can have been more salutary than the voyage of the *Marigold* in 1595: near the south-west coast of France the ship was attacked by pirates and Richard Bird (brother of one of Liverpool's leading merchants) was transferred to a Spanish man-of-war. He was never heard of again.[44]

There was, of course, the contrary side to this activity. In 1563 a Lancashire pirate, Thomas Wolfall, arrived off Anglesey with a foreign bark he had captured in the English Channel; he claimed to be operating under letters of marque from the earl of Warwick. During the 1580s Humphrey Brooke of Liverpool captained the privateer, the *Relief,* which had been commissioned by his brother Giles.[45] As well as this direct form of action, there was also rather quieter, illegal trade: smuggling. In an area like south-west Lancashire and Wirral peninsula, away from the direct supervision of the Chester and Liverpool customs officials, all sorts of evasion and fraud were possible. Ships, it was claimed, often departed and returned without making any customs entry for their goods. Liverpool ships used other anchorages for unloading, such as Wallasey, Frodsham and Otterspool. Indeed, Chester's deputy customer, Thomas Wickstead, who was based in Liverpool from 1573 was accused in 1581 of using his office to favour his own commercial affairs. He was part-owner of a ship, traded as a merchant, and had six or seven warehouses from which he discharged his goods 'at his pleasure and keepeth his original book private'. In particular, he was accused of receiving goods from London that he conveyed illegally to Ireland.[46] As well as evasion and fraud, outright smuggling was a possibility. A detailed account of such activity was provided by a Chester customs official in 1583. He claimed that at about 10 o'clock in the evening Giles Brooke and four other Liverpool merchants had kept watch in Liverpool chapelyard and had unlawfully unloaded a ship with three cartloads of barley and calf skins. In another incident the same year Giles Brooke, equipped with a pikestaff, and Nicholas Abraham, armed with a cudgel, had struck the customs official while illegally loading tallow on to the *Lantern*. Brooke was clearly exasperated by what he perceived as eavesdropping and spying, and he had threatened to cut off the official's ears if he found him there on another night.[47] The scale of this activity by one of the town's leading merchants is surely a reflection of the style of some trading and of the limited potential of a small town.

CHAPTER FIVE

Overseas trade

S EABORNE TRADE could certainly bring a wide range of opportunities, but for a small port town in Tudor England much depended
on location. Routine, mundane coastal traffic was likely to be of
considerable significance within the overall pattern of trade. Liverpool's
location dictated that the north-west counties of England, north Wales,
western Scotland and the Isle of Man were all potential trading directions. Not surprisingly, the Irish Sea area had been and remained
Liverpool's shipping focus throughout the Tudor period, with regular
connections to several Irish ports.[1] More distant European routes were
possible but difficult to sustain given Liverpool's handicap of distance
when competing with the ports of the south and east of England.

Coastal trade

There were few substantial English ports north of Liverpool, so there
was little to attract the town's shipping in that direction. Liverpool,
however, was a magnet for small vessels from these north-western
harbours. Lancastrian traffic from as far as Preston predominated, with
four or five different vessels from these ports making several trips a year
to Liverpool; in 1579, for instance, the *Jesus*, the *Trinity*, the *Mary*, the
Michael and the *Matthew* frequented the town. The dominant commodities were foodstuffs: peas, beans, barley and wheat that were shipped in
both directions in vessels usually of no more than 10 tons. Occasionally
imports from further afield into Liverpool, such as salt and iron, were
trans-shipped northwards.[2] The furthest Lancastrian port in this type
of trade was Milnthorpe.[3] Cumberland ports were also small fishing
villages. Every year Workington and Ravenglass pickards of 7, 8 or 9
tons brought herring into Liverpool. They returned with salt and mixed
cargoes. Only occasionally did Liverpool vessels venture to compete in
this direction with commodities such as salt, iron, nails, alum and wine.
In 1573 two Liverpool ships took grain and malt to Workington and
Milnthorpe, while the *Jesus* made a similar journey in 1581 laden with

iron, pitch, wine and assorted merchandise.[4] Details of this coastal trade
are limited in the port books, but there are indications that the volume
of this Cumberland trade was increasing in the last quarter of the
sixteenth century. In 1587 eight ships left Liverpool for the area whereas
between February and September 1594 twenty-one ships departed for
this area. In a twelve-month period between 1602 and 1603 twelve ships
left for Workington, twelve for Ravenglass and thirteen for Milnthorpe
with barley, oats, peas, beans, wheat, iron and pitch.[5] The nature of
the cargoes suggests that food supplies played an important part in this
increasing traffic, possibly a response to the opportunities created by the
severe harvests of the 1590s, rather than to any sustainable regular trade.
Kendal did have a woollen industry and Liverpool, although not exactly
convenient, was one of the nearest ports for distribution of this cloth,
Kendal cotton. Throughout the Tudor period some Kendal merchants
did trade through Liverpool, such as William Collinge in the 1530s, but
their fabrics never seem to have been more than a minor commodity
in the coastal trade. In 1586 the *Elizabeth* of Ravenglass did bring nails,
flocks and Kendal cotton into Liverpool, but this was a rare event.[6]

Further north still the Scottish west-coast ports were of little attraction
to Liverpool shipping with no substantial commodity to trade. Every
year a few Scottish fishing boats reached Liverpool, especially during
the autumn herring season: two pickards in 1561, two again in 1562,
and still at this level by the 1590s. Intermittently a larger Scottish vessel
visited the town – it would seem *en route* from elsewhere – for example
the 30-ton *James* in 1576 carrying bay salt from Brittany, and the *Grace of
God* in 1579 with a cargo of cod, sheep fells and old brass.[7] The infrequent
connection with Scotland remained during the Tudor period, but was
never more than inconsequential for Liverpool.

To the Isle of Man, however, Liverpool was of some importance
and just seventy miles away. The island was dependent on Liverpool
and Chester for supplies of all kinds; and exports from the island were
primary products such as sheep fells, wool, hides and herring. In 1597
a Liverpool ship returned with a typical cargo of wool, tallow, goose-
grease and puffins.[8] The Isle of Man had a political link with Liverpool
through the earls of Derby, with their governor's castle and residence
at Castletown. Imports for here and the island's population could,
therefore, be quite varied but occurred in only small volume: cloth, hats,
iron, coal, wine, salt, treen cups. Some of the trade was conducted in
Manx vessels, for instance in 1570 the *Katherine* at 4 tons, the *Margaret* at 6
tons, the *Mary* at 8 tons and the *Sunday* at 16 tons sailing out of Douglas
and Castletown. Sometimes the smaller Liverpool ships were involved
in this traffic, such as the 8-ton *Michael*.[9] During the Tudor period this

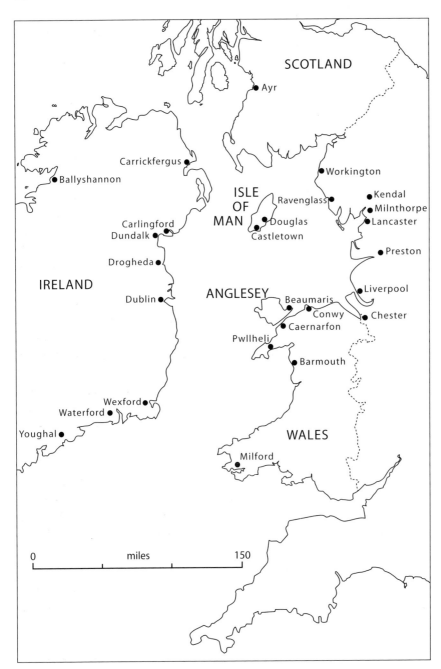

A map to indicate the regular trading area of Liverpool shipping in the sixteenth century. North Wales, the Isle of Man and north-west England provided the bulk of small-scale regional trade, whilst Irish ports, especially Dublin and Drogheda, provided routine more distant locations.

regular connection with the Isle of Man was sustained, but it remained of limited potential.

The Wirral peninsula and the north Wales coast were, likewise, areas of geographic proximity but restricted economic potential. In Tudor times these were sparsely populated coastlines with few communications inland; only Beaumaris on Anglesey had a population approaching 1,000. This had been a town of some local significance with its own overseas contacts with France and Spain, yet royal commissioners reported in 1595 that no foreign ship had visited the port for twenty years. A substantial part of Beaumaris' traffic had been taken by Liverpool and Chester ships.[10] Liverpool's interest extended to Conwy, Caernarfon, Pwllheli and Barmouth, although this activity involved only a few ships a year. Usually one or two Liverpool ships called at Beaumaris, such as the *Margaret* of 16 tons which called there in 1577 *en route* from Waterford in Ireland, or the 20-ton *Ellen* which stopped with 7 tons of salt, half a ton of iron and 8 tons of empty casks in 1597. Perhaps some of these visits were unplanned and enforced stoppages. By the later Tudor period the trade to the north Wales coast was more typically in foodstuffs: wheat, barley, oats, malt, peas, beans as well as some tons of coal. From Michaelmas 1602 until Michaelmas 1603 sixteen ships left Liverpool for this area: one to Conwy, two to Barmouth, three to Caernarfon and ten to Beaumaris. More distant contact with Wales appeared only intermittently, such as the *Julian* of Pembroke, which reached Liverpool in 1587, and the *George* of Milford which arrived with a cargo of herring in 1603.[11] Liverpool town books testify to persistent, modest Welsh contacts during the Tudor period: the men from Beaumaris in court in 1563; Welsh Alice (Alice Wynne) who achieved a degree of notoriety in the 1580s; and the painter from Ruthin in 1603.[12] There is, however, no real evidence to suggest major or developing trade and contact, beyond the established coasting routes.

Supplementing the regular pattern of traffic there were two limited opportunities for further coastal shipping. Very occasionally vessels from elsewhere in England reached Liverpool, but so singular was their arrival that they warranted special mention, such as the *Mary Grace* from the west country in 1585.[13] Also occasionally, the nobility and gentry of Lancashire chartered shipping for their own purposes. The earl of Derby did this for personal transport in order to reach the Isle of Man. In May 1583 the *Eagle*, the *Lantern* and the *Michael* were used to convey the fourth earl, his council, his household and his horses to the island. More usually the earl and the local gentry used small vessels to import household requirements. The *Mary* of 8 tons was used in 1570 to bring in bay salt, feathers and two pipes of muscadine for the earl of Derby, the *Michael* of 8 tons was commissioned in 1574 to transport rye and wine for Sir Richard Sherburne, while the *Mary John* brought in sack for Cuthbert Halsall esquire in 1598.[14] This chartering of vessels remained an intermittent and insubstantial feature of the coasting trade.

Irish trade

Notwithstanding the enduring feature of coastal trade, it was across the Irish Sea that Liverpool's main shipping interest lay. Irish routes formed the backbone of the commerce of Liverpool and Chester. Other English and Welsh ports, especially Bristol, were involved, but the two north-western ports dominated Irish traffic. Liverpool did possess two slight, but increasingly significant, advantages over Chester: its nearness to Dublin (125 miles) as well as its proximity to the textile industry of south-east Lancashire. During Henry VIII's reign John Leland had noted that Irish traders frequented Liverpool and that Manchester merchants bought their Irish yarn in the port. Leland perceptively noted a third advantage; that at Liverpool 'smaule custume payid', so that merchants increasingly chose to use the port in preference to Chester. In the mid sixteenth century the chantry commissioners reported Liverpool having 'grete concurse of strangers', while nearer the end of the Tudor period Camden reiterated the earlier opinion that the town was 'the most convenient and frequented place for setting sail into Ireland'.[15]

An important commodity from sixteenth-century Ireland was fish, and about four times a year Irish ships reached Liverpool to distribute cargoes of herring, salmon and cod.[16] Because of the nature of the Irish economy, hides from both wild and domesticated animals formed a second staple export: usually salted rather than cured. Some wool was available but mostly of inferior quality, and from 1522 to 1569 the export of wool from Ireland was prohibited by the English government. The export commodity that was increasing in importance during the Tudor period was linen yarn. Local Lancashire supplies were inadequate and accounted for a tiny proportion of the yarn supplies necessary for the textile activity in the Manchester area by the second half of the sixteenth century. This dependence on Irish imports had great consequence for Liverpool. Linen yarn, with some wool, sheep fells and calf fells, easily dominated Liverpool's imports. Demand from the Manchester linen weavers was sustained through to the end of the century. In 1565 some 358 packs of linen yarn had been unloaded at Liverpool; by 1593–94 this quantity had risen to 1,510½ packs brought in from Ireland.[17]

Despite its small population and internal distribution problems, Ireland was an ideal market for luxury products as well as more basic commodities.[18] Virtually every year wine, hops and malt were dispatched from Liverpool, as well as a variety of good quality cloth and less-expensive, serviceable materials, such as Manchester and Kendal cottons, kerseys and northern dozens. To accompany the fabrics all kinds of haberdashery items were sent: buttons, gloves, hats, stockings, combs, mirrors. Salt, iron, bags of nails and soap, both Flemish and Castilian, were important necessities for which there was a steady market. Many luxury items were available, usually in small quantities: pewter, pots and pans, cutlery especially Hallamshire knives, spices, paper, dyestuffs such as madder and ochre, alum, fish-hooks, chairs, treen cups, drinking glasses, and groceries such as prunes, aniseed, onions, ginger and liquorice.[19]

Important and commonplace as these mixed cargoes were for Liverpool ships *en route* to Ireland, it remained a characteristic that they were assembled from commodities obtained mostly from outside the town. The predominant local product that was exported was coal. Before the port books of the 1560s the annual quantities cannot be calculated, but certainly they were rising during the 1560s and 1570s. A period of stabilisation followed, with a substantial rise in the 1590s, which was probably associated with increasing military activity. Minor fluctuations in quantities may be due to inadequate record-keeping or to variable production levels, as well as to varying levels of demand in Ireland.[20] In the late 1560s over 300 tons were shipped *per annum*; during the 1580s 200–400 tons *per annum*; while in 1592–93 over 600 tons were sent. The coal was mined in the Prescot area, about ten miles from the port. It was then transported by road to Liverpool where it was shipped by the shipowner/master, rather than by the town's merchants or coal producers. Often coal provided the owner/master's part of a mixed cargo that was shared with other merchants. Quantities varied, but the smallest regular shipment of coal was 6 tons, with 10 or 12 tons being quite frequently conveyed; 20 tons formed the largest regular consignment. Exceptionally, greater quantities were possible, such as the 26 tons dispatched in one vessel in 1603. Demand during the 1590s was met with more voyages rather than with larger cargoes.[21]

Irish trade had the virtue for Liverpool of relative proximity; by the end of the Tudor period this turned out to be a mixed blessing. Ireland was not necessarily an easy area to trade with because it was relatively undeveloped economically and Ulster province, for example, was almost inaccessible by road. Fortunately, the principal towns lay on the coast, although Dublin, the main commercial and administrative centre with a population of about 5,000 by 1600, had a poor harbour. Drogheda, with a population of about 2,000 in 1600, was much more important

Table 7 *Numbers of ships leaving Liverpool for Irish ports*

	Dublin	Drogheda	Dundalk	Carrickfergus	Carlingford	Waterford	Ballyshannon	Total
1565–66	18	10						28
1569–70	15	15						30
1572–73	9	16		4				29
1573–74	11	14		10				35
1575–76	2	11		2		2		17
1579–80	13	28	1		1			43
1582–83	22	19	1					42
1590–91	12	14			3			29
1592–93	38	29	4		8			79
1593–94	34	28	6		4	2		74
1597–98	18	13		1	2			34
1602–03	18	18		2	6		2	46

Table 8 *Numbers of ships from Irish ports entering Livepool*

	Dublin	Drogheda	Dundalk	Carrickfergus	Carlingford	Waterford	Wexford	Youghal	Ballinhey	Ard	Lough Foyle	Total
1565–66	16	16				3	1					36
1569–70	21	13		2		1	3					40
1572–73	6	28	2	2	1		1					40
1575–76	9	19		2			2					32
1579–80	28	31	3				3					65
1582–83	34	17	2		3		2					58
1590–91	17	16	1		2	7	3					46
1592–93	41	27	7		4	4	1		1			85
1593–94	41	31	7		2	1						82
1597–98	13	11		1	5		2	1				33
1602–03	22	18	2	1	13		1		1	1	1	60

for trade from Liverpool, while several other Irish ports were of minor significance. Overwhelmingly Liverpool vessels used Drogheda and Dublin during the Tudor period; a pattern that did not change, although it was modified somewhat by military considerations towards the end of the century.[22]

Irish merchants from these towns used factors, associates and servants to obtain goods from the interior, usually through territorial agreements with provincial lords. Groups of Irish merchants then operated together using one Liverpool ship: a not unusual example being the twenty merchants from Drogheda using the *Bartholomew* in 1566 with a Liverpool master.[23] On Liverpool ships Irish merchants dominated the regular trade in exports and imports; a characteristic that remained unchanged in the Tudor period. Possibly restrictive practices emanating from Dublin were responsible for this. Protection for this imbalance was of concern to the Irish merchants and a challenge to the merchant community of the north-west of England. In 1575 so serious was a protracted dispute involving a group of Dublin merchants and John Crosse of Liverpool that the earl of Derby was ordered to liaise with Lancashire magistrates to settle the affair. By the late 1590s so many Irish merchants were using Liverpool that the town's assembly ordered them to pay hallage tolls in the future.[24] Despite the predominant position of the Irish merchants and a measure of rivalry, there was also an element of co-operation; Liverpool merchants could act as factors for their Irish counterparts, and the reverse was true. In 1539 a Liverpool merchant used a 'servant' in Drogheda to sell his London silks and kersey. William Golborne in the 1560s distributed goods in Liverpool on behalf of a group of Dublin and Drogheda merchants. For over twenty years Thomas Bavand served as factor in Liverpool for a variety of Irish traders.[25]

In 1534 Henry VIII used Liverpool for the same purpose which King John seems to have had in mind in the early thirteenth century: he dispatched troops to Ireland. To Elizabeth I later in the century Ireland was, in some respects, an unwelcome inheritance which she wished to keep secure but upon which she was unwilling to spend money. However, events forced the continuing attention of Tudor government to Ireland resulting, eventually, in military activity that had considerable significance for Liverpool. In 1559 the activity of Shane O'Neill prompted the dispatch to Ireland of the earl of Sussex as Lord Deputy with 600–700 men. A level of military engagement ensued with his Ulster campaigns of 1561 and 1563. In the 1560s further plantation development was authorised, and in 1565 a new Lord Deputy, Sir Henry Sidney was appointed. By this time it was clear that Liverpool was being used quite regularly for the transport of personnel, including the Lord Deputy himself, his horses, fine apparel, treasure and staff. Regular provisions were important and new destinations could be explored. For instance, supplies for 1,000 men were dispatched to Carrickfergus through Liverpool over a three-month period in 1567; this was a destination hitherto little used from the town. The level of activity subsided and then revived from time to time, with disturbances in Munster and on-going colonisation schemes.[26]

During much of the 1570s and up until about 1583 Liverpool's involvement with military commitment in Ireland remained. In August 1573 the earl of Essex, as Captain-General, sailed for the town of Carrickfergus with 200 horsemen and 400 footmen in seventeen Liverpool ships. Supplies of wheat, malt, barley, oats, beer and biscuits followed.

Reinforcements were necessary from Lancashire and further afield: for example 600 Lancastrians in October 1573, and London footmen in July 1574. Wounded men were returned to Liverpool and their stories together with the experience of the Liverpool vessel, the *Swan*, must have brought home to a small town the reality of the situation in Ireland. The *Swan* belonged to the brothers John and Thomas Winstanley; it was wrecked off the coast of Ireland in February 1574 and the crew, according to the town books, 'most viliounouslie murthered, slayne, and cut in peces as the vilyst kynd of fleshe'.[27] Until the suppression of the Desmond rebellion in 1582–83 the level of activity generated in Liverpool scarcely abated. Supplies continued to be sent through the town and contingents of troops, from time to time, were dispatched. Carpenters and masons were also sent to construct, improve and repair fortifications in Ireland.[28]

For a decade from 1583 to 1593 the level of military activity and Liverpool's support role subsided somewhat, although it never disappeared. From 1593 onwards a new phase and level of commitment is evident. By the summer of that year shipping in Liverpool had been 'stayed' on orders of the Privy Council to transport new levies of men. On one occasion this provides some indication of the scale of operation: two 40-ton vessels were used to take 120 men each, three 28-ton vessels took 100 men each, and one 28-ton ship took a further 80 men. In conjunction with Chester, the mid-1590s saw almost unrelieved effort to support the military campaigns in Ireland. In 1595, for instance, the small town had to cope with 1,000 troops at a time: no mean undertaking. Provisions from Liverpool were shipped to Dublin, Drogheda and Carlingford. By March 1596 the mayor of Liverpool wrote to Chester's mayor to protest that he could no longer 'stay' shipping simply because none was available and there were not five seafaring men left in the town. Yet in April nearly 1,300 men were transported from Liverpool, although 200 had to be left behind. Several more thousands of men followed in the next few months. It was Lord Deputy Burgh's opinion in 1597 that 'the conveniency of shipping commonly serveth at Liverpool rather than the river of Chester'.[29] The small town can only have been too well aware of its convenience by this time.

During 1598–99 more reinforcements than ever were sent as activity in Ireland moved to Lough Foyle following the English disaster at Yellowford and the appointment of the earl of Essex as Lord Deputy. In February 1599 Captain Davies reported from Liverpool the dispatch of 2,300 men and over 500 horses. With the appointment of Lord Mountjoy in 1600 even winter campaigns were organised. Shipping by this time was operating on a shuttle basis, with ships returning to collect men left behind in Liverpool.[30] As activity intensified, unfamiliar locations brought dangers of their own, such as the Liverpool ship that ran aground at Lough Foyle in May 1600 through lack of pilots. The level of shipping demanded by royal officials and the desirability of using Liverpool as the departure port were not as popular as they had been some years earlier. The mayor of Liverpool complained bitterly that for the Lough Foyle campaign twenty ships from the small town had been used, but only two from Chester.[31]

Local merchants had been significant beneficiaries for much of the century in providing the bulk of supplies; the mayor of Chester in 1580 had been ordered specifically to use only traders from his city, from Liverpool and from north Wales. From 1574 onwards Thomas Bavand of Liverpool had become established as a major victualler supplying, for instance, many of the ships to Carrickfergus with coal, biscuits, butter, cheese, barley, malt, wheat, oats and beer. He was referred to as Lord Deputy Sidney's 'servant' during the mid-1570s. Thomas Bavand surely profited handsomely from his victualling activity, although all did not always proceed smoothly. He was paid £500 in September 1580 for his dealings, yet by December he was complaining to the Queen's Lord Treasurer, Lord Burghley, that he had loaded a ship at his own expense with barley, malt and butter. Nevertheless, by 1585 he was still a substantial supplier of Her Majesty's garrison.[32]

With the new levels of activity during the 1590s demand for supplies expanded enormously in difficult harvest circumstances. The principal Liverpool victualler by this time was Giles Brooke, who used various ships such as the *Steven*, the *Valentine*, the *Gift of God*, the *James* and the *Christopher*. Supplies were the usual food commodities, but could involve a miscellany of extra goods: framed timber, unframed timber, joists and boards and even canvas to make biscuit bags. The 1603 probate inventory of John Bird reveals he had in Chester a veritable armoury: 43 headpieces, 20 muskets, 9 calivers, 13 breastplates, 15 backplates, 6 gorgets, 15 bandeliers, 9 musket rests, 6 flax and touchboxes, 2 swords without hilts, 1 sword, 1 rapier, 6 hilts and 4 pommels. Presumably this equipment was for dispatch to Ireland.[33]

As well as profit and opportunity for some, the military contact with Ireland brought inevitable problems to a small town. There had always been difficulties when shipping was delayed by bad or inappropriate weather. In 1567 one contingent of soldiers had been sent to Liverpool, re-directed to Chester, and then returned to Liverpool before finally embarking. Tempers must have been rather frayed. When 200 men were delayed in the town in 1574 the mayor had to make extra financial allowances to them. These tactics did not always work or were not

always available, and in 1581 so serious was this type of problem that
the mayor reported to the Privy Council the 'late mutynous disorder and
disobedience of certen solildyers' at Liverpool. The increased pressures
of transport during the 1590s together with harvest shortages brought
intensified and sustained problems. In March 1596 Liverpool's mayor
claimed that over the previous few years the town had been 'surcharged
with a multitude of soldiers' and that the return of poor and sick soldiers
'did so infect a number of houses with the diseases of that country'.
Perhaps in the absence of a response to these complaints when more
soldiers were delayed for five weeks by adverse weather in December
1596, the mayor ordered that they should no longer be victualled, gave
them all 20d. and a passport to Chester; he kept the captains' horses
to defray the outstanding costs, discharged the shipping and gave the
saddles to the shipowners to offset their loss of earnings. Even these
tactics could not influence the weather, and in 1601 there were more
serious protests and claims that no more than 700 men could be lodged
in the town at one time while awaiting favourable sailing conditions.[34]

To suit the interests of the town and its inhabitants, there must have
been exaggerated claims made from time to time. However, it is hard
to escape the conclusion that a small town of Liverpool's size must, at
times, have been overwhelmed by the numbers of troops embarking and
disembarking at the port. The wars in Ireland had, at first, provided
Liverpool shipping with a dangerous, yet welcome, supplement to their
regular trading across the Irish Sea. By the 1590s it is arguable that the
military support activity had become a serious burden to a small town
and a disruption to long-standing and regular trading patterns.

Continental trade

Notwithstanding the dominance of localised distributive trade, Tudor
Liverpool could also support longer-distance enterprises. By the late
sixteenth century great changes were under way nationally in both the
character and direction of overseas trade; new trading companies were
operating to new destinations. The majority of this trade was still routed
through London, so there was little prospect that Liverpool would
play a significant part in these developments.[35] Provincial ports were
all affected by their locations and the geographic opportunities these
offered. Liverpool's major directional advantage, as has been seen, lay
with the Irish Sea and with access to the Atlantic. This did afford some
contact with the western seaboard of Europe, particularly France and
Spain.[36] Similar opportunities, of course, applied to Chester, Bristol and
other ports of south-west England.

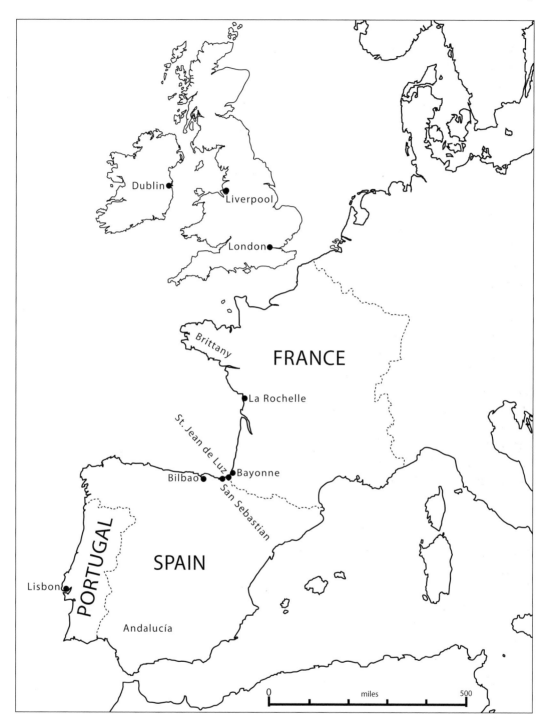

Liverpool shipping in the sixteenth century had little experience of distances greater than the Irish Sea, except for small summer expeditions to the Basque coast of northern Spain (Castile) and south-western France. Here Lancashire textiles were exchanged for cargoes of iron and whale oil.

Spain was the most important continental trading location for Tudor Liverpool. After national encouragement in the mid-fifteenth and early sixteenth centuries, such as the treaty of Medina del Campo of 1489 and the marriage of Catherine of Aragon to, firstly, Prince Arthur and then to Henry VIII, reasonable levels of English trade with Spain (or, more accurately, Castile) had been established.[37] A Spanish merchant was first recorded in Chester in 1444–45; Spanish iron was imported into Chester in 1464–65; and in 1473 the first Spanish vessel was recorded there.[38] By the early Tudor period Liverpool merchants were beginning to share in this overseas activity. They are not readily identifiable in the Chester port books at this time, but from the 1530s they do appear in local Spanish records, for instance for Lekeitio on the Basque coast. In 1553 a Spanish merchant discharged 60 tuns of wine in Liverpool.[39] The mid-sixteenth-century reign of Mary I and her marriage to Philip II of Spain provided renewed encouragement to this trade. By the early years of the reign of Elizabeth I Liverpool had established a regular, if modest, commercial connection with Iberia. In 1565 George Rainford had sufficient contacts to ship into Chester three tons of iron on board the *Santa Maria de Tolaia* of Bermeo and to send out a consignment of Manchester cottons on the same vessel. John Hewitt of Liverpool operated as a resident factor in Bilbao for eighteen months on behalf of Thomas Sekerston of Liverpool and a Salford merchant, a practice that had become quite common among English merchants by this time. In 1564 John Crosse sent his younger brother, Christopher, to buy and sell for him in Spain.[40] During 1565–66 four Liverpool ships made the journey to Spain and one to Lisbon in Portugal.[41]

Table 9 *Voyages by Liverpool ships to continental ports*

	Spain	Portugal	France
1565–66	4	1	2
1569–70			2
1572–53	2		4
1575–56	3		1
1579–80	4		1
1582–83	9		1
1584–85	8		1

From early in the reign of Queen Elizabeth I, however, this recently established trade became increasingly difficult to sustain. This was not through problems associated with the journey, but rather through political circumstances and relations between Catholic Spain and Protestant England. In 1561 the estates of the province of Vizcaya in northern Spain tried to restrict access for foreign shipping to its ports. During the following two years there was considerable piracy off this Basque coast, and in January 1564 all English shipping at these ports was seized: in all about thirty ships and one thousand mariners. From 1563 to 1564 and again from 1569 to 1573 English retaliation placed an embargo on trade with Spain.[42] A graphic sign of this changing climate must have been the arrival in Liverpool in 1565 of the 70-ton Spanish ship, the *Santa Maria de Bignonia*; she had been captured as a pirate by the Queen's ship *Sacar*.[43]

The Liverpool port books record no Spanish vessels visiting Liverpool from 1565 onwards. Liverpool ship owners and merchants, however, struggled for twenty more years to maintain this Iberian trade. Despite the embargo, two voyages were made in 1572–73 and three in 1575–76. These ventures typically involved small groups of Liverpool merchants, together with two or three Chester men: such as John Gellibrand, Robert Corbet, Ralph Burscough and Robert Wytter in 1566, and also in the same year William Halewood, Ralph Sekerston, William Secum, Alexander Garnet, Peter Starkey and Thomas Bavand.[44] Most of the town's more substantial merchants were involved, often in just one of these rather speculative voyages in any year. Almost exclusively the Liverpool merchants sent quantities of Manchester cottons to Spain. On rare occasions they supplemented the cargo with cloth of northern

The Basque area that crossed the Spanish/French border lay in a location that could be used to advantage by Liverpool's mariners in the sixteenth century when faced with a complex and changing international situation. Portugalete, Bermeo, Lekeitio, Mutriku, Deba, San Sebastian, Renteria and St Jean de Luz were all visited by Liverpool ships during the Tudor period.

dozens and herrings. Usually the voyages were to the vicinity of Bilbao: small Basque harbours such as Deba, Portugalete, Lekeitio, Bermeo and Renteria. From here the return cargoes were principally iron and train (whale) oil. The iron was highly prized for its quality and until the seventeenth century there were no Spanish duties on its export. The oil was used for lighting and for processing practices in the leather industry. Occasionally the imports into Liverpool included small amounts of pitch, liquorice and Castile soap. On just three occasions the voyages went to the adjacent port of San Sebastian where, in addition to the regular commodities, oranges and lemons were obtained. Just once, in 1573, a ship left Liverpool for Andalucía; it may, however, have been a Chester vessel with the cargo of Manchester cottons shared by five Chester and two Liverpool merchants.[45]

Although this trade survived during the first half of Elizabeth I's reign, it cannot have been easy in the political circumstances; as early as 1567 Ralph Sekerston claimed that the king of Spain was preparing for an invasion of England.[46] The trade, however, was profitable and this lay behind the formation in 1577 of the Spanish Company to control all trade with the Iberian peninsula. The company was based in London, but with members in Hull, Southampton, Exeter and Bristol. By 1578 the company was in correspondence with Liverpool merchants and was trying to get its officer in Chester to enforce its monopoly. From 1578 to 1580 Liverpool contested this situation with some vigour and with a combination of intercession and negotiation the Liverpool merchants were successful in gaining exemption from the authority of the Spanish Company.[47] Unfortunately, considerable effort had been expended to protect the Iberian trade which proved to be of limited future potential.

From 1579 until 1585 trade with Spain flourished for Liverpool. About twelve merchants participated each year and they continued to export Manchester cottons while importing the iron and train oil. The international situation was, however, deteriorating fast and hostilities in 1586 saw the collapse of this trade.[48] In July 1586 Nicholas Abraham, a

RIGHT

Speke Hall lay well outside the Tudor town of Liverpool. The fine half-timbered house was constructed by several generations of the landed gentry Norris family during this period. The overall size of the house and the surviving Tudor design of the great hall and parlour provide evidence of the lifestyle that was possible for the Tudor gentry. The wealth and influence of these families impacted seriously on a small town such as Tudor Liverpool. Edward Norris was mayor of the town from 1521/2 and from 1532/3, while William Norris was mayor 1554/55.

PHOTOGRAPH: CARNEGIE, BY KIND PERMISSION OF THE NATIONAL TRUST

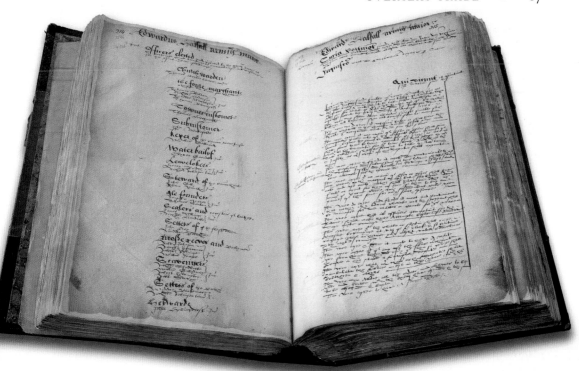

Pages from the Liverpool town books, dating from 1586. On the left-hand page is a list of officers elected at the portmoot court.

LIVRO, 352 MIN/COU 2, LIVERPOOL TOWN BOOK, VOLUME 2 1576-1624

The parlour at Speke Hall contains a wonderful carved overmantel (*above*) which testifies to the wealth of the family that commissioned it. The design also provides detail of the Norris family genealogy during the Tudor period. William Norris (died 1568) with his two wives are shown in the upper section of the overmanel with their numerous children immediately below – seven to the right and twelve to the left, although not all of them survived childhood (*see detail, below*). William Norris' father, Henry, with his wife and children are to the left, while William's son, Edward, and his wife and two children are to the right. This suggests that the carving was done in about 1560, before Edward had more of his children.

The following text appears within the map illustration:

The freres

KRAGFARGVS·
TOWNE·

KRAGFARGVS
CASTELL·

This map of the castle and settlement at Carrickfergus, Ireland, was produced early in the reign of Elizabeth I. The stone castle, stone churches and stone houses contrast with the smaller structures. The anchorage beside the castle is very evident and appears to be under construction or repair. The two small ships may well be the only contemporary illustration of vessels that may have sailed from Tudor Liverpool.

Liverpool merchant, and John Lambert, a Liverpool seaman, testified before the mayor of Weymouth that they had been kept as prisoners in Bilbao for over twelve months; they also reported the preparation of '700 sailles of shippes' to invade England.[49] After 1585 no further direct shipping from Liverpool to Spain was recorded in the port books. The defeat of the Armada and the prolonged conflict with England was also a blow to Basque shipping and trade. During the 1590s some Spanish products continued to reach Liverpool via rather circuitous routes. The first recorded trans-shipment of Spanish iron arrived on a ship from Drogheda in 1590, along with the more usual cargo of yarn, skins and wheat.[50] Almost every year thereafter quantities of iron arrived from Dublin or Drogheda; usually only a ton at a time but with as many as twelve Liverpool ships carrying this amount. In the main, the transactions were undertaken by the same merchants, such as John Bird and Giles Brooke, who had been involved formerly in the direct Spanish trade.[51] Reminders of the dangers of continuing contact with Spain were present: Robert Kettle, master of a Liverpool ship, was captured in 1595 and served fourteen weeks in a Spanish galley before release in Mount's Bay.[52] A measure of the inadequacy of the supplies from Ireland is provided by the arrival in Liverpool in 1603 of seven tons of 'Dansk' iron shipped via the Isle of Man.[53]

By the end of the Tudor period, not only had Iberian trade virtually disappeared from Liverpool but the other continental market of earlier in the century had also evaporated. During the earlier part of the sixteenth century some French traders had frequented Liverpool, probably as an extension of their wine trade to Chester. In 1559 two French ships laden with wine had reached the Mersey and the masters had bartered with Liverpool merchants for Manchester cottons. Other traders appeared in 1561 and 1562, and five French ships reached Liverpool during 1569–70. At this time just a few Liverpool ships made voyages to France, such as the *Michael*'s voyage from la Rochelle in 1566.[54] Political circumstances dictated that this trade was not entirely trouble-free. England

LEFT
Rural Sefton parish lay to the north of Liverpool and was the home of the Molyneux family, landed gentry who held a number of royal appointments in south Lancashire during the Tudor period. The Molyneux family provided the funds for a substantial rebuilding of Sefton church, including very fine woodcarving – right on the eve of the Reformation in King Henry VIII's reign. The arches on the rood screen were originally round, but were altered in the nineteenth century to the then-fashionable 'gothic' shape that we see today. As hereditary constables of Liverpool castle the Molyneux had immediate influence in the town which grew as the family acquired property in the town from the dissolution of the chantries and after 1537 control of the fee farm with its access to marketing and anchorage tolls.
BY KIND PERMISSION OF THE RECTOR, ST HELEN'S SEFTON

was involved in some assistance, including a military expedition to Le Havre, to aid the Protestant French Huguenots. This may explain the French prize that was brought into Liverpool in 1563; it certainly made an impression when it 'shot off a noble peall of gones ... the lyke never herd in thiese parties'.[55] Perhaps as some form of retaliation a vessel from Waterford was chased by the French into Liverpool the following year. In 1565 another French ship from St-Jean-de-Luz was taken at sea and brought into Liverpool, although it was later released.[56]

Despite these difficulties some French trade was sustained. French vessels usually brought Breton salt, for instance 26 tons of it in 1566. They returned with cargoes of Manchester cottons and coal: the same two commodities that were taken by Liverpool merchants to France. The majority of Liverpool ships traded with the Atlantic French ports of Saint-Jean-de-Luz and, to a lesser extent, with Bayonne and La Rochelle. At all of these ports it was possible to obtain cargoes of iron, pitch, resin and train oil. Some of these commodities, especially the iron, were undoubtedly of Spanish origin and had been provided by local coastal ships from Bermeo and Fuenterrabia. The train oil came from Basque whalers who might have originated on either side of the Franco-Spanish border. Three Basque provinces lay north of the Pyrenees and four to the south; the Franco-Spanish border was a recent and uncertain phenomena.[57] The principal Liverpool merchants operating in this part of France were, not surprisingly, the same men involved in the Spanish trade: John Crosse, John Gellibrand, Thomas Sekerston, Ralph Sekerston, George Rainford, Robert Wytter, Giles Brooke. The destinations may have been 'technically' French but this region and its trade was closely inter-related with that of Spain. Political circumstances ensured that Liverpool trade to this area declined at the same time as that to Spain. By the late 1570s and up to 1585 there were just a few voyages a year. By the late 1580s and 1590s direct contact with France had all but disappeared; only indirect communication through Ireland allowed the import of some French wine to continue. During the 1570s several Liverpool merchants had been accused of landing wine before it could be gauged and of storing it illegally in their houses: sack, Gascon claret and white wine.[58] By 1585 supplies of wine began to reach the town from Ireland and other English ports.[59]

By the end of the Tudor period the French and Spanish trade had gone from Liverpool; it was not replaced by alternative continental destinations. There are a few isolated references to trade with or from other areas, but these vessels seem to have reached Liverpool only in exceptional circumstances. For instance, a Hull ship arrived with rye from Denmark in 1563, and a Hamburg merchant had a similar cargo.

In 1564 some of Liverpool's merchants were required to appraise an old Flemish bark that had arrived in the town. An initiative in 1566 resulted in a Liverpool vessel taking goods from seven of the town's merchants to Lisbon in Portugal, but the enterprise was not repeated.[60] Geographical constraint of location together with the limitations of its hinterland ensured that Liverpool's foreign trade remained, at best, modest throughout the Tudor period and, because of political developments, it had disappeared by the end of the sixteenth century.

Limitations of wealth in the society of south Lancashire and in the merchant community in a small town hindered investment on a scale significant enough to have redirected this trade. From the mid sixteenth century onwards London witnessed considerable acceleration of investment by merchants and gentry, particularly through the new trading companies, even if this support may have been sporadic and short-term.[61] Liverpool men, but not ships, had reached the Guinea coast of west Africa in the mid Tudor period. A collection of wills from sailors who died on five voyages financed by London merchants in the 1550s contains several references to Liverpool mariners: Nicholas Bray, Henry Stevenson, possibly John Tarse and Ralph Bailey, a merchant.[62] These contacts, however, do not appear to have been developed at this time.

Trade across the Atlantic was perhaps a more likely direction for diversification. Propaganda for Atlantic travel and colonising schemes abounded in the 1570s and 1580s, and certainly some Lancashire individuals invested in Sir Humphrey Gilbert's north American plans.[63] These schemes collapsed, but one ship, the *Golden Hind*, returned from the Newfoundland area in 1583 captained by Edward Heyes of Liverpool. He had worked for Humphrey Gilbert since 1578. He returned in 1583 believing that Newfoundland offered great possibilities, and during the next decade approached those with influence in government, such as Lord Burghley, with his ideas. Little came of his projects and by the 1590s he was operating as a privateer. Shortly before his death in 1602 Edward Heyes did turn his attention back to north America with Bartholomew Gosnold's venture. The profits of these activities allowed Heyes to buy property in Essex and Sussex before settling in London. His 1602 will, however, describes him as a gentleman of Liverpool.[64] He was related to the Liverpool merchant John Mainwaring, and it is hard to conceive that Heyes' voyages and plans did not provoke a little interest in his home town. Another Atlantic connection lay with the Molyneux family of Croxteth. Anthony, the youngest son of Sir Richard Molyneux, spent part of his career sailing with Sir Francis Drake, and Anthony's sister was married to the eldest son of Sir Humphrey Gilbert.[65] A Liverpool mariner, John Young, served as a privateer in the West Indies in the early 1590s.[66] These tentative links with the New World indicate a certain willingness in Liverpool to diversify overseas interests; the extent of participation demonstrates the limited resources and ability of the town to engage in a significant way at this time.

Small town trade

To Liverpudlians in the Tudor period the size and success of the town's fleet of ships was of considerable moment in the local rivalry with Chester. Beyond the region this rivalry was, in all likelihood, a matter of no consequence; to the two towns it was of singular importance. From the thirteenth century Liverpool had not been regarded as a 'port' in its own right; rather, it had been designated for trading and customs purposes as an out-port, or creek, of Chester. Chester's jurisdiction stretched from Barmouth and north Wales to the Scottish border. The head-port at Chester had the appropriate customs officials for all of the area. By the Tudor period a series of deputy officials had been established and it was these, the deputy customer, the deputy controller and the deputy searcher, who operated from Liverpool.[67] The arrangements applied only to customs administration, but could be interpreted to cover control of shipping and cargoes: an involvement that could be regarded as a challenge to Liverpool's independence and status which had particular application in the later Tudor period when the government commandeered shipping for military duty in Ireland.

The issue was not new and it was perceived very keenly throughout the sixteenth century. In 1550 Chester's assembly ordered that none of its citizens should take their goods to the port of Liverpool, on penalty of the considerable fine of £40. As far as the port books evidence is concerned, no Chester ship did use Liverpool before the end of the century. The rationalisation of record-keeping with the inception of port books at Liverpool from 1565 onwards testifies to a growing independence. Chester responded by trying to invoke its traditional pre-eminence. Matters were perceived so seriously that Liverpool mayor, Robert Corbet, and Member of Parliament, Ralph Sekerston, attended the Duchy of Lancaster courts in London in an attempt to safeguard their town's interests. The issue simmered until the formation of the Spanish Company in 1578, which provided Liverpool with another opportunity to claim independence and Chester with the chance to assert its supervision. On a local basis the issue was hotly contested for several years. A special rate was collected in Liverpool to finance the correspondence and personal communication with London. Advice was sought from the earl of Derby and his contacts with members of the Privy Council proved invaluable. Liverpool did establish its exemption from the requirements of the Spanish Company and from control by Chester in this matter. Ironically, the small town that wished so keenly to challenge the superiority of Chester was described by the earl in 1581 as 'that poor town'.[68]

During the sixteenth century silting of the River Dee was having some effect on Chester's trade, although the extent of its impact remains debateable. Certainly a new haven, or quay, was under construction by the 1540s at Neston in the Wirral peninsula, some ten miles from Chester, to help the problem, although it was only nearing completion in 1569. By early in the seventeenth century Neston no longer sufficed and the quay was moved a mile further north to Parkgate.[69] The problems of anchorage and trans-shipment of cargoes to the town cannot have helped Chester's viability.

At the same time Liverpool's local financial duties on goods entering and leaving the town were less onerous than those at Chester. The official duties on wine, iron and leather may have been consistent to both ports (although maybe evasion was easier in Liverpool), but port dues and market tolls were a matter for each individual town. Throughout the Tudor period Liverpool was noted for its lower rates. In the early 1530s Dublin merchants were involved in a dispute over customs' duties and complained of the 'extortion' suffered at Chester and, in consequence, 'go of their own accord to Liverpool'.

Undoubtedly Chester was the larger town, and had more ships. By the Tudor period, however, it seems probable that in order to sustain its position Chester was including with its shipping the vessels from elsewhere within its customs area, particularly from Wirral. By the reign of Elizabeth I there were about twenty-four ships operating from small ports such as Neston, Heswall, West Kirby and Wallasey, and these accounted for thirty-nine per cent of Chester's Irish trade.[70] It is likely that by the end of the Tudor period, in difficult times for both towns, that the volume of Liverpool's trade had surpassed that of Chester. In 1586 Liverpool's customs were £272 3s. 9d., whereas Chester's (including Conwy, Beaumaris and elsewhere) were £211 4s. 8d.[71] Not all goods were taxed, yet the customs dues may be indicative of the balance of trade shifting to Liverpool and the fact that Irish ships preferred to use that port. Liverpool certainly believed that this was the situation. In 1601 Liverpool's mayor complained bitterly to the Privy Council that Chester was abusing its position to direct the stay of shipping: 'they will so insult over us as now they term us to be a member of Chester, and by that means challenge a superiority over us'.[72]

By this time this North West rivalry had probably reached something of a stalemate. During the Tudor period some changes had taken place:

Liverpool ships no longer went to Spain and France; local coal had become an increasingly valued exportable commodity; and the transport of troops and their supplies to Ireland had reached overwhelming proportions. Yet a very great deal had not changed: the predominant export and import commodities remained unchanged; coastal traffic and the Irish trade remained at the heart of Liverpool's trading activity; and overall quantities of goods remained modest. During 1565–66 twelve Liverpool vessels were recorded making voyages, other than coastal ones. During 1602–03, again, twelve Liverpool ships were recorded making voyages to Ireland. International, national and local circumstances during the Tudor period did not favour the development of continental trade, and there was little basis for mercantile expansion and prosperity in this area. There was little incentive to acquire more or larger vessels, and so by the end of the sixteenth century Liverpool's fleet was little different to what it had been throughout. In consequence, there was little need to expand or improve the anchorage facilities. Liverpool remained a small port.

CHAPTER SIX

Urban identity and status

T HE RESTRICTED MEANS OF COMMUNICATION in the Tudor
period and significant regionalism did not necessarily mean that
small towns such as Liverpool were totally isolated and inward-looking.
Those with mercantile interests and sufficient wealth could and did
travel in northern England, to the Midlands and to London. Those
with this opportunity to travel remained, however, a restricted group
since more general economic development and growth in Liverpool
at this time was so limited. One consequence of this situation was the
attention that merchants and burgesses were able to pay to their town's
administration, regulation and environment, if only to help ensure
their own social and commercial survival. In a small town what might
seem superficially trivial details of both personal and urban status
were of considerable moment. Civic affairs in Tudor Liverpool were
dominated by the few that had some wealth and opportunity for contact
beyond the town; their small numbers meant that the co-operation and
assistance from other members of the community were essential. A small
population also ensured that the attentions of local gentry and the earl
of Derby were hard to evade.

Town government and administration

Tudor merchants typically formed small, compact and financially
dominant élites within their towns. In Exeter, one of the larger Tudor
towns, just twenty-six families provided the fifty mayors that were
chosen during the reign of Elizabeth I.[1] In Liverpool St Luke's Day, 18
October, was election day and marked the commencement of the civic
year in Liverpool. The mayor was elected and sworn into office, the
people's bailiff was elected, and then the newly chosen mayor nominated
his choice for the other bailiff. The mayor also chose a sergeant-at-mace.
On Monday following election day the Great Portmoot, an assembly
of the town's freemen, was held, with the second Portmoot taking
place on the Thursday following. Usually three more meetings of the

Portmoot were held during the next twelve months.[2] On the face of it these arrangements in Liverpool sound reasonably open to the male population of the town. An indication of participation is provided by the reference to 'the late disordered assemblies of whole commons' that was noted in early 1580. In response, an attempt was made to establish a re-ordered council to govern the town. The new council was to consist of the mayor, twelve aldermen and twenty-four councillors like, it was claimed, many other contemporary towns. In order to achieve the twelve aldermen, two men who had not previously served as mayor were chosen, and the twenty-four councillors were nominated. These offices were to be held for life, with vacancies filled by council members as and when necessary. The proposed plan left the Portmoot, the assembly of all freemen, with powers to elect the mayor, to choose one of the two bailiffs and to participate in discussing bye-laws.[3]

The plan of 1580 indicates where the views and preferences of some of the town's élite lay. Almost immediately that it came into existence the new council had to contend with the jurisdictional claims of the recently formed Spanish Company, and by 1581 the council was proposing the collection of a special rate to finance the defence of the town's and, no doubt, the élite merchants' interests. The assembly of freemen refused to co-operate in the collection of a tax that it had not sanctioned, and the new-style council was last heard of in June 1582.[4] For the remainder of the Tudor period the government of Liverpool reverted to the hands of the freemen. In all likelihood the level of office-holding proposed for the new council was in itself difficult to sustain in a small town, and some participation by freemen in matters of interest and concern hard to deny in an environment of just seven streets.

During the period 1550–1603, when the town books permit identification with certainty, there were thirty different mayors in Liverpool; they came from just twenty-two families. One man, Robert Corbet, held the office on five separate occasions, and Robert More served at four different times. More typically five individuals had three terms as mayor, and five men had two terms. None of these individuals ever served in consecutive years. A further eighteen men held the office just once, although six of these appointments could be regarded as honorific. Aside from these six, all other mayors came from the Liverpool merchant community. Identification during the first half of the sixteenth century is more sporadic, and dependent mainly on surviving family archives. Nonetheless there does appear to be the suggestion that local gentry control of the mayoralty was declining during the Tudor period.[5] The appointment cannot have been other than time-consuming during the year of office; in addition to the Portmoot, the mayor presided over his own minor court held about every three weeks, and he supervised all of the daily administration in the town.[6]

The posts of the two bailiffs were also dominated by the merchant families, although from a somewhat wider financial spectrum than those who became mayor. For instance, Thomas Bastwell, the owner of a small vessel, served as mayor's bailiff in 1555–57, again in 1561–62, and again in 1573–74, yet he never achieved the dignity of mayor. Many mayors, however, did have the earlier experience as bailiff. Giles Brooke was bailiff in 1584–85 before serving as mayor in 1592–93 and again in 1601–02. John Bird was mayor's bailiff in 1579–80, the people's choice as bailiff in 1583–84 and then mayor in 1590–91, 1594–95 and again in 1600–01.[7] In a small town the office of bailiff provided the opportunity for most merchants to participate very significantly in civic administration. The office served also as a form of apprenticeship for those men who would become mayor. The virtual absence of craft gilds meant that civic office-holding had the undivided attention of the small merchant community in Liverpool.

The burgess rolls of the town provide some guide to the number of potentially active participants in the wider administration within Tudor Liverpool. Soon after its foundation in the thirteenth century there had been provision for 168 burgages.[8] The few rolls that survive and are preserved with the town books from the first half of the reign of Elizabeth I suggest only a very slight rise in numbers at this time followed by a period of stabilisation or even stagnation towards the end of the reign. Some admissions to freedom through completed apprenticeship, purchase or patrimony are recorded in the town books, but the entries provide only a partial picture and no detailed freemen rolls survive. Since even labourers were admitted to freedom and in view of the total size of the town's population, it can be supposed that quite a high proportion of the adult male townsmen were technically freemen.[9] The steady rise in the proportion of 'foreign' or non-resident burgesses in the later part of the Tudor period appears to demonstrate the attractiveness of the town's facilities to outsiders, while increasingly concentrating the administrative responsibility on a few.[10] It may also be a reflection of the precarious viability of the town that non-residents had to be tolerated to the extent of comprising between thirty and forty per cent of burgesses.

As in other Tudor towns, the operation of civic administration required participation by a number of local officials. The individuals were appointed by the Portmoot and their names recorded annually in the town books. By the middle of the sixteenth century this team usually comprised: a clerk, two chapelwardens, a supervisor for the town's warehouse, two stewards for the common hall, two leavelookers (to supervise weights and measures), four rate assessors and appraisers, two collectors for dues owed by 'foreign' traders coming into the town, one water bailiff to collect anchorage and wharfage dues from non-freemen, two supervisors for the butchers' stalls, two alefounders (to supervise licensed and unlicensed brewing), one hayward and two moss reeves who had duties associated with pasturing of animals and collection of turf from the town field and heath. From 1556 four supervisors of street-cleansing were added to this list and from 1583 two more officers to oversee the siting of market stalls.[11] The majority of these officials were closely involved with supervision of marketing and trading activities of the town and the impact these may have had on the environment. Throughout the Tudor period the appointment and operation of these posts remained quite routine and provided the annual opportunity for about thirty individuals to participate actively in civic administration – at a rather mundane level. The offices of mayor and bailiffs were reserved to the merchant community, but the other jobs were available to the adult males of the town. The annual listings of names suggest that some form of rota was in operation and that, in such a small town, the overall participation rate was high. The supervisors of the butchers' stalls, the hayward, the water bailiff and the clerk usually served for a number of consecutive years, presumably on a part-time basis, such as Oliver Garnet the water bailiff from 1573 until 1591. The other jobs were normally undertaken for one year at a time. Enforcing local regulations among neighbours and acquaintances cannot have been always easy or popular and the merchant élite exercised authority only with a significant level of co-operation from the adult male population of the small town.

Most official duties concerned the trade and environment of the town; financial administration is notable by its absence. As a borough Liverpool did hold some property, but relatively little and insufficient to provide much independence. By the Tudor period the town property amounted to one burgage in Dale Street, another in Water Street, two half-burgages, eighteen pieces of land in the town field, the rent charge on a house, some land near Edge Lane just outside the town, and a tenement in Garston a few miles away. These assets generated the grand sum of just over £5 a year.[12] The town was able to collect some other revenue such as fees for admission to freedom and local tolls but all sources of revenue did not amount to a great deal, unlike Chester where income could be in excess of £100.[13] Annual income was modest and so special leys (rates) were collected when necessary for particular and abnormal expenditure. An indication of the style of financial operation is evident in November 1561 when 'the great wynde and stormes' damaged the harbour. A town meeting was, and could be, called to assemble in the chapel on Sunday. A collection of 13s. 9d. was taken up and a work rota arranged. The money presumably paid for materials since labour was to be provided for a month by an individual from every house in the town through a system of street rota.[14] Such a style of organisation and participation was possible only in a town as small as Liverpool. Only a few other facilities were maintained and repaired by the town: the stone bridge over the stream at the end of the Pool, the butts by the castle, the stocks near the high cross and the common hall.[15] Civic financial administration may have remained modest, but even so a significant degree of self-government and regulation provided Liverpool with a measure of identity in which a high proportion of the male population participated.

In view of the size of Tudor Liverpool, the common hall could indeed serve as a community centre, and certainly it was used for wedding dinners and dancing.[16] In a small town corporate and communal entertainments were real possibilities. On 17 November 1576 mayor Thomas Bavand made arrangements to celebrate Elizabeth I's accession day, the first recorded indication of this in Liverpool. He arranged for one bonfire to be constructed in the market place near to the high cross, for another to be built outside his own house, and encouraged other householders to do likewise. A banquet, perhaps for fellow councillors, took place at Ralph Burscough's house and it was concluded with white wine, sack and sugar at the mayor's house. Thomas Bavand did have the foresight to ask the two bailiffs to see that all fires were later quenched.[17] Modest celebrations these may have been compared with some that were being organised by this date elsewhere, but at least they were easy to organise and to attend in a small town.

Waits had been employed by some towns as official civic musicians since the fifteenth century. By the Tudor period in the larger towns they could comprise reasonably sized groups of musicians with their apprentices.[18] Liverpool aspired to this civic dignity, albeit with some difficulty of provision and continuity. By the mid sixteenth century the one town wait had to provide four sureties before receiving his silver badge of office. He was required to play every morning and evening except Sundays. By the early 1560s these duties had been enlarged to include attending upon the mayor on market days and on fair and festival days. The likelihood seems to be, in this part of the country, that the wait was either a harper or a piper, perhaps playing a form of bagpipe.[19] Notwithstanding the additional duties, it proved difficult in Liverpool to recruit and retain the one musician. James Atherton was dismissed, for unspecified reasons, in 1565 and Henry Halewood had his badge of office removed in 1572 for his lewd behaviour at the fair. A short while later the badge was returned to him but a year later he was in gaol for violent behaviour. Probably the official duties of wait did not warrant much income and maybe attracted 'unsuitable' characters. The only indication of remuneration is the permission for them to collect in the town from door to door.[20] In 1579 Henry Halewood reappeared as the town's wait despite damaging the windows of the common hall and his involvement in an assault. He was replaced again, but the replacement disappeared from the area and allowed the troublesome Henry Halewood yet another stint as wait during the 1580s.[21] The one wait was evidently regarded as a desirable acquisition for the town despite the repeated difficulties in finding satisfactory personnel. The limited resources of the town would appear to have inhibited the sophistication and continuity of musical provision.

In a small town community activity and civic sociability were possible through local entertainment. The restricted nature and scale of Tudor Liverpool's administration and communal gatherings reflect the small town environment. Opportunities existed for substantial merchant participation and domination in civic affairs, yet their role was circumscribed. With just seven streets in the town every household must have been identifiable. The town's routine administration may have been somewhat unsophisticated yet it required quite wide participation and co-operation from the male population. Local contact, communication, persuasion, conciliation, and even coercion, provided the components of the administrative machine in a face-to-face environment.

The local nobility and gentry

Three hundred years after acquiring borough status the level of independence and recognition achieved by Liverpool in the Tudor period were still uncertain.[22] With a population of less than 1,000 and in a fairly isolated location in the north-west of England Tudor Liverpool faced a hinterland dominated by the traditional influence of landed wealth. The immediate locality contained one noble family, one major gentry family of county status, and a dozen or more lesser gentry families. All of these families were anxious to protect and enhance their own positions; Liverpool was well within their horizons and interests.[23]

Throughout the Tudor period successive earls of Derby dominated south Lancashire politically, economically and socially. As major landowners the Stanleys wielded immense power in a predominantly rural environment and, as the pivot of local government and administration, controlled patronage and local politics. The earls had an immediate and real presence in the county, aside from any significance they may have had nationally. During the sixteenth century their role and status in the area was uncontested.[24] By the time of his death in 1504 the first earl had become the greatest landowner in Lancashire, with considerable holdings also in Cheshire, the Welsh borders and elsewhere. Some of this property lay very close to Liverpool: Roby, Childwall, Kirkby, Knowsley and the lease of Toxteth Park. Throughout the century, despite minorities, the family maintained and exploited their position. Their principal houses (in addition to a London property) were at Knowsley and Lathom, both not more than twelve miles from Liverpool. Edward, the third earl, served as a military commander for Henry VIII, was created a Knight of the Garter by Edward VI, and became a privy councillor and Lord High Steward to Mary I. He and his sons held the commission of lieutenancy in Lancashire from the 1530s until 1594. The earl and/or his eldest son invariably headed the Lancashire Commission of the Peace.[25]

This geographic proximity and influence was reinforced by property in Liverpool itself. The Tower was the Stanleys' early fifteenth-century stone house on the waterfront. The Tudor earls were accustomed to spending some months in any one year in London and at court but on a regular basis they visited their Lancashire houses. Usually the family arrived in Lancashire some time after the Garter ceremonies in April and remained in residence until the autumn. Their household was a vehicle and reflection of their status with its own council, officers and servants; the list compiled at Lathom in 1587 recorded 118 household staff. The mayor of Liverpool, along with Chester's mayor, took his place in the impressive funeral processions of the third and fourth earls; the heraldic display and hierarchical processions testified to the status of the earls and to Liverpool's position within the regional hierarchy.[26] Not surprisingly, the earls were treated with considerable respect by Liverpool. They and their sons were usually freemen.

On a visit to the town in August 1566 the third earl with two of his sons, a number of local gentry and a group of the earl's officers were met at the boundary of the town by the mayor, bailiffs and burgesses. The earl had arrived in a vehicle for which the scribe of the town books was unable to find an appropriate word. Almost certainly this was a coach since it was pulled by two large horses. Undoubtedly it was designed to impress; the like had probably never been seen in the vicinity of Liverpool. The procession was escorted into the town to the Tower and later the mayor provided refreshments for the earl's party.[27] This visit characterises the intermittent occasions on which the earls passed through Liverpool and perhaps stayed for a few days at the Tower while waiting for suitable weather to sail to the Isle of Man. At times the earls could make plain their influence, such as when Henry, the fourth earl, summoned the mayor to attend him in the Tower to arrange to have his four sons installed as freemen – immediately.[28]

It was the fourth earl who provided Liverpool with the opportunity to witness the increasingly elaborate ceremonies associated with the Order of the Garter and St George's Day. The earl had become a Garter Knight in 1574 and in April 1577 found himself in Liverpool *en route* to the Isle of Man; he had to wait nearly two weeks for an appropriate wind and thus had time to prepare suitable ceremonial. He supervised the siting of the cloth of state (to represent the Queen) in St Nicholas' chapel along with other rich ornaments and cloth of gold. Liverpool men, with Thomas Inglefield as captain and leader, were used to form a guard of honour. During the evening prior to the feast day a service attended by the earl, mayor Thomas Bavand, aldermen, bailiffs and townspeople was held in the chapel. A procession was formed with the earl in red-purple robes, his household staff and civic dignatories. After the service there were volleys of gunshot from the guard of honour in the chapelyard and from ships moored in the river. On St George's Day itself the guard performed drill and exercises on the shore before another procession to the chapel. This time the earl's chaplain conducted the service and provided a sermon. As the party left the chapel more volleys of shot were fired from at least 1,200 calivers (according to the clerk). This was followed by a banquet and, when it was dark, by 'squybbes', fireworks prepared by a gunner. On the following day another service and sermon were arranged with the earl appearing in yet more new robes. Entertainments and morris dancing were provided 'the lyke wherof was never sene or knowen to be done in this said towne of Liverpole'.[29]

The presence and influence of the earls can scarcely have seemed greater. Liverpool's officers, however, were more than prepared to use the relationship with the earls for their advice and connections. In 1560 the town took advice from one of the earl's officials over arrangements for the national debasement of the coinage. In 1572 the town appealed to Lord Strange, during his father's illness, to intervene on its behalf in a customs dispute with Chester. The town's bailiff, William Golborne, was sent to Knowsley and Lathom on several occasions over a period of a few months to pursue the case. Advice was again sought in 1578, and so seriously was the threat from the Spanish Company perceived that the mayor and senior townsmen went *en masse* to Knowsley in 1581. On some occasions the earl's intervention was useful and successful; in

1581 Sir Francis Walsingham replied to the earl as 'the chiefe person in these partes and patrone of that poore town'.[30] The earl and the town had both recognised their respective places.

The earls of Derby took their influence seriously and were anxious to protect it; they could show considerable displeasure when arrangements or decisions made by the town did not suit them. In 1561 bad weather caused a Dublin vessel to run aground in the River Mersey. Liverpool's mayor prevented the vessel being taken by the earl's steward to the Cheshire side of the river. Soon afterwards the same mayor and his officers received a very curt reception at Lathom and were required to hand over the ship and its contents. Later in the same year the earl forbade Liverpool people from using Toxteth Park for pasture. A special town meeting was convened and a letter of apology dispatched to the earl in London.[31] These relations with the earl testify to Liverpool's weak political situation and to an awareness of the town's own vulnerability. The attitude of the town's merchant community was not, however, so different from that in many other Tudor towns; the earl of Leicester, for instance, dominated Warwick with a population of over 2,000.[32] Liverpool could not escape the influence of the earls of Derby and, inevitably at times, tried to use it.

Not only the earls of Derby, but many south Lancashire gentry had significant interest in the royal borough of Liverpool; since many of them owned burgages they were hard to ignore. The Molyneux family of Croxteth and Sefton was the most prominent local gentry family during the Tudor period. By the time of his death in 1548 Sir William Molyneux held property all around the town: at Croxteth, Sefton, Kirkby, Walton, Fazakerley and Kirkdale. During the 1530s he had gained control of the fee-farm of Liverpool. In the late fifteenth century it had been granted by Henry VII to one of his Welsh followers, David ap Griffiths, and Henry VIII had re-leased it to the widow and her son-in-law, Henry Ackers, steward of the royal manor of West Derby.[33] In 1537 the fee-farm was re-assigned to Sir William Molyneux and his family then held the lease for the rest of the Tudor period. The fee-farm provided control over the Mersey ferry, the shambles for butchers, stallage and market tolls, fair tolls, anchorage dues and the perquisites of courts.[34] Disputes between the town and the Molyneux family were frequent, particularly during the 1550s. Eventually the contest reached the Duchy of Lancaster courts in London, occasioning a special ley to be collected in Liverpool to fund the expenses of the mayor on several trips to the courts during the period from 1554 to 1556. The Molyneux family defended their interests with some vigour, although the town did have its charter confirmed by Mary I.[35]

In addition to the fee-farm the Molyneux family had long held the constableship of Liverpool castle, although by 1559 the castle was reported to be in 'greate ruin and decay'. Nothing was repaired, so that when the castle was re-surveyed in 1588 it was considered ruinous.[36] The family also leased the town's mills from the crown: another source of potential profit and dispute, as was evident during the 1580s.[37] The influence of the Molyneux family in Liverpool was considerable and was enhanced by the prompt acquisition of the properties of three of the four Liverpool chantries at the time of their dissolution. The properties were initially obtained in 1548 and by the time the family conducted a rental twenty years later it had 60 tenants in the town.[38] With this investment the Molyneux family exerted a very real and immediate influence among the population of the town. The town's authorities did not have the resources to exert their independence permanently and, at times, were undoubtedly forced to placate the family with, for instance, a banquet in 1559.[39] The rivalry was recognised and mostly controlled; it would resurface again in the seventeenth century.[40]

The Molyneux family may have been the most prominent local gentry family but it was by no means the only such family with which the town had to contend. In the immediate vicinity of the town the More family held considerable property and burgages in Liverpool itself. At his death in 1541 William More esquire held the manors of Kirkdale and Bootle as well as lands in Fazakerley, West Derby, Linacre, Litherland, Little Crosby, Ditton and Orrell. By the time of a rental in 1565 the family had 21 tenants on its Liverpool property and this was steadily being augmented; by 1576 there were 48 tenants and by 1592 there were 53 tenants in the town. This alone must have conveyed significant influence that was reaffirmed by the family ownership of Bootle and Kirkdale and residence at Bank Hall.[41] The More family acquired income from their urban as well as rural rents, and used some of their assets to provide commercial opportunities for younger sons. Thomas, son of William More (died 1541) became a successful merchant in the town, while two brothers pursued careers in the church. Later in the century three sons of John More esquire (died 1571) were each endowed with seven or eight tenancies in the town and went on to quite successful trading careers.[42]

Other gentry held substantially less property in Liverpool than the Molyneux and More families, but together they constituted a further significant influence that showed little sign of declining. In 1558 Richard Blundell esquire of Little Crosby had just one burgage in the town and bought half of another in Castle Street in 1580. Robert Blundell esquire of Ince Blundell had two houses in the town in 1586. Richard

Bold esquire of Bold, Roger Breres gentleman of Walton and Robert Fazakerley gentleman of Fazakerley all held just one burgage each. Richard Gellibrand gentleman of Lathom had one burgage in the town in 1570 but by 1610 the family had five properties in the town. Many other gentry families, for instance the Norrises of Speke and the Ecclestons of Eccleston, held small amounts of urban land.[43] The other reasonably substantial gentry property-owner was the Crosse family; James Crosse esquire held 12 burgages in 1558 and by 1619 the family had expanded their interest to 20 burgages. John Crosse esquire (who died in 1575) chose to live in Liverpool at Crosse Hall and to pursue an extensive commercial career.[44] The influence these families were able to exert as burgage holders must have been reinforced by their marriage connections with each other. John Crosse (died 1575) married three times and on each occasion into the families of south Lancashire gentry. His son John married the daughter of John More esquire of Bank Hall. Another daughter of John More married Nicholas Fazakerley gentleman, and another son married into a further south Lancashire gentry family. John More's eldest son and heir married a daughter of Sir Richard Molyneux.[45] Relations among these gentry were not always harmonious and rivalry could be keen, but family links and identity of interest ensured that to the end of the Tudor period the gentry retained their influence in a small town.

Many of the 'foreign' (non-resident) freemen in Tudor Liverpool were in fact gentry from south Lancashire. The 1565 list of burgesses includes, for example, Sir Richard Molyneux, William Norris esquire, the heirs of Richard Bold esquire, Richard Blundell esquire and William Fazakerley gentleman. By 1572 the earl of Derby and four of his sons were all recorded.[46] Foreign burgesses were expected to contribute to town leys and sometimes did attend town assemblies, as did Sir Richard Molyneux, William Norris and John More in 1563. In 1568 the town even fined some of them for non-attendance, although whether the fines were paid is not clear.[47] Gentry influence was substantial and immediate and their spending powers must have been of keen concern to the merchants of the town. The appointment of some gentry as mayor of the town testifies to a wish, or perhaps a need, to maintain close formal relationships. The appointment of members of the More family and of William Norris may have resulted from a wish by the town to secure additional weight in its rivalry with the Molyneux family, particularly over the terms of the fee-farm lease. The choice could, however, fall further afield such as the choice of Sir William Hesketh of Rufford in 1577–78. The considerable presence of the Molyneux family was recognised with the mayoralty of Sir Richard in 1588–89, while the ultimate testimony of deference to landed interests must be the choice of two sons of the third earl of Derby in the consecutive years 1568–69 and 1569–1570 and the eldest son of the fourth earl in 1585–86. Undoubtedly these appointments were intended to be largely honorific since the recipients must have been very frequently absent from Liverpool, but they were also a very blatant recognition of prevailing status and influence. The relationship was reciprocal; a small town needed and used local friends and allies. The local gentry had no wish to crush the economic vitality and potential of the town; they wished to share its success.

Parliamentary representation

During the Tudor period considerable strides were made in the status, identity and significance of Parliament, in particular the House of Commons, thanks largely to Henry VIII's legislation concerning religion and the succession. Seats in the Commons became increasingly desirable for various individuals and groups; fifteenth-century statutes concerning residence of MPs in their boroughs were almost totally ignored. The limited number of county seats remained dominated by the landed county élites; boroughs became the target for gentry, lawyers and minor officials seeking a seat in Parliament. Frequently small boroughs had to respond to the requests and preferences of local magnates.[48]

Liverpool had sent representatives to the Parliaments of 1295 and 1307, but thereafter had no parliamentary representation until 1545. From this time the choice of the small town's two MPs became greatly influenced by the earl of Derby and the Chancellor of the Duchy of Lancaster.[49] The earl was demonstrating his significant patronage and status in south Lancashire, while the Chancellor was a royal appointee able to marshal the considerable patronage of the Duchy organisation, albeit from a distance in London. The Duchy Chancellors usually held office for some years, such as Sir Ambrose Cave from 1559 to 1568 and Sir Ralph Sadler from 1568 to 1587. During their time in office they were able to make their presence felt in the north-west of England. The selection of the parliamentary representatives for the Lancashire boroughs provided opportunity for both elements of patronage to be wielded and demonstrated. In Lancaster the Chancellor had a strong influence and, for instance, the sons of the Chancellor and the Vice-Chancellor of the Duchy were chosen. In Preston, Clitheroe, Wigan and Liverpool the Chancellor and the earl of Derby tended to share the patronage since there were two seats allotted to each borough. The earl, like the Chancellor, used the opportunity to advance his household officers and favourable gentry.[50]

In a town as small as Tudor Liverpool this combined influence must have been hard to resist, whereas Chester was able to choose their MPs with greater independence: usually their recorder and one alderman.[51] In 1555 the town books refer to the apparently accepted Liverpool practice of holding an assembly in the common hall to seal the town's reply to the sheriff's writ requesting the nominations; one of the Members was to be Sir Richard Sherburne (steward of the third earl of Derby), and the other place was left open for 'thother to be nominatyd' by the Chancellor of the Duchy, as no specific information had been received from him.[52] The shared patronage was openly recognised. Late in 1558, at the commencement of the reign of Elizabeth I, writs were sent out for a new Parliament. In January 1559, since instructions had not been received from the Chancellor again, the town tried to nominate one of its own merchants, Ralph Sekerston, and the meeting agreed to support him with limited expenses. In the event, the Chancellor did make a last-minute choice and Ralph Sekerston's name was erased from the parliamentary return.[53]

Ralph Sekerston was an alderman of the town who had served as mayor in 1550–51, and was to do so again in 1560–61. As one of the principal merchants he must have been moderately wealthy by the standards of Liverpool and he was experienced in civic affairs. He was also persistent. For the second Parliament of Queen Elizabeth's reign in late 1562 the town was 'evyll trobled abourte the election'; the town chose a younger son of Sir Richard Molyneux and reserved the other choice for the earl of Derby, 'merveylying muche that he send not to the towne'.[54] Several meetings were held in this vacuum of instruction and eventually the mayor replied to the sheriff, as returning officer, that no choice had been made since no information had been forthcoming from the earl, 'when always wee were moost naturallye beholdyn and bound to him'. In these circumstances Ralph Sekerston was again nominated 'one daye and disapoynted another daye'; the sheriff refused the certificate from the town. Another town meeting agreed to send Ralph Sekerston to London. 'He roode almoost poost and toke the sayd cerificat wyth him' in an attempt to secure the earl's approval. The Chancellor 'in his fumous' summoned Liverpool's mayor to Westminster and tried to oppose the choice but, with the earl of Derby's approval, Ralph Sekerston finally took his seat in the House of Commons.[55]

Ralph Sekerston's determination and speed of journey to London secured his nomination, although he was to cost Liverpool dearly. The disputed selection put the town to 'great charge' so that 'a sesse was leyd and gathered throughe the towne and send up to London for the charges of him after ii*s*. a daye'. Ralph Sekerston attended the parliamentary sessions and 'stode up after the maner theare and was speaker hymsellffe, to the great grief of mayster chauncellour'. 'All this whylis nothing was herd of what mayster Richard Molineux dyd.'[56] The town, for the first time, funded its own Member of Parliament and clearly took an interest in the proceedings; during the adjournment in 1567 Ralph Sekerston explained 'openlie his doyngs in this last parliament' to a town assembly and claimed that he had presented a petition on behalf of the town.[57] Ralph Sekerston and the town seemed pleased with the new opportunity.

Not surprisingly, at the elections of 1571 and 1572 Ralph Sekerston was returned as MP for Liverpool, with the approval of the earl of Derby. The town returned their choice to the sheriff and left blank the Chancellor's nomination.[58] With his little experience, Sekerston became quite an active parliamentarian; in 1571 he served on three committees for dress regulation, on tillage and, very appropriately, on navigation. He also introduced a private member's bill 'for erectyage of a parish church at Lyverpole'.[59] There can have been little dearer to the aspirations of Liverpool's small population. Unfortunately there was no time for the bill's completion, as with so many private bills in each session. In 1572 Ralph Sekerston returned to Westminster with equal enthusiasm. He served on just one committee, on cloth, but he was a frequent speaker on a variety of economic and social issues. He spoke, for instance, in the debate concerning poor law revision and claimed the bill was 'very parciall. London and other greate cities provided for. But no provision for Lipoole and other smale boroughes'. In addition, Sekerston's rather blunt attack on lords, gentlemen and bishops for keeping too few servants created some opposition, notably from Lord Burghley himself. Perhaps inevitably a few days later when the Liverpool MP returned to his plan for a parish church in the town (with Sir Richard Molyneux and his successors as patrons) he obtained insufficient support. He claimed that the town's chapel was 'fairer' than the mother church at Walton but, without wider political support, his private bill did not proceed beyond its second reading.[60]

During the remainder of the session Ralph Sekerston continued his parliamentary participation. He spoke against the proposal to limit the export of leather and probably further antagonised royal ministers by speaking of the abuses of the Lord Admiral's privateering licences. On these types of topic the Liverpool MP had particular knowledge and/or views, as he had on the proposal to limit imports by royal proclamation. This bill was supported by Lord Burghley, yet Sekerston claimed that 'this bill altogether for the benefit of the City [London]', and that Liverpool would suffer from restrictions limiting the import of Spanish iron and oil. Sekerston did associate himself with the interests of other localities, such as Stafford, but primarily he saw himself as a representative of his town and its concerns. In the debate on the bill for sea marks and buoys he approved of the main provisions yet complained that all of the forfeitures would go to Trinity House; perceptively he said 'every man now seeketh all commodities to come to London, as though all the knightes and burgesses of the rest of the realme come in vayne'.[61]

Two months later in August 1572 Ralph Sekerston was back in Liverpool explaining his 'doyngs in this parliament', and passing on first-hand information about the provisions of the new poor law.[62] Liverpool and its MP could scarcely have seemed more closely linked. Personal tragedy, however, followed soon; Sekerston's two married daughters and only son died later in the same year. Sometime within the next two or three years Ralph Sekerston himself died.[63] His blaze of independence as Liverpool's own representative in Parliament also died. For the rest of the Tudor period the two MPs from the town were again 'outsiders' nominated by the earl of Derby and the Chancellor of the Duchy.[64] In 1583 the town wrote to one of these Members, Arthur Autye who was secretary to the earl of Leicester, explaining that Liverpool was too 'poore to perfourme anie reward'.[65] The town was indeed neither large nor wealthy, but for their own merchant they had paid the two shillings a day allowance; for an 'outsider' it was a different matter.

Ralph Sekerston may have had a parliamentary career of only a decade, yet he had shown what was possible, albeit with the co-operation of the earl of Derby. A Liverpool merchant of fairly moderate means could and did travel regularly to Westminster to sit in the House of Commons; he could even debate policy with the Queen's treasurer, Lord Burghley. Sekerston knew of national policy and helped to pass national legislation; he also retained and enunciated his local interests and concerns. Not until 1603–04 did another Liverpool merchant sit in Parliament: Giles Brooke, former mayor and alderman. Ralph Sekerston's parliamentary excursion testifies to the potential for national participation by a small town. It also demonstrates Liverpool's unimportant and insignificant role at this level. Sekerston may have made a valiant personal contribution but he was politically isolated and without support from other social and economic interests. The small town flexed its parliamentary muscles, briefly, yet was unable to sustain the activity. It may be that Liverpool's show of independence happened to suit the interests of the earl of Derby in reminding the South East of the regional strength of the North West. Liverpool's small population did perceive themselves to have a corporate identity; their borough status provided a degree of self-government that was supported by a high level of participation in town meetings and offices. The merchant élite controlled the council and the mayoralty, but they did live in the same seven streets as everyone else. The earls of Derby and local gentry retained traditional influence in the town yet their interest could be amicable and advantageous. A measure of suitable deference oiled the wheels of co-operation in matters of common regional interest.

CHAPTER SEVEN

Social contact

I n Tudor Liverpool a face-to-face society was inevitable; seven
streets cannot have taken long to perambulate. The adult male
population must have known virtually all other men by sight, probably
had commercial contact with many, interacted with each other for civic
administrative purposes, and met each other on a fairly regular basis at
town assemblies. The very notion that a town meeting could be called
at short notice to debate emergency decisions and actions, such as the
harbour repair after the fierce storm, highlights the nature and scale
of community contact. Less obvious from surviving sixteenth-century
records, but surely with equal facility, the adult female population must
have known each other in such a restricted environment. The mundane,
everyday domestic necessities must have ensured contact with one
another: fetching water from the town's wells or buying food supplies
at the Saturday market, for instance. Indeed, a significant proportion
of the population in Tudor Liverpool must have been related to their
neighbours, although the absence of chapel registers in this period
makes it difficult to reconstruct the complexity of this. The children of
the small town grew up knowing at least the appearance and identity of
their contemporaries. In a community of this size such social distinction
as existed must have been very evident and ever present.[1]

The social order

Nowhere can the Tudor social order have been more visible than
in Liverpool's one chapel. St Nicholas' chapel was the one building
that came closest to accommodating the majority of the small town's
population. There was the concern, exhibited through MP Ralph
Sekerston, to enhance the status of the chapel to full parochial rank, but
during the sixteenth century there is no evidence of any wish or incentive
to build another ecclesiastical structure. Rather, all attention and civic
pride was focused on the one chapel on the waterfront at the centre of
the town. The mayor had long had a separate stall in the chancel. In

1572 this was refurbished with a new pew and, in conformity with the new religious arrangements, the royal coat of arms was mounted above it in 'fayre guylding or other pleasant colors'.[2] The location of the mayor's pew was just the most prominent of seating arrangements in the chapel. By 1587 the town books reported that 'some contraversie, contencion and variance hath bene had and moved amongeste diverse women, as well the bailiffes wyves nowe beinge, as others whose husbandes have heretofore supplied the same office, and chieflie for and aboutes theire places of kneelinge or sittinge in the church'. The town assembly had to deal with this issue and took the decision that, by seniority of office, those whose husbands had been mayor were to sit and kneel at the uppermost form or nearest to the mayor. Those whose husbands were then bailiffs were to have the next form and the remainder were to sit next according to the anciency of holding the office. A similar arrangement was decreed for aldermen's wives. All of this was to be accomplished with the proviso that if the forms were not 'sufficente and large enough to conteine theim all', then the youngest in office was to remove herself to some other convenient place.[3] Petty as these seating disputes may seem, they must have involved and have been witnessed by many in the town. Precedence, place and the illusion of stability were undoubtedly of major concern to Tudor Liverpudlians.

In the town some merchants and officials claimed gentleman status. The Secum family of merchants probably based their view on their status as freeholders within the town. Peter Starkey, the town's customs official (from Great Budworth in Cheshire), and Thomas Wickstead, the deputy customer, both traded as merchants but used the title of 'gentleman'; presumably in view of their official capacities.[4] William More esquire of Bank Hall used his resources to found mercantile careers for his younger sons by providing them with seven or eight tenements in the town. These sons continued to refer to themselves as gentlemen while pursuing very active trading operations.[5] At least two of the gentlemen in Tudor Liverpool had followed military careers. George Ackers (from West Derby) had served as a captain under the earl of Essex in France, Flanders and Ireland. His probate inventory (1588) testifies to his former military interests with its three calivers (small hand guns), four flax and touchboxes, one target (shield), three morions (helmets), two bandoliers, one sword, a buckler, two rapiers and two daggers. By the time of his death, however, he had invested in a number of trading ventures and had a half share in the *Eagle*.[6] Captain John Gifford (alias Wardell) gentleman had served primarily under the auspices of the earl of Derby; in the 1570s he had trained the militia throughout south Lancashire. By the 1590s he had settled, somewhat impecuniously, in Liverpool.[7]

Ferdinando, fifth earl of Derby, by a follower of Marcus Gheerhaerts the Younger, (c.1594), oil on canvas, 30 × 24½ ins. Ferdinando Stanley, 5th earl of Derby (born 1559, died 1594) was one of the leading aristocrats of the later sixteenth century. His family had houses in Lancashire, Cheshire and London and, although he was regularly at the royal court, he also frequently visited Knowsley. During the 1580s Ferdinando was especially involved with patronage of theatre companies in London. He was mayor of Liverpool from 1585 until 1586.

BY COURTESY OF THE DERBY COLLECTION, KNOWSLEY, K258

The fine collection of Molyneux brasses at Sefton testify to the wealth and influence of the landed gentry. Sir William Molyneux (died 1548) had served King Henry VIII on three expeditions to Scotland and he is commemorated wearing armour, while the brasses of his two wives (Jane Rugge and Elizabeth Clifton) provide some detail of early Tudor costume for the wealthy. His son Richard was mayor of Liverpool 1541/42. The Molyneux coat of arms appears in Sefton church in a number of memorials.

Above: the Molyneux coat of arms on the floor, beneath the brasses of Sir William and his wives.

Right: Sir William Molyneux (died 1548).

Far right: Elizabeth Clifton, wife of Sir William.

PHOTOGRAPHS: CARNEGIE, BY COURTESY OF THE RECTOR, ST HELEN'S CHURCH, SEFTON

Probate inventories for women are relatively rare, produced only for spinsters and widows, since married women at this time were deemed to have no possessions in their own right. Jane Nicholson appears to be among the poorest inhabitants of Liverpool, possibly lodging with other family members or elsewhere in the town. The items recorded in the inventory belonged solely to her, and provide an indication of an existence at the margins of society.

LRO, WCW JANE NICHOLSON, LIVERPOOL, 1593

An inventory of the goods and chattells of Jane Nicolson
late deceased, praysed the 15 of June 1593 by William Eccleston,
Raffe Chamner, Richard Whitfield and Myles Kyrkdale.

Imprimis: vi old sheep & ii lambes with certaine wole	xx s.
It: in old brass & pewter	iii s. 4 d.
It: in barley upon the ground	xx s.
It: in otes, beans & pease & fitches	xiiii s.
It: parsneps & and flax upon the ground	xii s.
It: a dishbord, one folding table & one form & one chere & bords	ii s.
It: in treen ware	xx d.
It: one byll, a pair of tonges & a candle pane	xiiiid
It: bedding linen and wollen	v s.
It: in apparel linen and wollen	v s.

Summa totalis £iiii iiii s. ii d.

Birth, inherited wealth, occupation, legal status, civic rank and lifestyle all contributed to contemporaries' perceptions of social rank; local elements and traditions also played a part. At levels of society below that of the would-be gentlemen and of the mayor and civic officers these perceptions are difficult to discern.[8] In Tudor Liverpool many of the town's population were probably quite similar to each other in living standards, available wealth and lifestyles. There was the small élite of more prosperous merchants but, following them, the financial resources of ships' masters, the other tradesmen, the craftsmen and the service providers cannot have been very different from each other. Perhaps this proximity of status explains the interest in a visible ranking made possible by the civic seating arrangements in the chapel. Exact social gradations at this level of society may have had a degree of clarity to contemporaries; mostly they now elude the historian.

In a small town those individuals that did not readily fit into the established social pattern must have been very noticeable: in particular those that could be perceived as representing potential instability or in some way causing a possible charge on the resources of the town. There was, therefore, an incentive to minimise disruption and to ensure the preservation of an ordered community. The 'deserving' poor were not a discovery of sixteenth-century legislation; they had long existed and been recognised. The orphan, the aged, the incurably ill and the disabled all deserved assistance and charity since, through no fault of their own, they could not maintain themselves. Family support may well have hidden much of this activity, particularly in a small, reasonably stable community. The elderly may have been at least partially supported by children and orphans cared for by aunts and uncles or even older siblings. Random references suggest that the town did recognise some responsibility for these deserving cases when immediate familial assistance was not available. A town assembly agreed, for instance, to lease to Henry Wirral, 'a verie poore man', a cottage, yard and garden in More Street at an exceptionally low rent.[9] Certainly there were elements of self-interest, with a desire to avoid future expenditure in this type of provision; probably also these was some measure of willingness to assist those perceived to be 'deserving'.

Illegitimate children were a less clear category for concern. Many wills from south Lancashire testify to recognition of illegitimate children and an attempt by at least one parent to make some provision for them. John Gifford gentleman (1598) left the bulk of his possessions to his illegitimate daughter in Liverpool. Thomas Bolton (1597) made provision for apparently all of his children; he shared his assets among three legitimate daughters, a legitimate son, and two illegitimate sons.

Quite frequently a division of an inheritance among legitimate and illegitimate offspring was chosen by testators. As an only surviving child illegitimacy was no great barrier to sole inheritance. Presumably these children that were recognised in wills had, in any event, been provided with some previous regular maintenance. Illegitimacy appears to have represented the dubious fringe of the deserving, but hopefully, avoidable poor; in a small town acceptance of responsibilities must have been hard to avoid.

In addition to the various categories of deserving poor, who were ever present, there was also the real possibility during the Tudor period of some natural disaster creating additional local distress. High mortality, where the death rate rose to double or treble the norm, could be very disruptive to a community by removing wage-earners, interrupting local trade and interfering with routine agricultural practices. Widows and young children could be left without immediate financial support. Though serious and traumatic at the time, these disturbances were often of short-term duration but were, nonetheless, feared in urban areas.[10] It is clear that before the 1540s Liverpool had considered measures to adopt at times of epidemic disease. The main plank of the plan was an attempt at isolation by housing all actual and suspected victims in cabins on the heath just outside the perimeter of the town until the mayor considered it safe enough to allow them to return.[11]

A serious outbreak of disease (referred to as plague, although it may have coincided with the sweating sickness) occurred in 1558 when 'great sicknesse' was reported in all parts of Lancashire. It was claimed by the Liverpool scribe that the infection had been carried from Manchester by an Irishman trading in linen cloth. Beginning in August, the outbreak 'encresyd dayle and dayle to a gret numbre that died'; perhaps about 250 people by mid November. A disaster on this scale in a town of Liverpool's size must have had enormous personal impact as well as causing considerable disruption to the local economy. The weekly market was abandoned and the annual fair cancelled. Nervousness was understandably still evident in January 1559, when Ellen Denton was forced to avoid the town because she was believed to have the disease.[12] Not until 1578 was plague or other epidemic sickness mentioned again in the vicinity of Liverpool and a watch was kept at the boundaries of the town; apparently with success.[13] Not until after the end of the century, in 1610, did a return of the plague necessitate special decisions and cabins on the heath.[14] The isolation arrangements may or may not have been entirely efficacious, but their implementation does testify to a degree of organisation and control throughout the population of Tudor Liverpool.

For those with inadequate, insufficient or uncertain employment, or indeed no employment at all, food prices were of crucial importance; high prices and/or paucity of supply could create the potential for instability and riot. Wheat was usually the key crop, although in the north-west of England oats and barley and even the fodder crops of peas and beans were of significance. A harvest could be considered deficient when the price of wheat rose to 10–25 per cent above a thirty-one year average; it could be considered bad if the price rose to 25–50 per cent above this average; and it could be considered to be a state of dearth when the price got above 50 per cent more than the average.[15] Evidence is limited and patchy, but it is clear that by the 1590s food prices in Lancashire were rising rapidly. In isolated years this had happened previously, for instance in 1578 when corn was at 'an excessive price', and in 1580 when little wheat was to be had in all of Lancashire and Cheshire.[16] The 1590s, however, were undoubtedly the worst consecutive harvest years of the century, and it is possible to speculate that dearth may have appeared earlier in this area than in the rest of England since there was high mortality from 1591 onwards. By March 1596 Liverpool's mayor was complaining to the mayor of Chester that 'the dearth considered' Liverpool could not cope with the multitudes of soldiers in the vicinity of the town. He also commentated that many householders were recently dead. By October of 1596 it was reported to Lord Burghley from Chester that no wheat or rye could be obtained at any price, and even by 1600 there was still great scarcity of wheat.[17]

Evidence for prices is extremely patchy and not necessarily consistent, but local sources do provide some particular instances. In south Lancashire wheat had been costing 3s.–4s. a windle (a large measure) during the 1580s. By the 1590s it was costing 5s. for the same amount and by 1602 this had risen to 6s. Rye had cost 13s. 4d. for a bushel in the 1580s had risen to over 30s. by the mid and late 1590s. Barley and oats had, likewise, more than doubled in price and in individual years had exceeded this rate of increase.[18] In view of the potential for distress and disorder occasioned by these inflated food prices, Liverpool's authorities do seem to have had a regard to ensure supplies to all of the town's population. In 1560 a decision of the Portmoot restricted the sale of corn at the market to no more than six windles to any one person on one day. In 1577 the permitted quantity was reduced to four windles, and early in 1578, in view of the excessive price of grain, the water bailiff was empowered to search boats for anyone attempting to transport grain to Wales and other places. As the harvest situation eased and supplies became more available during the 1580s a distinction was still enforced at Liverpool's market between the quantity of grain a townsman could buy and what was available to 'foreigners' from outside the town. From 1588 onwards the distribution to 'foreigners' was further reduced, including the guests of householders in the town. In 1595 quantities to both towns-people and outsiders were again reduced.[19] Such was the scarcity of supply by this time that the assembly took the decision to remit all tolls on any corn brought to the market by outsiders. It became necessary to instruct the leavelookers to carry halberds when supervising the market; whether for their own defence and/or to maintain order and supervise the specified rationing is not clear. There is also indication during the last few years of the century that a few individuals were presented at court for indeed attempting to purchase more than the permitted quota of grain: three people in 1598, and six in 1599.[20] The marketing of fish was similarly controlled by the town to ensure that supplies reached all of the population. When vessels landed in Liverpool during the herring season the water bailiff was instructed to see that all poor people were served with just 1d. or 2d. worth of fish.[21]

This paternalistic attitude by the civic authorities may well have had a significant impact in a small town for much of the time. It was reinforced by individual recognition that some individuals, through various circumstances, were unable to support themselves. Exact defini-tions of the 'poor' probably elude precision, and poverty was and is a relative concept.[22] Testamentary evidence provides an indication of contemporary recognition that some of the town's population needed help; twenty-three per cent of Liverpool wills from the later Tudor period provided a cash bequest to the poor. The amount was usually quite small, but was presumably made in the belief that the deserving poor could be identified and the bequest adequately distributed. In a small town perhaps this was a realistic assumption. Bequests ranged from Reginald Melling's 6s. 8d. in 1572 to Anne More's £8 3s. 4d. in 1589. Most gifts were of about £1. There is no sign of more elaborate provision such as almshouses, stocks of materials, subsidies to fund education or apprenticeships.[23] Nor is there surviving evidence of donations and support that may have been provided during individuals' lifetimes to those that they perceived to be deserving of relief.

In a variety of ways the prevailing social order was recognised, maintained and protected during the Tudor period in Liverpool; in a small town there was little sign of significant change.

Female perspectives

The Tudor perception of the status of half of the adult population, the women, is demonstrated by two phenomena; firstly by their relative, although by no means total, absence from surviving documentation, and secondly by the continuing use in south-west Lancashire of patronymics in the designation of females. In surviving parish register evidence from this area the use of the suffixes 'daughter' and 'wife' remain until the end of the Tudor period. At Childwall in 1563 Ellen Hamnet's daughter and Catherine Henry's daughter were both baptized, while in 1565 Elizabeth William's daughter was married. In Liverpool's parish of Walton-on-the-Hill the last recorded use of 'daughter' was in 1602.[24] Certainly the frequency of use of these appellations was diminishing, but their residual appearance in this period suggests a traditional and conservative view of the status of women by the male scribes. This prevailing opinion was bolstered by the authority of law, which continued to restrict severely female participation in legal and administrative processes.[25]

Needless to say, women had virtually no opportunity to participate in the civic administration of Liverpool. Their absence from formal records may, however, tend to diminish their status to a greater extent than was evident to contemporaries. The male clerk of the town books in 1587 blamed the wives of the civic dignitaries for the seating dispute in chapel; he may or may not have been accurate in where he attributed blame but presumably he was correct in recording the women in prominent positions in church. According to the 1587 rental details of forty-six properties in the town that belonged to the More family 22 per cent had female tenants. Another rental of 1598 of the forty-nine former chantry properties recorded 16 per cent in the hands of women.[26] These details would suggest that in any one year females formed a significant minority of heads of households responsible for their properties and their families, and in practice a number of other women must have functioned as heads of their households when husbands or fathers were away at sea.[27]

The 1565 assessment roll of contributions made in Liverpool for the repair costs at Walton parish church records 15 per cent of house-holds with a female head.[28] Sixteen of these twenty-six women were listed as widows, using that mode of description with the surname of their former husbands. Some of them ranked (with many of the men) among the poorest contributors, assessed at 1d. or 2d., but others were rated to pay rather more: widow Bailey in Water Street at 8d., and widow Fairclough in the same street at 16d. The other ten women were identified by forename and surname, with no indication of marital status; in the context it seems likely that they were unmarried at the time of the compilation of the list. All of these women were assessed at only 1d., except for Joan Mosse of Dale Street who was rated at 2d. It was evidently more important to ensure contributions from all eligible households in the town than to ignore the minority of females who, through force of circumstance, found themselves heads of households.

Provision for widows was less open to personal decision than provision for daughters; common law in the Tudor period required that for life a widow was entitled to maintenance from one third of her deceased husband's assets, and to provision of accommodation, albeit in one third of her former home.[29] In addition to this legal expectation, other arrangements might well have been made during the lifetimes of various couples so that testamentary evidence might well represent the wishes of only those with some specific reason beyond the routine to make a will. Probably provision for widows was influenced by numbers of surviving children and their ages as much as by actual wealth; Robert Wolfall's widow in 1578 appears to have inherited almost all of her husband's assets in order to help her cope with a young family. During widowhood some women could achieve a measure of independence, although if they were to remarry this disappeared.

There is no surviving evidence from Liverpool that women participated in organised trading or commercial activities beyond transactions at the weekly market, yet it is inconceivable that some did not do so indirectly through the activities of their sons or factors. The most notable surviving indication of widows maintaining the occupational activity of their former husbands appears to be with the operation of the ferry-boat across the River Mersey. For some years during the 1560s the widows of Peter Gregory and Ralph Oliver continued the joint venture after the deaths of their husbands. This may have been an exceptional case that was intended to provide both women with a means of livelihood in the short term, similar to the decision in 1576 by the town's assembly to allow Catherine Diall to operate an alehouse during her widowhood in order to maintain herself and her family.[30] For the majority of females in Tudor Liverpool there was little economic independence. Part-time, rather marginal, activity such as keeping an illegal alehouse was the most many women could achieve. Even widow Ward, the town's midwife, can scarcely have made a fortune.[31]

Neighbourliness

With just seven streets and one chapel Tudor Liverpool surely constituted one community: one concentration of people who could identify, talk to and meet each other. Parochial identity and gild associations were unknown phenomena and occupational groupings were too small to generate significant identity.[32] Nonetheless, the potential for disruption and disorder existed even in small places, particularly port towns.

Evidence from the town books during the second half of the sixteenth century bears testimony to unrest, disturbance, violence and crime, yet rarely was this kind of activity co-ordinated, organised or sustained. Co-existence and neighbourliness usually prevailed.

Provision to deal with disorder was not elaborate. The sergeant had a bill as a symbol of his office but there was little other means of enforcement available to the town's officials, other than for voluntary assistance from other townspeople.[33] There were no other constables or law enforcement officials in the town. In 1579 the town books refer to the inconvenience of not having a gaol in the town; when necessary the ground floor of the common hall served the purpose. Alan Gogney offered his newly built house near the sea to the town, but there is no evidence that the lack of a gaol prompted expenditure on the purchase of such a property. A pair of stocks provided the most regularly used form of punishment for minor misbehaviour and at intervals they were repaired. There is mention of a cuckstool (ducking stool) needing repair in 1578 and this supposes a willingness to use it.[34]

The records of the mayor's Court of Passage do not survive from the Tudor period but the town books suggest that theft was not a widespread crime. The scale of the environment in a small town may well have increased the likelihood of detection and reduced the opportunities for handling and concealing stolen goods. John Mole was apprehended in 1585 for stealing a goose, while in the same year John Owen and his wife were accused of being 'sly robbers'. They were probably not residents and were ordered to be expelled from the town. Margaret Griffiths alias Rees was found guilty of stealing linen and woollen clothing from the house of the former mayor Robert Corbet; her punishment was a whipping.[35] Perhaps as a deterrent to others, the punishment meted out in 1565 to two pickpockets apprehended in the house of Reginald Melling was more severe. The one from Chester was to be nailed by the ear to a post by the butchers' stalls in the market (presumably on market day), then stripped and beaten out of the town by boys with rods. His accomplice from Liverpool was to be secured with an iron chain and horse-lock to a block of wood for several days, as well as being ordered to make restitution of 5s. 4d.[36] Punishment appears to have been short, sharp and summary; and the incidents appear to have been sufficiently unusual to warrant special mention in the town books.

The enforcement of national provisions against unlawful pastimes and leisure activities must have presented much more of a dilemma to civic authorities in such a small community. The town's officers were required to suppress behaviour that supposedly had the potential for disturbance, but among some of the population these self-same activities must have been welcome and endemic, particularly in a port town. In compliance with official policy Liverpool's bye-laws throughout the Tudor period prohibited servants and apprentices from indulging in cards, dice, bowls and other unlawful games 'inventid or to be inventyd', thus covering all eventualities. In an attempt to enforce these prohibitions apprentices were ordered not to leave their masters' premises after 8.00 p.m. unless out on authorised business.[37] Despite the regulations, the proscribed activities are evident throughout the Tudor period with perhaps only token attempts at effective suppression. In a small town neighbours and the town's officials must have been well informed about group activity and behaviour. Alehouse-keepers were warned to suppress the illegal games, especially dice, and the ale and tippling houses were blamed for being 'greate norisshers of idlenes'. Bonds and sureties were taken from time to time in an attempt to control the pastimes; a measure of supervision was perhaps achieved, but not suppression.[38] It must have been impossible to regulate activities in private houses and quite hard to conceal them totally in just seven streets. Richard Dobbe had servants and apprentices gambling at his house in 1566; the wife of Thomas Harker kept a bowling alley and welcomed servants and youths to use it in 1591.[39] Keeping part-time and unlicensed alehouses provided much welcome supplementary income. It seems doubtful that the suppression of these leisure activities was pursued with great determination and consistency; sufficient will did not exist among the town's authorities.

Interest was more acute if and when these same activities contributed to disturbance and disorder. Throughout the Tudor period a level of personal lawlessness was ever-present in Liverpool although there is no sign that it increased in severity or got out of control. Small-scale affrays involving up to six or eight men occurred periodically, and usually bonds to keep the peace were the response and other forms of punishment were not invoked. Brawling, in this restricted sense, seems to have been a part of life in Tudor Liverpool. The largest number of men involved in one incident occurred in 1587 when fourteen names were recorded in the town books.[40] Virtually no explanation of these incidents is given, although a clue may be provided by the date of the disturbance in 1565: the day after Twelfth Night. Twelve youths were involved and the town's wait James Atherton was discharged from his post since he appeared to have been the 'captain' of the offenders.[41] In a port town it is inconceivable that the return of various ships, albeit with small numbers of crew, did not provide the occasion for meetings in alehouses and a degree of celebration. Commercial dispute seems to lie behind the raid on the premises of merchant Alexander Garnet in 1564 when quantities of cloth were seized by other merchants: all senior members of the town.[42] The only sign of organised or orchestrated disorder occurred earlier in the sixteenth century when local gentry used the town to pursue their family rivalries. There had been an altercation over rent payments, and animals had been impounded in lieu. These animals were released and together with thirty rioters caused a commotion 'up and downe the stretes' of Liverpool. The depositions of evidence produced for the Duchy of Lancaster Court make it plain that the participants had 'assembled' in Liverpool and were the tenants of Sir William Molyneux and William More esquire.[43] The town seems to have been the location of the disturbance rather than the occasion.

Only occasionally were women involved in disorder. Four women were presented to the court in 1589 for scolding (arguing) in the town's street to the provocation of their neighbours; the punishment for this disruptive behaviour was a significant fine of 10s. 0d. or ten days in gaol, without benefit of wine, beer or ale at meal-times.[44] Actual violence and use of weapons associated with these affrays are only infrequently mentioned. Alice, the wife of Edward Wilson, was sufficently motivated to beat with a staff the wife of Robert Davy, the wife of Robert Johnson and their daughter, while merchants Richard Andleser, Thomas Secum, Thomas More and Ralph Sekerston all recoursed to use of their daggers in 1563 and 1564. Likewise, George Rainford was sufficiently provoked to draw his dagger on Thomas Bavand in 1584.[45] Evidence of serious injury seems, however, rare. The face-to-face society of a small town kept disturbance and behaviour within acceptable bounds.

Tudor Liverpool did have to contend with one enormous additional problem that presented an immediate threat to the ordered operation of the town: the conveyance of English troops to and from Ireland. The logistics of transport and victualling created their own difficulties which were exacerbated by the actual passage of considerable numbers of men, many of whom were reluctant participants. Contrary winds which caused delay in embarkation resulted in serious difficulty for the town. During the winter months of 1565 Sir Henry Sidney's company was delayed and there was actual bloodshed before the men finally departed. In 1572 the town was 'verie evill vexed and troubled' before the soldiers of the earl of Essex's expedition eventually vacated the port. The unrest continued into the next year when the only way to ensure punishment of a soldier was to have twelve billmen from the town guard him in the stocks. Retaliation was envisaged and on the Sunday following townsfolk assembled on the heath with their best weapons 'egar as lions' in 'batell arey' to provide a show of strength to the awaiting soldiers.[46] Quite extreme action had been necessary to preserve control in the town.

The other aspect of this troop transport was the return journey. In 1573 the town was burdened with many poor soldiers; some were sick and wounded, and some of those who died had to be buried at the town's expense. After the misfortunes at Carrickfergus in the following year Liverpool's schoolhouse (formerly St Mary del Quay) was pressed into use as a temporary hospital for the sick soldiers.[47] In 1581 the 'late mutynous disorder and disobedience of certen solildyers' was reported to the Privy Council and it was recommended that an example be made of the 300 troops involved at Liverpool.[48] Serious as these military disturbances had been, they had been of relatively short duration, until the 1590s, when the level of continuous activity in Ireland must have almost overwhelmed the small town. Soldiers were billeted throughout the town and a multitude of sick, wounded and disbanded soldiers remained. In March 1596 the mayor claimed that for several years Liverpool had been 'surcharged' with these troops.[49] Some attempt had been made since 1593 at national provision for the relief of returning seamen and soldiers through a system of parish collections. Whether south Lancashire benefited in any way from these collections is not clear, although certainly Prescot parish was collecting the money in 1594 and the Lancashire magistrates were urging more substantial collections from larger parishes in 1595.[50] Liverpool's neighbourliness must have been tested greatly by the increasing incidence of large numbers of soldiers in its midst. For such a small town several hundreds of men provided welcome transport work and supply opportunities, but their presence in the town for any length of time brought very real issues of order and control.

The immediate difficulties of coping with departing and returning soldiers may have deflected interest from the ever-present sixteenth-century problem of vagrancy. Tudor writers stressed the dangers and threats posed by vagrancy, although presumably the incidence of actual vagrants was more acute in areas of high unemployment and locations that were convenient and attractive to travellers.[51] In Liverpool evidence of the more disreputable activities of vagrants is sparse, possibly because the numbers involved were not great in this area. During the later part of the Tudor period, however, there was increasing interest in ensuring that there was little opportunity for travellers to lodge and settle in the town. As a port Liverpool could have attracted such vagrants as were to be found in south Lancashire. With the limitations of the available evidence it is hard always to distinguish offences that involved outsiders. Contemporary attitudes are, however, plain. In 1572 'noe players of interludes ... jugglers and gesters, or wandring people brynning any monstrous or straunge beastes' were to be allowed into the town without a licence from the mayor. Possibly in response to this measure of control, a year later two wanderers and performers with hobby-horses were put in the stocks at the high cross.[52] Not until this same year, 1573, was the issue of begging specifically mentioned in the town books; a woman and her five children were ordered not to beg at the chapel at service time. Comment two years later would suggest that this particular problem was on the increase since action had to be taken 'to advoyde the evill example of the griedie beggars and petie pikers', and by 1580 the clerk noted 'the multitude of idle and loytringe persons'. In 1581 it was claimed that many of these vagrants came from the Isle of Man, Ireland and the North, in addition to Welsh Alice who was to be expelled from the town.[53]

For the last two decades of the sixteenth century Liverpool does appear to have pursued more concerted activity against the vagrants in the town. In 1584 a three-year residence qualification was specified for recognition of settlement, otherwise vagrants were to spend two days and nights in the stocks before eviction from the town. Renewed activity was directed against beggars. The culmination of the campaign was the decision in 1596 to produce a catalogue of all lodgers in Liverpool; those without the appropriate residence qualification were to be expelled or maintained at the cost of those with whom they lodged.[54] These attempts to undertake firmer action against vagrants, at a time of the influx of soldiers *en route* to and from Ireland, highlighted the issue of illegal accommodation being provided by the inhabitants of Liverpool. Throughout the Tudor period townspeople were not supposed to house those who might be perceived to be beggars or vagrants; the fine was fixed at 6*s.* 8*d.* Only intermittently had offences been noted until the 1580s. Anyone with a guest staying more than one night was supposed to inform the mayor. For many Liverpudlians additional income, however small, from permitting lodgers to remain must have been very tempting. William Golborne was accused of keeping 'diverse and manie tenantes on the back sydes of his tenementes', and throughout the 1590s many 'strangers' were received as tenants by townspeople. There was a fear that children might be born to vagrants and able to claim a settlement right in the town.[55] It would appear that efforts to control lodgers met with passive resistance. Many of the under-tenants and lodgers were not necessarily perceived as troublesome vagrants and their presence must have been well known along Liverpool's seven streets. Many found accommodation where there was space available in alehouses and with widows. The town authorities, however, did increasingly regard lodgers as potentially or actually unemployed and likely to be a charge to the town if they were allowed to remain.

Until the 1580s and 1590s Liverpool had not felt the acute problems associated with poverty and unemployment apparent in other towns. In south Lancashire land tenure and inheritance patterns do not seem to have created unrest and insecurity until an increasing population towards the end of the Tudor period started to put pressure on agricultural employment. Likewise, the much-maligned enclosure activities of the century had little impact on farming practice and employment in this area.[56] In consequence, serious unemployment was not a major issue in the vicinity of Liverpool; rather, the whole area was relatively poor. One small indication of this lies with the valuations of probate inventories. Wills known as *infra* wills had valuations of £40 or less, which allowed them to be processed more cheaply by rural deans rather than through the diocesan probate machinery. By this determinant 52 per cent of the surviving Liverpool probate inventories from the Tudor period were of *infra* status. Indeed, this proportion is marginally better than for the immediate area around the town; in Walton parish 56 per cent of probate valuations were of *infra* status.[57] Low valuations for these probate inventories are by no means conclusive, but these *infra* wills would appear to represent testators who left few, low-value items. Since the poorer section of society is undoubtedly under-represented by will-makers, Tudor Liverpool was a poor town. Yet, in a contradictory way Liverpool did not have the urgent and insurmountable problems associated with poverty and experienced by some urban locations at this time.[58] The eventual deteriorating situation in Liverpool late in the Tudor period probably accounts for the increasing interest in the town in implementing the provisions of national legislation.

The 1531 poor law had assumed that the deserving poor would be dealt with by their own communities through charitable giving. The 1563 legislation made the additional provision of an organised collection for poor relief: in effect, a voluntary rate. No evidence survives to indicate that this rate was ever collected in Liverpool; the low numbers of 'designated' poor perhaps rendered the organised collection unnecessary, at least in the eyes of the civic authorities, and in any event Liverpool chapel-goers were perhaps unwilling to contribute to the poor of Walton parish. A poor box was not provided in St Nicholas' chapel until 1598. There is no suggestion that the whipping campaign and searches for vagrants directed by the Privy Council during the 1560s had any impact in this locality.[59] The 1572 poor law distinguished carefully between the deserving poor, who would be maintained by the provision of a compulsory rate, and a tighter definition of vagrants who would be strictly punished. The complementary act of 1576 made provision of stocks of material to provide work for the unemployed and the designation of one or more houses of correction in each county. This package of provisions remained in force until almost the end of the sixteenth century. In Liverpool consideration was given to the new arrangements since the town's MP, Ralph Sekerston, was able to report in person to the civic authorities and his neighbours. By August 1572 the town books could report that 'it was provided for the poore folke, according to this estatute parliament'. Liverpool appears to have done its duty with great alacrity, but it is hard to believe that compulsory, regular collections of a poor rate were introduced and went unrecorded. Local circumstances perhaps did not warrant full implementation, and certainly by 1578 the town did not have a collector for the poor rate.[60]

Not until 1580 was it decided, because of the large number of 'idle and loytringe persons', to invoke the provisions of the 1576 act and to tax the town £20 in order to provide materials for employment and to repair the stocks. The rather naïve belief was expressed that the materials might be replenished by charitable donation. In addition to this a few, probably local, unemployed were found modest employment by the town: two, and later four, men were hired as shepherds and swineherds for the town.[61] After initial enthusiasm the scheme to provide materials for employment collapsed either through lack of support or because it was found unnecessary. After 1586 there is no mention of it and it remains doubtful that a compulsory poor rate was ever collected. The only sustained interest was in identifying lodgers and in conveying vagrants out of the town, if necessary.

Nationally the inadequacy of the existing legislation was recognised during the 1590s and three statutes of 1598 were intended to ensure some uniformity and consistency of provision.[62] The acts were intended to be systematic in application, rather than permissive, and by this date Liverpool's authorities were prepared to respond more decisively. In June 1598 an assembly discussed the provision for the poor people of the town and decided on the acquisition of a house of correction. Robert More was approached to let his Pool House at the bottom of Castle Street to the town for a rent of 20s. a year, although by 1599 the rent had not yet been paid. Only those identified and listed as deserving poor were to be allowed to remain in the town. All begging was to cease and all vagrants were to be punished strictly. How effective these intentions proved is impossible to assess. New determination by the town's authorities seems evident; the town books reported in 1599 that persons assisted with relief the previous year were to continue to receive attention; and in 1600 the rent on Pool House was paid at last.[63]

In comparison with levels of action undertaken in other towns, Liverpool's treatment of the poor was limited in scope and late in development. Many towns, for instance London, Norwich and Ipswich, had launched local experiments and schemes well in advance of the requirements of national legislation. The authorities in Chester and Lincoln had considered vagrancy an issue in the 1540s and had sought to control begging. Action in Norwich had been seriously expanded and co-ordinated during the 1560s and 1570s.[64] Beyond restricting the settlement of outsiders, Liverpool had done little until the late 1590s. The reason for this delayed action is not readily apparent. Did Liverpool really have fewer poor or fewer problem poor? In Norwich during the second half of the sixteenth century it has been estimated that between one quarter and one third of the population were close to poverty. In Warwick it has been calculated that one in nine families could be classified as poor in good times and one in four in bad times.[65] If the *infra* probate records are any guide then a sizeable proportion of Liverpool's population was poor. Poverty may have been so endemic that contemporaries may not have perceived the need for elaborate poor relief schemes until very late in the Tudor period. It may have been that the predominance of a mixed rural economy in the area around Liverpool together with the survival of the town field and heath meant that many of the urban population were able to maintain themselves most of the time. The mixed pattern of farming was some help in counteracting the effects of bad harvests, and the multiplicity of part-time employment in a port created something of a cushion in difficult times. A paternalistic community-wide concern was sufficient for those known and deserving poor who were unable to support themselves.

Disorder was present throughout the Tudor period in Liverpool, but not at unmanageable or unacceptable levels. Only the plague outbreak of 1558 caused the weekly market and annual fair to be abandoned. Otherwise sufficient control was maintained for commercial and civic activities to operate. At no time did the town's authorities lose control. Only during the final decade of the sixteenth century were there signs that the small town did not have the resources, both human and financial, to cope. The combination of nationwide economic distress and substantial participation in the provision of troop transport to Ireland did occasion severe pressure for the town, albeit mostly of a temporary nature. The Tudor population of the seven streets in Liverpool must have recognised each other and known each others' strengths and failings. Personal familiarity bred a degree of social cohesion that was reinforced by the operation of the town assembly and town council. The town's social order remained and survived considerable strain.

CHAPTER EIGHT

Learning and godliness

ONE CONSEQUENCE of living in a small town was that the facilities and opportunities for education and wider cultural activities were quite limited. This was at a time during the Tudor period when England witnessed profound and perplexing religious change associated with the early phases of the Reformation. The speed and extent of the impact of this change have been the subjects of considerable debate.[1] In this context Liverpool presents an interesting case-study. It was distant both from royal decision-making in London, and also from ecclesiastical authority. As a port and a market town Liverpool sustained some modest contact beyond its immediate locality and in a small town personal dissemination of ideas and opinions cannot have been too difficult. Yet Liverpool was located in what was to become recognised as one of the most religiously conservative parts of the country where by the end of the sixteenth century there was a marked reluctance to embrace much or any of the new Protestant religious opinion. In the Tudor period the relationship between educational opportunity, literacy and religious opinion was an intangible, but immensely important, aspect of life for everyone.

Schooling

By the sixteenth century formal education may have been available in several ways, not now always easily differentiated. 'Petty' schools provided elementary teaching; 'free' or 'common' schools tended to provide a somewhat more elaborate curricula; while true grammar schools delivered a genuinely classical regime.[2] South Lancashire had several schools founded early in the Tudor period, such as at Farnworth near Widnes in 1507.[3] Liverpool's school dated to 1515; it was established through the provisions of the will of John Crosse, a native of the town who became rector of St Nicholas' church in Newgate Street, London. He bequeathed several pieces of land and tenements in Liverpool to finance the priest of St Katherine's chantry with the specific duty of keeping

a grammar school. From the early 1520s until the 1540s Humphrey
Crosse (possibly from the same family) was the priest/schoolmaster
in Liverpool. The suppression of the chantries during the late 1540s
occasioned considerable negotiation about the school's future during the
1550s. By 1565 it had been established on a clear basis with the Crosse
bequest funding the schoolmaster's wages and the mayor and burgesses
responsible for the appointment of the appropriate individual.[4]

Availability of education in the Tudor period depended both on
the cost of attendance and on the location of the school. In Liverpool
the town's boys can have had no difficulty in reaching the school but,
as was usual at this time, there was no provision for girls. Before the
1570s the school met in the chapel of St Mary del Quay, not far from
St Nicholas' chapel. From 1572 this building was leased as the town's
warehouse and the school was transferred to, or had already moved to,
the chapel of St Nicholas itself. At this time there were about 36 pupils
in the school.[5] No surviving records mention any cost for attendance,
although the town books have plenty to report concerning the schoolmaster's salary. It seems likely that for Liverpool boys the tuition was
free. An indication of wider interest is also evident in the bequest
of Robert Ballard in 1580. He was a husbandman from West Derby
who apparently was unable to sign his own name, yet he invested £7,
which was to bring in 9s. 4d. a year to augment the teacher's salary
at the 'comen scole within Lyverpole'. For a decade at least this sum
was paid and suggests that perhaps pupils from surrounding townships
might attend Liverpool's school.[6]

During the second half of the Tudor period the schoolmaster had
his salary paid by Duchy of Lancaster officials at Halton Castle near
Runcorn, since the revenue came from confiscated chantry property.
The salary, however, was augmented by a ley (tax) collected annually in
the town.[7] Early in 1565 Ralph Higginson from Everton was the schoolmaster, but he had left before the end of the year. He seems to have
been teaching in a temporary capacity before going to the University of
Oxford where he obtained his BA in 1569. He eventually became curate
and schoolmaster at West Derby chapel.[8] There was an attempt to recruit
a replacement for him by four of the town's aldermen when they were
in London; they hired John Ore for a salary of £10 a year. Probably he
never actually reached the town, since the curate of St Nicholas' chapel
had to supervise the school until 1568 when John Ryle was licensed by
the bishop of Chester as Liverpool's schoolmaster. Ryle was an 'outsider'
but he did settle in the town, married and leased a house from the town
in Dale Street. His salary continued at £10 a year, with an additional
£1 15s. 0d. for serving the office of clerk in the chapel; a post that Ryle

reluctantly accepted in 1572. Ryle continued in the position of school-master until 1583 when he was replaced by Richard Welling.[9]

Welling was a former pupil of Farnworth school. He came from a yeoman family at Upton near Widnes; aged twenty-one, he had attended the University of Oxford in 1578. Liverpool was his first permanent post. He remained for ten years until illness forced his premature retirement, prior to his death in 1594.[10] His successor was another newly qualified BA graduate, Richard Baker. His tenure of the job was brief, until 1598, when it proved difficult to find any replacement at all. Again the curate had to agree to oversee the school 'untill God sende us some sufficient learned man'.[11] A ley collected in 1600 suggests that the post had been filled, and by 1602 Hamlet Webster, another former pupil of Farnworth, was in post until 1616 when he moved to his own former school.[12]

Quite a number of teachers in south Lancashire were local products, mostly of the school at Farnworth. In more favoured parts of the country the quality of schoolmasters could be high because of the surplus of university graduates, but there was little to attract them as far as the North West.[13] In Liverpool there is evidence of only BA degrees and even that qualification was hard to obtain. The available salary was insufficient to attract better-qualified MA candidates, and so local men were often the only possibilities. The academic reputation of the school must have depended on the quality of its one teacher and on the curriculum he could provide. In all likelihood the school in Tudor Liverpool had its limitations by contemporary standards. A further indication of this is provided by the decision to choose an alternative school and 'table out' (or board) children by those that could afford. One specific example of this is provided by John More esquire of Bank Hall on the edge of Liverpool. He chose to send his 'lytell boyse' (James, Thomas and Robert) to Farnworth school. The boys, aged between 10 and 14, were boarded first with John Lister, a yeoman from Denton in Widnes, and later with John Fazakerley's wife.[14] It is probable that John More's decision was an indication, in his view, of the relative reputa-tions of Liverpool and Farnworth schools during the 1550s, although it is possible that at this time the Liverpool school was undergoing a period of instability following the loss of the chantry priest/schoolmaster.

Scholarship provision ensured a connection between south Lancashire and the University of Oxford, particularly Brasenose College.[15] With the aid of scholarships, or even without, it was possible for the sons of yeomen and husbandmen to attend university although, in view of the cost, it was no doubt easier for the gentry to cope with the expense. Various estimates have been made of this cost, ranging from £20 to £50 a year, but it is not always easy to discern what has been included in the calculation.[16] John More esquire of Bank Hall kept a careful record of the allowances he sent to his son William at Brasenose College. All sums of money were sent by carrier to the principal for use by William. During the academic year 1553–54 some £4 6s. 8d. was sent while, probably more accurately, in 1554–55 £12 2s. 0d. was accounted for. In 1564 John More's fourth son, Robert, also entered Brasenose and again there is some record of the cash outlay and of goods that were sent.[17] Over a three-year period between £9 10s. 0d. and £12 0s. 0d. a year was dispatched. In addition, Robert may have carried money himself. The residence at university certainly necessitated a stream of articles being sent from Liverpool. At the beginning of the term in October 1564 a new feather bed, a bolster, a pillow, a pillowcase, three new sheets 'markyd with his mother's marke', two blankets, two coverlets, two kerchiefs 'of new cloth with letters ffor his name', six books and an old hair brush were all transported. Three months later a shirt and a pair of shoes were sent, and the carrier was reimbursed for purchasing a pair of bedstocks for Robert. In another three months black cloth for hose was required, and in the summer a cap, a doublet, a pair of hose and another pair of shoes followed. During the next two years more clothing and material was sent, but no additional bedding. In 1566, for example, over a yard of russet fustian, one and a half yards of broadcloth, three yards of lining and twenty-four black silk buttons were dispatched for a coat.

In addition to attendance at the universities at Oxford and Cambridge it was possible at this time to continue education by gaining admittance to the Inns of Court in London, ultimately for a complete legal training but possibly for two or three years of preliminary study. Accommodation and tuition in London cost even more than at the universities, so when Robert More moved from Oxford to Gray's Inn in 1568 his father had to increase his expenditure. From 1568 until 1574 between £18 and £25 a year was necessary.[18] Undoubtedly the More family was exceptional during the Tudor period in the Liverpool area in its patronage of school and higher education. Robert More gentleman did return from his extensive education to a mercantile career in Liverpool; he was bailiff in 1577–78 and mayor in 1591–92, 1595–96 and 1599–1600. Education for most boys was infinitely more restricted. The quality for most was probably rather indifferent and for many any wider educational possibilities remained unexploited.

Apprenticeship

An alternative or complementary route to training and some education lay with the apprenticeship system, again predominantly for boys.

Certainly apprenticeship was recognised and practised but the surviving evidence is of a somewhat limited nature; records survive for only some years and then not necessarily in a systematic way. The five new apprentices of 1584 appear to be the largest entry in any one year, although there were enough apprentices in total in Liverpool for them to be regarded as a distinct group. Usually they were the subjects of various regulatory codes; from 1564, for instance, they were to be confined to their masters' houses after 8.00 p.m.[19] Predominantly the apprentices came from the town or from adjacent parishes. Beyond this area a variety of places in the north-west of England provided just a few recruits: from elsewhere in Lancashire, from Cumbria, from Cheshire, north Wales and the Isle of Man. The length of indenture varied; seven years was most common, although some apprentices served shorter periods: three, four, five or six years, and some a greater length of time: eight, ten, thirteen, and, exceptionally, fifteen years. These variations seem dependent on the starting age of the apprentice, so that age at completion of the indenture was quite uniform. Seven girls were also recorded as apprentices to Liverpool merchants and their wives; probably they served as household servants until reaching the age of twenty-one.

While serving their apprenticeships it is not a straightforward matter to classify these children and young people among the town's population. Their economic circumstances were very basic and their assets virtually non-existent, yet some had enough money to buy goods such as salt for trade on their own account.[20] Some apprentices eventually became freemen of the town, leading merchants and future mayors, such as Ralph Burscough, Giles Brooke and John Bird. For others their apprenticeship was little more than enforced exploitation and a form of cheap labour. Apprenticeship for some did provide an occupational training and some education. The presumption must have been that future merchants had or acquired literacy and numeracy. Peter Williamson's apprenticeship arrangements in 1602, although apparently as only a mariner, permitted him to carry two barrels of the best commodity on each voyage. Thomas Johnson was also apprenticed to a mariner; his indenture provided for a year to be spent in France learning the language, albeit his father having to fund his food and lodgings.[21]

Beyond the limited economic resources of Liverpool much more diverse apprenticeship opportunity existed throughout Tudor England. Through a combination of poor communications, lack of employment pressure in the south Lancashire area and the costs involved, only a few individuals, however, placed their sons in more distant apprenticeships. For instance, opportunity in London was considerable yet few

Liverpool apprentices made their way there in the Tudor period. One Liverpool boy was apprenticed to the London Carpenters in 1588, but this scarcely represents a headlong flight.[22] His father was recorded as a husbandman, so it seems likely that if he could send his son to London others from Liverpool could have done so had they wished. The apprenticeship was for seven years, but John Potter was scarcely a boy when he went to London. He was at least 18 years old and it therefore cannot have been parental choice alone which took him to the capital. Provincial towns appear to have offered as little attraction as London for Liverpool apprentices. Norwich never seems to have attracted any recruits from Liverpool. Bristol was the chosen destination of five apprentices in the period from 1533 to 1542 but none in the following decade. Chester was a much more accessible town with undoubted contacts with Liverpool. Nonetheless, apprentices in Chester rarely came from Lancashire, let alone from Liverpool.[23] Perhaps local rivalry prevailed over local proximity. Apprenticeship within Liverpool, after perhaps some attendance at the town's school, was the most likely course of training and education for boys from the town.

Through apprenticeship and/or the school in the town a basic form of education was available for many boys; the extent of literacy, however, remains debatable. Tracing literacy in the Tudor period is quite difficult; for much of the period it may have been regarded as a specific skill necessary for only certain occupations. A proportion of men may well have operated on the margins of literacy.[24] Usually only the ability or inability to write a signature can be used as an indicator of literacy, and even then few comprehensive lists of signatures remain. Ownership of books is another possible indicator, but few probate listings of possessions survive. Several specialist stationers traded in Chester and other general merchants may well have handled books. The Wigan mercer, Mathew Markland (died 1617), had books, horn books, card and paper among his shop supplies; he operated as grocer, chemist, stationer and bookseller.[25] Much the same function was performed by a few of the Liverpool merchants. Certainly John Bird (who died in 1603) had supplies of stationery equipment: paper, parchment, sealing wax, pens, inkhorns and books. When needed these materials were certainly available in Tudor Liverpool.

Only five of the Liverpool probate inventories from the last quarter of the sixteenth century specifically mention book ownership, and even these may be atypical of the will-making section of society. Edward Heyes, gentleman (died 1602) had a Bible and William Secum, merchant (died 1592) had two books valued at 6s. 8d. Perhaps one or two books was the usual extent of literary material. George Ackers, gentleman (died

1588) had a veritable library; he had thirty-one books valued at 34s. 4d. in total. The only other two inventories to mention books are explicable by the occupations of the deceased. James Seddon (died 1588) had been curate of St Nicholas' chapel; he had 10s. worth of books. Schoolmaster Richard Welling (died 1592) had a larger collection of reading material since it was valued at 40s.

In truth, statistics of the levels of literacy remain elusive. Writing material and paper existed in Liverpool, available to those that could afford it. A free school existed for most of the Tudor period, as did apprenticeship opportunities, making the possibility of a limited education available to many boys, providing a teacher could be persuaded to reside in Liverpool and the value of the opportunity was recognised. The school and the level of the schoolmaster's salary were of concern to the civic authorities, and the Tudor period did witness a significant growth in the keeping of town records, as testified by the town books. In the event it seems likely that few females in Tudor Liverpool were literate, although records are too sparse to draw firm conclusions. A significant proportion of the male population, however, was literate at least to the extent of signing their own names. During the second half of the sixteenth century 11.5 per cent of known merchants marked rather than signed surviving documents, 47 per cent did sign some material and, unfortunately, in the case of 41.5 per cent the ability to record a signature is unknown.[26]

In a small town the extent or absence of formal education must have been very noticeable at this time. The ultimate range of opportunity was considerable. Robert More attended Farnworth school, the University of Oxford and the Inns of Court in London. Some of his contemporaries in Liverpool, even by the end of the Tudor period, may have received no formal education at all. Literacy was a skill of perhaps dubious immediate value for many in the town. Awareness of prevailing cultural mores and styles could have been acquired through other channels. The Liverpool schoolboys are known to have performed plays during 1574–75 and the local nobleman, the earl of Derby, provided well-testified support for drama both in London and through touring companies that visited south Lancashire: the earl's company and the earl of Oxford's men both did so in 1582.[27] Inevitably a small town offered limited educational opportunities, but for many individuals learning may not have been limited and by the end of the sixteenth century education had become linked inextricably to the religious changes of the Tudor period.

Reformation changes

The Tudor period witnessed momentous changes in religious ideas and practices. From half-way through the reign of Henry VIII royal direction of religious matters became increasingly evident and Protestant opinion gained support among growing numbers of the population. Some towns with greater concentrations of literate individuals than the surrounding rural areas found themselves at the forefront in the introduction of the new ideas. Differential speeds of change between parishes and the impact of the influence of different clergy meant that towns could well be the focus for religious debate and dispute. As a small town, Liverpool had a far less complicated religious infrastructure than many urban centres. It had no monastery, no friary and no quantity of parish churches. Chester had nine parishes, a large Benedictine monastery, a nunnery and three friaries. London had over one hundred parish churches and over fifty religious houses.[28] Liverpool had just one ecclesiastical building in which the town's population could gather and one small chapel beside it; diversity of belief must have been a very public phenomenon.

St Nicholas' chapel was part of the larger parish of Walton-on-the-Hill, but the town had always had a very direct and particular association with its one chapel. By the commencement of the Tudor period, and well before the circulation of any Reformed opinion, Liverpool in effect controlled its chapel. It provided the only clergy in the town, the only meeting place and the only burial location, as for instance anticipated by William More in his will of 1537.[29] The chapelwardens were listed annually in the town books along with the secular town officials. The four chantries were modestly endowed with property mostly in the town. Three of the chantries were fourteenth-century foundations: St Mary's chantry at the high altar, St Nicholas' chantry and St John's chantry. All had endowments of six or seven burgages, several cottages and various rental income from land within the town and the town field. Well into the Tudor period these chantries were still well supported, such as by a 1509 bequest to St Mary's, and William More's bequest for masses in St John's chantry in 1537.[30] So popular and part of the religious fabric were these chantries that a fourth was established in 1515 with the generous bequest of John Crosse. His will provided for the foundation of St Katherine's chantry with the requirement that the chantry priests provide the teaching for a school. Four burgages and other rental income ensured an income nearly as great as that for the other three chantries.[31]

Maintenance and repair were accustomed civic responsibilities. Notebooks kept by William More esquire, probably during a tenure as

Liverpool's mayor in the period 1510–12, demonstrate the civic direction of repairs and necessary funding at both Liverpool chapel and the mother-church at Walton.[32] Reformation change made little difference to this duty. In 1555 a church-ale was held to raise funds for the 'new adorning' of the chapel: presumably a reference to internal decoration in accordance with the Catholic dictates of Mary I's reign.[33] The wisdom of change and consequent refurbishment may have been the objects of debate, but not the responsibility and provision of funding. More mundane attention continued during the reign of Elizabeth I. In 1564 the chapel walls and the wooden roof on the steeple were attended to. Unfortunately winter storms in 1565 did considerable damage and a double rate was necessary in the town in order to raise the £30 necessary for further repairs. A stone mason had to be hired specially. Only a few years later the entire chapel was slated. In addition the chapelyard required attention. In 1578 the porch on the south side was flagged so that the elderly and infirm could enter more easily, and a year later the chapelyard wall required £20 to deal with its collapsed state. The curate, James Seddon, was in trouble in 1585 for allowing swine to do considerable damage to the chapelyard, while his successor Hugh Janion was not popular for cutting down the 'greate thorne' there in 1593 in order to graze his horse and cattle.[34] Within limits, the Liverpool authorities do seem to have sustained a continuing interest in their chapel and achieved a state of maintenance at least sufficient to avoid criticism at visitations. If the level of the four chantry endowments can be taken as an indicator, then Liverpool chapel was better provided for and better maintained than many other Lancashire church buildings.[35]

The town's involvement with its chapel was heightened by its distance away from ecclesiastical control and/or influence. Early in the Tudor period the diocesan centre had been at Lichfield in Staffordshire: too far away for regular supervision. In 1539 legislation promoted by Henry VIII established Chester as one of six new dioceses. It came into existence in 1541: it was nearer than Lichfield, but poorly endowed and slow to establish effective administration.[36] The parish church at Walton-on-the-Hill might, in theory, have exercised some control over its chapel in Liverpool, but in the Tudor period this seems doubtful. The local Molyneux family of Croxteth and Sefton had purchased the advowson of Walton rectory in 1470 and, in consequence, throughout the sixteenth century a member of that family held the post. Anthony Molyneux DD was instituted in 1543 and held the rectory until his death in 1557. His godson, Anthony Molyneux BA, succeeded him. Alexander Molyneux, aged ten, the youngest son of the patron Sir Richard Molyneux, was presented to the living in 1565 and held office for sixty-six years. He did not become a deacon until 1574, and was still 'no preacher' in 1590. He was described as unlearned and unaccustomed to say service or administer the sacraments. Like his predecessor, he was non-resident.[37] The rector of Walton scarcely presented any challenge to Liverpool's control of its chapel, other than for the presence of the tithe barn on the edge of the town for his income. In the absence of the rector, conceivably the vicar at Walton might have shown some interest in Liverpool's chapel. However, he had other chapels at Kirkby, West Derby and Formby in the parish and, other than for financial contributions to the mother church such as the 1565 ley, he had little influence over the more substantial community in Liverpool.[38]

The clergy in Liverpool had long been susceptible to the preferences and wishes of the civic authorities in the town. Early in the Tudor period the chapel had its team of four or five priests but, with the dissolution of the chantries, just one curate remained as the sole religious official. By the later Tudor period the curate at St Nicholas was chosen by the town and the appointment confirmed by the Chancellor of the Duchy of Lancaster. Towards the end of the sixteenth century the word 'elected' was used in the town books.[39] Many individuals were local products, as were many of the Lancashire clergy. Few outsiders were able to find patronage in the area. From 1515 the chantry priest who ran the school, Humphrey Crosse, was from the family in the town. His contemporary, Thomas Rainford was the brother of a town merchant.[40] From 1557 until 1563 Evan Thomasson alias Nicholson, the younger son of a local burgess, served as curate, apparently to the satisfaction of his congregation. The town books reported that 'he hath well and diligentlie served as minister', but shortly before his death he was accused of using rosary beads and ordered to say services only from the newly authorised Protestant prayer book. In his private possession, but presumably available for use, he kept a large Catholic service book.[41]

Probably at this time a replacement was not easy to find with the deprivations and vacancies that arose early in the reign of Elizabeth I. A replacement is not recorded until John Milner officiated briefly from 1572 until his death in 1574. He was replaced in October of that year by another local man, James Seddon; his brother and sister both lived nearby. Indications in the town books suggest that he was considered unfit for his duties by 1584 and a successor was considered, but James Seddon continued in office until his death during the winter of 1588–89.[42] It seems likely that even in good health his qualities were considered inadequate for one of the 'big' occasions in Liverpool chapel, such as the St George's Day celebrations in 1577 when the earl of Derby arranged the extensive festivities and used two of his own chaplains to preach the sermons.[43] Hugh Janion ministered in the town from 1590 until 1594, when the town was again exercised about the unsatisfactory qualities of the curate. Six months' notice was discussed but in the event Janion remained until his death in 1596.[44] Ralph Bentley was 'elected' by the town's assembly to succeed as curate, yet by only 1598 he was called upon to explain 'whether he be mynded to continewe in his place as minister here'. Bentley claimed that he had already been discharged by the mayor and had found himself another post. With the consent of the bishop, the town appointed Thomas Wainwright who previously served as curate just a few miles away at West Derby chapel. His personality and religious persuasion must have been known, and he was also a product of Farnworth school. In 1604 he was referred to as 'a reading minister', and evidently gave reasonable satisfaction in his new chapel.[45]

The standard of the living available to these Liverpool clergy is hard to assess with precision. There were many poor livings in the Tudor church and often clergy supplemented their incomes with teaching, preaching, scribing or other writing activity. The situation did improve slowly during the sixteenth century, but mainly in the south of England; Lancashire was probably scarcely affected.[46] The curate in Liverpool was paid £4 17s. 5d. per year as his stipend; this had to be collected from the Duchy of Lancaster officials at Halton Castle near Runcorn. Deductions were made for fees, portage, the acquittance and the clerk's work, leaving £4 5s. 7d., which was augmented by £8 0s. 0d. collected annually by Liverpool.[47] The collection of this money must have made abundantly clear the clergyman's dependent position, and created a very direct interest by the population in 'their' chapel. In view of the level of inflation, the value of the total stipend available to the Liverpool curate must also have been deteriorating in real terms by the latter part of the Tudor period.[48] Not surprisingly, in dress, housing and culture there was little to differentiate the clergymen and the majority of the town's population. With the level of income available luxury features of life were scarcely possible. The probate inventory of James Seddon (died 1588) reveals goods totalling only £6 5s. 0d. He had just a few household items, clothing worth just 11s. 0d. and books worth 10s. 0d. One of his successors, Thomas Wainwright (died 1625) left goods which totalled £31 5s. 0d. and £8 0s. 0d. of this was accounted for by his books. From these two examples and the level of the annual stipend, it seems likely that the standard of living for the town's clergy was on a par with husbandmen and poorer craftsmen.

These clergy of limited income and limited education had to officiate through a period of considerable religious upheaval. The dissolution of the monasteries and friaries late in the reign of Henry VIII cannot have caused much more than a ripple in Liverpool since, other than for the ferry tolls and a granary in Water Street (already rented out) which belonged to Birkenhead Priory, there was no monastic property, individuals or resources involved in the town. The dissolution of the chantry chapels and pensioning of chantry priests (Ralph Hayward, Richard Frodsham, John Hurde and Humphrey Crosse) must have brought home to Liverpool the local impact of royal religious policy.[49] Whether other aspects of new Protestant opinion, such as an English Bible or the 1549 Prayer Book, surfaced in the town during the 1540s and early 1550s are impossible to discern in the absence of suitable records, unless the phrase 'new adorning' of the chapel in the town books of 1555 refers to work to restore images which had been whitewashed and concealed in the early years of reformation.[50] It seems unlikely in view of the town's location in the north-west of England that Protestant opinion had much opportunity to make headway before the reign of Elizabeth. Even then progress must have been slow with traditionally trained local clergy of limited educational experience and the limited direction and supervision by the bishop of Chester.

In a small, one-chapel town the clergyman's personal qualities and religious opinions must have been open always to close scrutiny by his congregation and, potentially, of very real significance in the direction and persuasion of his flock.[51] In 1562 the town books recorded a decision by the mayor that services were to be held in the chapel every Wednesday, Friday and Saturday evenings, in addition to Sundays. In 1572 the seventy-eight organ pipes were removed and lodged with a chapelwarden, while at the same time a decision was taken to use the fabric from two copes for costumes in a pageant. By 1584 the siting of the pulpit in the chapel was another decision taken by the town's assembly.[52] All of these actions indicate a measure of town influence over the speed and implementation of changing religious practice. By 1590 it had been decided that the first and second lessons should be read in the nave of the chapel; the new curate, Hugh Janion, did not concur and the mayor was reprimanded for not enforcing the town's wishes. In 1592 the instruction had to be reiterated.[53] Also at this time the town decided to contribute financially to support the appointment of a preacher: new in Liverpool, but a practice adopted in some towns from the 1570s. From 1591 until 1593 voluntary contributions raised £4 a quarter to pay Mr Carter who, it was said, preached with great zeal, often and diligently. The annual fee was greater than that received by the town's curate. This preacher was almost certainly Oliver Carter BD from Manchester College who was patronised also by the earl of Derby.[54]

The Protestant preaching initiative does not seem to have been sustained through the town's economic difficulties of the 1590s. Over a twenty-year period from about 1570 Protestant opinion had probably made steady, but essentially limited, progress in Liverpool. The town's curates had perhaps contributed little since they were scarcely well informed or, it would seem, enthusiastic supporters of the new opinions, and they provided little decisive leadership in new directions. More likely some of the congregation's views had been changed slowly by awareness of developments elsewhere in England, by some wish for conformity to the established doctrine, by the local influence of the fourth earl of Derby, and by the appointment during the 1580s of a few well-trained Protestant clergy to better livings in Lancashire, such as Thomas Meade at Prescot, John Nutter at Sefton and Edward Fleetwood at Wigan.[55] Control of the town's chapel by Liverpool's population was not new, but the style of service wanted by the majority may have been by the 1590s. The meagre endowment of the curate's stipend at Liverpool's one chapel was a serious factor inhibiting more rapid advancement by Protestant preaching clergy.

Many scholars have written at some length of the survival of Catholicism in northern England and in Lancashire in particular. Christopher Haigh speaks of the county by the end of the reign of Elizabeth as 'by far the most Catholic in England', while John Bossy comments that there were 'more Catholics in this relatively small area than in the rest of the north put together'.[56] However, it is difficult to be precise about Catholic survival and the development of recusancy (the refusal to attend Protestant church services). It must have taken at least a decade for Catholics, particularly in the north of England, to realise fully that they could no longer attend their parish churches and chapels. Indeed, for some time after 1559 Catholicism must have continued as the religion of the majority and there was probably no need for resistance to the new arrangements providing the 1559 Protestant settlement was enforced casually.[57] The 1559 legislation provided a 12d. fine payable for non-attendance at the established services. The duty of collection lay with the churchwardens. Especially in the north of the country, it is probable that from 1559 until about 1580 'religious conservatism was very prevalent, but outright Catholic nonconformity was relatively rare'.[58] There was no need for widespread recusancy.

The type of society was also a contributory factor to the continuation of Catholicism. In an area of social conservatism the numerous gentry were able to play a significant role in supporting the 'old faith'. The gentry were able to maintain domestic chaplains who could continue to hold traditional services for the rest of their lives, while in the later

Tudor period gentry households might provide shelter and support for the 'new' priests trained abroad. The gentry had the resources for this sustained commitment.[59] The gentry were also important because of their role in local government where their co-operation was essential for the enforcement of legislation within their locality. By 1570 the gentry's significance had been recognised and a letter to Lord Burghley reported that in Lancashire 'in some houses of great men ... no service hath been said in the English tongue'.[60] Some of the conservative inclinations of the Lancashire gentry must have had an impact for some time in the small town of Liverpool where their influence was so strong.

In 1564 it was reported to the government that Liverpool was 'full of Papists' and that two priests were at large, Sir William More and Sir Robert More; they both did 'much hurt and prate openly'. It was claimed that they had not attended church at all since the beginning of Elizabeth's reign.[61] As the younger brothers of John More esquire of Bank Hall these two Catholic priests were well housed and protected, and able to provide the necessary sacraments for Liverpool's Catholic population. William More was still alive in 1571. In all likelihood there were other 'old' priests that had been ordained in Henry VIII's or Mary's reigns and who were alive and available within the vicinity of Liverpool. David Rose from West Derby, an 'old priest, now Papist, was owed a debt from Liverpool in 1574.[62] In Liverpool and south Lancashire there was little enthusiasm or organisation to track down and to apprehend old priests. They must have contributed immeasurably to sustaining the Catholic faith after 1559. They ensured continuity, familiarity and local identity. They also provided an overlap with the arrival of 'new' priests, reinforcements trained in seminaries abroad. The first arrived in England in 1574 and were augmented after 1580 by some Jesuits. Many of these new priests originated from Lancashire. William Wilson was born in about 1571, educated at the seminary at Valladolid in Spain and returned to England in 1595; his brother John lived in Liverpool. The priest Robert Hawkesworth was arrested in Liverpool in 1595; he had been educated at Blackburn grammar school and had trained at Rheims and Rome before returning to England in 1594.[63] Queen Elizabeth's government was unable to sever contacts with Europe, and remote Liverpool must have been well placed for the conveying of these Lancashire recruits to their training overseas. By the 1580s and 1590s the total number of available priests is uncertain, but for the population of Liverpool some cannot have been too far away.

By the late 1560s and early 1570s the political implications of recusancy were becoming more evident and the bishop of Chester was being urged to be more diligent in his supervision of his diocese. So serious, however, were the failings of Bishop Downham that the bishop of Carlisle was ordered to visit Chester diocese.[64] The developing political situation in the country transformed official attitudes to Catholics. From 1571 legislation began to tighten control, although in 1574 Lancashire was still 'the very sincke of Poperie'.[65] More vigorous government action did persuade Bishop Chadderton to improve the listing of recusants, yet much of the 'activity' may have been rather superficial in nature. Correspondence at this time attempted to ascertain the suitability of the earl of Derby's Liverpool house (the Tower) as a recusant gaol. In the event it was decided to site the gaol at the New Fleet in Salford, well away from the coast and where the inhabitants were considered 'well affected'.[66] The decision reflects the highly impractical nature of the proposed Liverpool location. In the town non-attendance at the Protestant services in the chapel may have been waning, but there must have been a great many Catholic sympathisers who were, perhaps, unconvinced and infrequent attenders at the chapel.

By the 1590s Catholic practices had survived, such as weddings where the parties were brought to church with piping and a day of entertainment which included dancing. Henry Halewood, the Liverpool wait, was accused in 1590 of piping at weddings in Walton parish.[67] Burials could be even more sensitive events. In the small town the only consecrated burial ground was at St Nicholas' chapel. The wish to use this or the chapel for burial with traditional Catholic rites could create conflict in the community.[68] In 1592 the Privy Council urged the earl of Derby to take greater action to suppress May games, morris dances, plays, bear-baitings and Sunday ales by those 'evily affected' in religion. Quite frequently recusants, their friends and sympathisers might disrupt the Protestant services with, for instance, blatant lack of attention and talking or piping in the churchyard. In Liverpool the town's authorities were still trying to suppress piping and dancing during the time of evening service in 1598.[69]

Outward conformity was possible at times for Catholic sympathisers while the 'trappings' of the old faith remained enticing for many in a conservative, remote area.[70] It was reported in 1590 that Sir Richard Molyneux of Walton parish 'maketh shew of good conformitie, but many of his companie are in evell note'.[71] Liverpool by the last decade of the sixteenth century had perhaps greater attachment to the established Protestant church than much of the area, and had at least installed a Protestant preacher, but the port maintained easy access with Catholic Ireland and Spain. During the 1590s the mayor and prominent townsmen frequently lodged foreign, especially Irish, merchants who refused to attend the chapel on Sundays.[72] This did not make the mayor and his associates into Catholics, but it did reflect an attitude of sympathy and an unwillingness to take action against non-attenders at chapel. There must have been a substantial proportion of the town's population which had direct contact with Catholics.

When enumerating recusants we are left with the question: who is to be counted? In south Lancashire and Walton parish in particular the totals recorded in the later Tudor period were almost certainly greatly under-estimated. During the 1590s nine individuals from Liverpool were named specifically as recusants, including Thomas Walker gentleman and Catherine the wife of Ralph Secum gentleman. William More esquire and John Crosse esquire were both cited as non-communicants.[73] By this time a degree of outward conformity may have been desirable in a one-chapel town for those interested in participation in civic affairs. When such prominent Liverpool families as the Secum, More and Crosse were not attending and/or communicating at chapel a significant example must have been provided for others of similar religious opinion. The services of a priest were surely available to these families. The other named recusants were Alice Pepper, the wife of Robert Ryding (the ferryman), William Scarisbrick (mercer), Elizabeth Rose (spinster), Evan Thomasson, William Thomasson and his wife.[74] Conformity may have carried overtones of political and civic respectability by the end of the Tudor period but, despite the attentions of a Puritan preacher, the new, established Protestant services can have been only beginning to make serious headway in Liverpool. Catholicism and religious conservatism were almost indistinguishable and still an integral part of the locality. Attachment to St Nicholas' chapel and burial ground faded slowly for those with Catholic sympathy. Through commercial activity, civic responsibility, neighbourhood proximity, friendship and kinship those of Catholic, those of Protestant, and those of indifferent and uncertain persuasion must have been in close association with each other up until the end of the century. In a small town that was remote from central government, with inferior clergy and uncertain episcopal leadership[75], who was to enforce conformity? In a crime with no obvious victim there must have been considerable reluctance to take action. Neglect of chapel attendance cannot have been a priority in the town as long as stability prevailed. This attitude, however, continued only until the early years of the seventeenth century; demands for religious conformity through politics, financial penalties, and other outside pressures eventually forced a hardening of attitudes.[76]

CHAPTER NINE

Conclusion

OR CENTURIES AFTER ITS FOUNDATION Liverpool remained
F a small town; it exhibited the basic functions of an urban location,
yet its size scarcely changed. Indeed, with a population of less than
1,000, some historians have regarded Liverpool's credentials as a town
to be somewhat dubious.[1] This small size, however, was the reality for
so many urban dwellers throughout England at this time. Liverpool's
Tudor population would have been sure that they lived in a royal
borough, that they had their own local administration and government,
and that they had an economy distinctive to that of surrounding rural
Lancashire. This does not mean that their lifestyle and the culture were
radically different from that of the rural population nearby; how could
they be in such a small place? But there was a distinctive character and
a sense of identity about the small town.

Within just seven streets Liverpool's residents undoubtedly felt the
impact of geographic proximity and the operation of the local economy
concentrated the interaction of people. The degree of co-operation
required for local marketing and overseas trading activities fostered
collaboration as well as rivalry. Knowledge of local issues and involvement
in local affairs were unavoidable when the town assembly was still a
significant aspect of civic administration. Tudor Liverpool had a face-to-
face society where identities were known, the annual civic offices required
quite wide male participation and the mayor lived, at most, only a few
streets away. There was little possibility that male, and female, heads
of households escaped their civic responsibilities and duties. The mixed
agricultural economy of south Lancashire provided a reasonably stable
environment in the sixteenth century so that migration in Liverpool's
locality was relatively restricted in scale. In consequence, Liverpool's
population struggled to maintain itself and significant development was
elusive. Friendship and kinship networks must have been very strong
factors in providing the economic and social horizons of most people.

As a small town, Tudor Liverpool remained a part of the social and
economic fabric of south Lancashire; it was neither separated from it

nor able to dominate it. The townfield, the heath and the exploitation of Toxteth Park continued to provide many of the town's population with agricultural interests. No real specialisation characterised the town; essentially Liverpool was the market place for a small region. Only the port and the opportunity to go to sea provided a degree of distinctiveness within this locality. The characteristics of Tudor society and the relative isolation of the North West allowed the local landowning families to require a degree of deference from, and to exercise considerable influence within, the town. The earls of Derby sustained their uncontested dominance of Lancashire society. Tudor central government was distant and remote; local administration 'fell into the hands' of the Stanley family.[2] Through their fund of patronage, connection and potential coercion the earls were an influence in Liverpool, as were many of the south Lancashire gentry. This was true, however, for many small towns. Liverpool was not a seigneurial borough; it had its royal status which was not contested. Noble and gentry influence had their limitations and could at times prove valuable.

During the Tudor period Liverpool lay away from many of the major national, political and economic interests: the wool trade to Europe, the French wine trade, Henry VIII's Scottish campaigns, the route and possible landing of the Spanish Armada. Coastal trade and the Irish Sea were the major influences on Liverpool's shipping activities. Local circumstances were determining factors. The natural advantages of the harbour at the Pool and the open Mersey estuary sustained most sixteenth-century trade. Numbers and size of ships remained modest, and port facilities were extremely limited but the Crown's demands for transport of troops and supplies to Ireland, particularly towards the end of the Tudor period, provided the extra opportunity that many of Liverpool's shipowners and merchants required. National policy resulted eventually in the collapse of the Iberian trade. This had never been substantial, but it had provided mariners and merchants from the town with long-distance experience and overseas commodities. Substantial involvement in Irish transport provided an alternative outlet and was significant in sustaining Liverpool's long rivalry with Chester. Beyond the region this rivalry was of little consequence, but for the traders of both towns it was of real concern. It was unlikely that two ports so close together could both flourish given the restrictions of their hinterlands. By the end of the Tudor period Chester remained much the larger and more imposing town, with its superior and complex administrative status and its new diocesan role yet, crucially for future development, its trading base was becoming curtailed. The volume of trade from the out-port of Liverpool had just surpassed that of its head-port at Chester.[3]

To contemporaries at the end of the sixteenth century the significance of this may have seemed slight, but future opportunity lay with the accessible harbour, proximity to Ireland, and an outlook to the west – to north America and the Caribbean.

Since economic development had been so restricted during the Tudor period the fabric of the town had changed little. The seven medieval streets remained, together with the one town chapel. Even the aspirations for parochial status had failed. The castle was in a state of ruin and the Tower was an ageing, little-used structure. Few communal facilities existed: the common hall and the street market. The school still met in the chapel and animals wandering in the streets were still of intermittent concern to the civic authorities. Much of Liverpool's experience must have been replicated in the many small towns in Tudor England. Liverpool's location in the north-west of the country did mean that there was little reason or incentive for many outsiders to visit the town. It lay beyond the easy surveillance of central government and officials. Yet Liverpool's trade, however limited, did provide the catalyst for its merchants to travel and sustain contacts beyond their immediate locality. Liverpool merchants had regular business with Manchester linen dealers, Yorkshire fairs, London merchants and Irish traders.

Insularity was more apparent than real. By the end of the Tudor period a consumer society was appearing among some in society: the gentry, merchants and yeomen. For those with some surplus money a range of luxury goods was available in Liverpool. Perhaps the most tantalising glimpse of goods available in the town is provided by the cargo carried by Thomas Knype from Liverpool in 1594.[4] Shortly after leaving the port on 11 August his ship foundered with all hands; some goods were washed ashore along the coast between Formby and Liverpool. Much was retrieved and an inventory (of what remained to be put in custody) was made for the Court of Admiralty. Depositions before the court explained that the goods had originated in London, that they had then been dispatched by carrier to Liverpool, and that they were being conveyed by Knype to a Dundalk merchant. The list comprised a hamper containing felt, velvet, ruffs, taffeta, a doublet and 43 hat bands; another hamper with 40 treen cups, 9 piggens, 22 knives, 9 pairs of spurs, 5 damask sword hilts, 4 pommels, 32 sword handles and 132 wool cards; a third hamper with 74 treen cups, 1 bent ladle, 14 sword handles and 144 wool cards. A portmanteau was said to contain a shirt, 3 falling bands, 2 ruffle bands, a handkerchief, 7 knives and 2 purses. A fardel contained 26 wooden bottles, 2 bags of nails, 1 lantern and a copper pan. Further metal goods were located including 24 spurs, 24 flat locks, 10 round locks, 12 case locks, 2 clout needles, 24 locks and a small bag of brass. There were also a further 24 treen cups and 56 earthern cups. The principal receptacle was a chest containing cloth breeches, a cloak, 4 bolts of silk, pieces of fustian, 2 papers of round silk girdles, a paper of shot silk, 6 velvet girdles, 6 French silk girdles, 10 papers of lace, 7 pieces of velvet lace, a hank of silk lace, a paper of black silk, a paper of coloured silk, 216 silver buttons, 72 gold buttons, 576 silk buttons, 12 pairs of gloves, 12 silk purses, 24 children's purses, 48 small purses, 24 small looking glasses, 6 broken looking glasses, 12 fine knives, 156 knives, 24 silk tassels for knives, 22 sword blades, 24 pens and inkhorns, 2 bolts of crewel garters and 36 French garters. There was also a bag of hops worth nothing after its excursion into the sea and it was cast on the dunghill. Tudor Liverpool was not isolated from the rest of England; but the rest of England had little reason to know or visit Liverpool.

Community is an elusive, possibly illusory, concept.[5] Participation in activities shared by the community, such as town assemblies, and identification with the community, for instance when large numbers of troops were passing through the town, must have been commonplace in Tudor Liverpool. A collective identity was present and surely understood by the small population. The parish has often been seen as the locale for the expression of community;[6] Liverpool had its chapel. A somewhat unusual characteristic of the town was the limited impact that Reformation changes had at this time. Early Tudor Liverpool was not a religious centre with a distinctive religious role. In the town there was little for legislation to remove: no monastery, no friary, no hospital, no religious fraternity or gild. The four chantries connected to the one chapel were suppressed, but the school survived. The relatively poorly endowed chapel attracted no enthusiastic Protestant preaching, and so awareness of and support for religious change came slowly during the sixteenth century. Religious persuasion and ideology had not divided the community of the small town. Even by the end of the Tudor period interaction among Catholics, Protestants and the indifferent prevailed.

The limitations of surviving archival material and the absence of other records affects the aspects of Tudor Liverpool which can be explored; for instance, the paucity of parochial/chapelry documents inhibits an understanding of the town's chapel and poor relief, and the commencement of the town books in 1550 biases comment towards the later Tudor period. Even so, something of Tudor Liverpool's character and characteristics can be recovered from the evidence which does remain, and some material from the parishes of south Lancashire contribute to an understanding of the small town in its locality. The medieval inheritance was prevalent in Liverpool throughout the sixteenth century and still much in evidence even by 1600. Small town concerns and features common to many small towns predominated: a secure and supervised market, clean water and a clean environment, law and order, protection from outside competition.

Yet each town was singular. Liverpool's distinctiveness lay in its location in the north-west of England and with a harbour that was yet to see its potential realised. Adversity during the 1590s had helped to focus co-operation and identity; and the difficulties proved to be of a temporary nature. A small town Liverpool may have remained at the end of the Tudor period, but the structure and privileges of a royal borough, the experience of shipping and overseas trade, together with the identity of its community were all factors that laid the foundations for expansion once westward opportunities were grasped.

Appendices

Appendix 1 *Liverpool ships, 1550–1603*

Name	Tonnage	Dates of operation	Owner(s)
Ann	14	1597–1599	
Anthony	20	1591	
Bartholomew	16	1563–1578	William Lawrence 1565–1578
Bartholomew	10	1592–1603	
Bee	6	1577–1585	
Butterfly	40	1592–1593	Lancelot Walker 1592
Eagle	30	1565–1594	Robert Corbet 1565–1573 Giles Brooke (½) 1582
Eagle	16	1590	
Edward	35	1573–1578	
Edward	10	1577–1590	
Elizabeth	36	1595–1603	Robert Pemberton 1600
Elizabeth	20	1600–1603	John Young 1600–1603
Elizabeth	14	1565–1581	Nicholas Richardson 1565–1581
Elizabeth	7	1584–1593	
Ellen	32	1593–1603	Giles Brooke 1593 Thomas Hubberstay 1600
Ellen	20	1572–1585	William Thomasson (½) 1582
Ellen	12	1592–1594 (wrecked)	Thomas Knype 1593–1594
Ellen	8	1591–1603	Cuthbert Lawrence 1593
Falcon	16	1565–1575	George Ashton 1565–1575
Flower de Luz	30	1573–1576	
George	30	1554–1574	John Winstanley (½) 1554–1569 Thomas Winstanley (½) 1559–1573
George	26	1592–1603	Edward Nicholson (½) 1593

Name	Tonnage	Dates of operation	Owner(s)
Gift of God (*Marigold*) 1585 >	16	1584–1603	Richard Bird (½) 1592 Henry Moneley (½) 1593 Evan Thomasson (½) 1595–1603
Good Luck	6	1565–1585	Thomas Bradshaw 1565–1585
Henry	26	1565–1566	
Henry	20	1593–1603	
Hope	36	1572–1602	William Kelly 1582 Thomas Tarleton 1595–1602
Hopewell	30	1595–1603	Walter Chambers (½) 1595–1603
James	20	1578–1585	Thomas Bolton 1580
James	18	1558–1569	Thomas More 1558
James	16	1599–1603	Richard Mather 1602
James	8	1592	
Jesus	6	1581–1585	Elizabeth Warton 1581
John	26	1594	Richard Mather 1594
John	16	1581–1583	Robert Wytter 1581–1583
John Baptist	20	1569–1570	
Lantern	26	1575–1583	
Luke		1573	
Margaret	9	1584–1594	Henry Shaw 1594
Mary	8	1569–1579	
Mary George	16	1565–1575	Thomas Fisher (½) 1565–1575 Richard Barber (½) 1565–1572
Matthew	10	1590–1592	Anthony More 1592
Michael	40	1579–1585	
Michael	26	1565–1582	Edward Nicholson (½) 1565–1580 John Williamson (½) 1565
Michael	20	1592–1603	William Thomasson 1592–1600
Michael	16	1572–1585	
Michael	12	1593–1594	Thomas Tarleton 1593
Michael	8	1578–1581 (seized in Scotland)	Robert Wyter 1578–1581
Peter	14	1565–1584	Peter Starkey 1565–1569 James Johnson 1580
Phoenix	26	1597–1603	John Bird 1603

Name	Tonnage	Dates of operation	Owner(s)
Samuel	8	1593	
Saviour	35	1558–1585	Thomas Uttyn 1558–1582
Saviour	24	1565–1566	
Speedwell	14	1592–1594	Henry Shaw 1592 Thomas Williamson 1593
Steven	26	1597–1603	
Strange	24	1580–1597	John Strange 1580–1586 Richard Mather (½) 1592
Sunday	24	1565–1576	
Sunday	14	1565–1586	William Walker (½) 1565–1576 Thomas Mason (½) 1565–1586
Swallow	8	1565–1581	Thomas Bastwell 1565–1581
Swan	10	1573–1574 (wrecked off Ireland)	John Winstanley (½) 1574 Thomas Winstanley (½) 1574
Toby	18	1582	
Trinity	16	1592–1594	John Gill 1593
Trinity		1573	
Valentine	26	1598–1603	
William	25	1563–1566	

Material has been collated from the port books, the town books, probate records and the High Court of Admiralty papers. Many vessels may have operated both before and after the period which is now identifiable from surviving records and ownership may have changed over time. Tonnages are those which are most commonly mentioned in the documents.

Appendix 2 *Tudor mayors of Liverpool*

Date	Name	Status/Occupation	Residence
1485–86			
1486–87			
1487–88			
1488–89			
1489–90			
1490–91	Evan Houghton		
1491–92			
1492–93			
1493–4			
1494–95			
1495–96			
1496–97			
1497–98			
1498–99			
1499–1500			
1500–01			
1501–02			
1502–03	David ap Griffiths		
1503–04	David ap Griffiths		
1504–05			
1505–06			
1506–07			
1507–08	William More	Esquire	Bank Hall
1508–09			
1509–10			
1510–11	William More	Esquire	Bank Hall
1511–12	William More	Esquire	Bank Hall
1512–13	William More	Esquire	Bank Hall
1513–14	David ap Griffiths		
1514–15			
1515–16			
1516–17	Robert Coudray		
1517–18	Thomas Walker	Merchant	
1518–19			
1519–20			
1520–21			
1521–22	Edward Norris	Esquire	Speke Hall
1522–23			
1523–24	William More	Esquire	Bank Hall
1524–25	Thomas Houghton		

Date	Name	Status/Occupation	Residence
1525–26			
1526–27	William More	Esquire	Bank Hall
1527–28			
1528–29			
1529–30	Thomas Houghton		
1530–31	Roger Fazakerley		
1531–32			
1532–33	Edward Norris	Esquire	Speke Hall
1533–34			
1534–35			
1535–36			
1536–37			
1537–38	Thomas Houghton		
1538–39			
1539–40	Christopher Houghton		
1540–41	Thomas Houghton		
1541–42	Richard Molyneux	Esquire	Croxteth Hall
1542–43			
1543–44			
1544–45	Thomas Fairclough		
1545–46	John More	Esquire	Bank Hall
1546–47	Thomas More	Gentleman/Merchant	
1547–48			
1548–49	Edward Gee		
1549–50			
1550–51	Ralph Sekerston	Merchant	Water Street
1551–52	Thomas More	Gentleman/Merchant	
1552–53	Ralph Bailey	Merchant	Water Street
1553–54	Roger Walker	Merchant	
1554–55	William Norris	Knight	Speke Hall
1555–56	Thomas More	Gentleman/Merchant	
1556–57	John More	Esquire	Bank Hall
1557–58	Thomas More	Gentleman/Merchant	
1558–59	Robert Corbet	Merchant	Water Street
1559–60	Alexander Garnet	Merchant	Water Street
1560–61	Ralph Sekerston	Merchant	Water Street
1561–62	Robert Corbet	Merchant	Water Street
1562–63	Thomas Secum	Merchant	Dale Street
1563–4	Robert Corbet	Merchant	Water Street
1564–65	Alexander Garnet	Merchant	Water Street
1565–66	John Crosse	Esquire	Dale Street
1566–67	Robert Corbet	Merchant	Water Street

Date	Name	Status/Occupation	Residence
1567–68	William Secum	Merchant	Castle Street
1568–69	Thomas Stanley	Son of earl	Knowsley Hall
1569–70	Henry Stanley	Son of earl	Knowsley Hall
1570–71	Ralph Burscough	Merchant	Dale Street
1571–72	Thomas Bavand	Merchant	Water Street
1572–73	John Crosse senior	Esquire	Dale Street
1573–74	Robert Corbet	Merchant	Water Street
1574–75	John Mainwaring	Merchant	Water Street
1575–76	William Secum	Merchant	Castle Street
1576–77	Thomas Bavand	Merchant	Water Street
1577–78	William Hesketh	Knight	Rufford Hall
1578–79	William More	Esquire	Bank Hall
1579–80	Edward Halsall	Esquire	Halsall
1580–81	Robert More	Gentleman/Merchant	Water Street
1581–82	John Crosse junior	Esquire	Dale Street
1582–83	William Secum	Merchant	Water Street
1583–84	Ralph Burscough	Merchant	Dale Street
1584–85	Thomas Bavand	Merchant	Water Street
1585–86	Ferdinando Stanley	Son of earl	Knowsley Hall
1586–87	Edward Halsall	Esquire	Halsall
1587–88	William More	Esquire	Bank Hall
1588–89	Richard Molyneux	Knight	Croxteth Hall
1589–90	Thomas Wickstead	Merchant	Water Street
1590–91	John Bird	Merchant	Water Street
1591–92	Robert More	Gentleman/Merchant	Water Street
1592–93	Giles Brooke	Merchant	Dale Street
1593–94	Robert Berry	Merchant	Water Street
1594–95	John Bird	Merchant	Water Street
1595–96	Robert More	Gentleman/Merchant	Water Street
1596–97	William More	Esquire	Bank Hall
1597–98	Richard Hodgson	Merchant	Castle Street
1598–99	William Dixon		
1599–1600	Robert More	Gentleman/Merchant	Water Street
1600–01	John Bird	Merchant	Water Street
1601–02	Giles Brooke	Merchant	Water Street
1602–03	Ralph Secum	Merchant	Water Street

Material collated from the town books, port books, probate records, and family archives. Previous efforts to compile a list of Liverpool's mayors resulted in many gaps in the record for the early sixteenth century. See T. Baines, *The History of the Commerce and Town of Liverpool* (London 1852), pp. 234–5 and J. Elton, 'Early Recorded Mayors of Liverpool', *THSLC* 54 (1903), pp. 119–30.

Appendix 3 *Tudor Members of Parliament for Liverpool*

Date	Duchy nomination			Earl of Derby's nomination		
1545–47	Sir Nicholas Cutlyer	Suffolk		Gilbert Gerrard esquire	Lancs	Royal official
1547–52	Francis Cave esquire	Leics	Brother of Chancellor of Duchy	Thomas Stanley esquire	Lancs	Relative of Earl of Derby
1553	William Bromley esquire	Salop		Ralph Assheton esquire	Lancs	Lancs gentry
1554	William Bromley esquire	Salop		Sir William Norris	Lancs	Lancs gentry
1554–55	William Bromley esquire	Salop		John Beamont esquire	Leics	
1555	John Beamont esquire	Leics	Royal official, friend of Chancellor	Sir Richard Sherburne	Lancs	Lancs gentry and officer Earl of Derby
1558	George White gentleman			William Stopforth gentleman		
1559	Ralph Browne gentleman	Derbys	Friend of Chancellor	Sir Thomas Smith	Essex	Royal official
1563, 1566– 1567	Richard Molyneux gentleman	Lancs	Friend of Chancellor, younger son of Sir Richard Molyneux	Ralph Sekerston	Liv	Liverpool merchant
1571	Thomas Avery esquire	Essex	Duchy official	Ralph Sekerston	Liv	Liverpool merchant
1572, 1576, 1581	Matthew Dale gentleman	London	Duchy official	Ralph Sekerston	Liv	Liverpool merchant
				Thomas Greenacres esquire	Lancs	Lancs gentry and officer Earl of Derby
1584–86	John Molyneux gentleman	Lancs	Friend of Chancellor, brother of Sir Richard Molyneux	Arthur Autye esquire	London	Secretary to Earl of Leicester, nominee Earl of Derby

Date	Duchy nomination			Earl of Derby's nomination		
1586–87	William Cavendish esquire	Derbys	Friend of Chancellor	John Poole gentleman	Chesh	Relative Earl of Derby
1589	Francis Bacon esquire	Herts	Royal official, friend of Chancellor	Sir Edward Warren	Lancs	Officer Earl of Derby
1592–93	John Wrothe gentleman	London	Duchy official	Michael Doughty	Lancs	Officer Earl of Derby
1597–98	Peter Proby	Hunts	Duchy official	Thomas Gerrard gentleman	Lancs	Lancs gentry
1601	Edward Anderson esquire	Beds	Relative of Chancellor	Hugh Calverley	Chesh	Son of sheriff of Cheshire, nominee Earl of Derby

See P.W. Hasler, *The House of Commons 1558–1603*, 3 vols (London, 1981).

Notes and references

Chapter 1.   The town and its population

1. J. Barry, (ed.), *The Tudor and Stuart Town 1530–1688* (Harlow, 1990), pp. 2–5; R. Britnell, *Britain and Ireland 1050–1530: Economy and Society* (Oxford, 2004); J. Chartres, *Agricultural Markets and Trade 1500–1750* (Cambridge, 1990), pp. 27–45; P. Clark (ed.), *Small Towns in Early Modern Europe* (Cambridge, 1995), pp. 1–14; C. Dyer, 'Small Towns 1270–1540' in D. M. Palliser (ed.), *The Cambridge Urban History of Britain, Vol. 1, 600–1540* (Cambridge, 2000), pp. 517–21; A. Dyer, 'Small Market Towns 1540–1700', in P. Clark (ed.), *The Cambridge Urban History of Britain, Vol. II, 1540–1840* (Cambridge, 2000), pp. 425–7.

2. T. Baines, *The History of the Commerce and Town of Liverpool, and the Rise of the Manufacturing Industry in the Adjoining Counties* (London, 1852); J. A. Picton, *Memorials of Liverpool*, vol. I and vol. II, (London, 1875); R. Muir and E. M. Platt, *A History of the Municipal Government in Liverpool from Earliest Times to the Municipal Reform Act of 1835* (Liverpool, 1906); R. Muir, *A History of Liverpool* (London, 1907); C. N. Parkinson, *The Rise of the Port of Liverpool* (Liverpool, 1952); J. I. Kermode, 'Northern Towns' in Palliser, *Cambridge Urban History I*, p. 667; J. I. Kermode, J. E. Hollinshead, J. M. Gratton, 'Small Beginnings: Liverpool 1207–1680' in J. Belchem (ed.), *Liverpool 800: Culture, Character and History* (Liverpool, 2007).

3. A. Crosby, 'The Towns of Medieval Lancashire: An Overview', *Bulletin of the Centre for North-West Regional Studies, Lancaster University* 1 (1994), pp. 13–14; G. H. Tupling, 'An Alphabetical List of the Markets and Fairs of Lancashire Recorded before the Year 1701', *TLCAS* 51 (1936), pp. 86–110.

4. J. Sheail, 'The Regional Distribution of Wealth in England as Indicated in the 1524–25 Lay Subsidy Returns', University of London Ph.D. thesis, 1968.

5. F. A. Walker, *Historical Geography of South-West Lancashire before the Industrial Revolution*, Chetham Society, new series 103 (1939), p. 15.

6. R. McKinley, *The Surnames of Lancashire* (London, 1981), pp. 2, 46, 77, 441–2; J. E. Hollinshead, 'The People of South-West Lancashire during the Second Half of the Sixteenth Century', University of Liverpool Ph.D. thesis, 1986.

7. Lancs RO, Blundell of Little Crosby DDBl 23/10–13; Derby of Knowsley DDK 471/56.

8. Muir, *History of Liverpool*, p. 3.

9. P. Clark, 'Small Towns in England 1550–1850: National and Regional Population Trends' in Clark (ed.), *Small Towns in Early Modern Europe*, pp. 90–120.

10. The usual Tudor spelling of More has been retained, although by the later seventeenth century Moore was in use.

11. J. A. Twemlow, (ed.), *Liverpool Town Books*, vol. I, 1550–1571 (Liverpool, 1918), vol. II 1572–1603 (Liverpool, 1935). The original records are housed in Liv RO 352 MIN/COU 1 1/1 and 1/2.

12. A. MacFarlane, *Reconstructing Historical Communities* (London, 1977), pp. 206–7.

13. *The History of Chantries within the County Palatine of Lancaster, Reports of the Chantry Commissioners*, F. R. Raines, (ed.), Chetham Society 59 (1862), pp. xxvii, 79, 84, 93, 98.

14. R. Sharpe France, 'A History of the Plague in Lancashire', *THSLC* 90 (1939), pp. 31–2.

15. *LTB* I, pp. 104–5.

16. BL, Harleian. Manuscripts 594, f. 101.

17. N. Goose, 'The Ecclesiastical Returns of 1563: A Cautionary Note', *Local Population Studies* 34 (1985), pp. 46–47; P. Clark, K. Gaskin, A. Wilson, *Population Estimates of English Small Towns 1550–1851* (Leicester, 1989), p. v.

18. *Registers of Walton-on-the-Hill, Prescot, Farnworth,*

Huyton, *Hale* and *Childwall*, Lancashire Parish Register Society 5 (1899), 76 (1938), 80 (1941), 85 (1946), 92 (1951), 106 (1967).

19. *LTB* I, pp. 436–40.

20. *LTB* I, pp. 441–5.

21. *LTB* I, pp. 820–2, 826–9.

22. Muir, *History of Liverpool*, p. 42.

23. Crosby, 'Towns of Medieval Lancashire', pp. 7–18; S. M. Jack, *Towns in Tudor and Stuart Britain* (Basingstoke, 1996), p. xiv.

24. J. T. Driver, *Cheshire in the Later Middle Ages, 1399–1540* (Chester, 1971), pp. 23–41; C. B. Phillips and J. H. Smith, *Lancashire and Cheshire from AD 1540* (London, 1994), p. 8; J. Boulton, 'London 1540–1700' in Clark (ed.), *Cambridge Urban History II*, p. 121; C. P. Lewis and A. T. Thacker (eds), *The History of the County of Chester, Vol. V Part 1: The City of Chester* (Woodbridge, 2003), pp. 53–71.

25. J. K. Walton, 'Northern Towns' in Clark (ed.), *Cambridge Urban History II*, p. 121.

26. Dale, Chapel, Castle, Water, More, Milne and Juggler (Bank) were the seven street names in use in the Tudor period. See *Calendar of Norris Deeds*, J. H. Lumby, (ed.), RSLC 93 (1939).

27. *LTB* II, pp. 824–6.

28. J. Langton, 'Residential Patterns in Pre-Industrial Cities: some case studies from 17th-century Britain', *Transactions of the Institute of British Geographers* 65 (1975), pp. 1–8; A. D. Dyer, *The City of Worcester in the Sixteenth Century* (Leicester, 1973), p. 163; A. B. Rosen, 'Economic and Social Aspects of the History of Winchester, 1520–1670', University of Oxford D. Phil. thesis, 1975, p. 127.

29. M. Gregson, *Portfolio of Fragments relative to the History and Antiquities, Topography and Genealogies of the County Palatine and Duchy of Lancaster* (Liverpool, 1817; 3rd edn, London, 1869), p. 351.

30. *John Leland's Itinerary of England and Wales*, L. Toulmin Smith (ed.), (London, 1907), p. 40; *Britannia*, W. Camden (facsimile rep. London, 1971), p. 790.

31. Lancs RO, Crosse of Shaw Hall Papers, DDSh 197.

32. *LTB* I, pp. 100, 398.

33. *LTB* I, pp. 150, 395; *LTB* II, p. 334.

34. *LTB* II, p. 218.

35. Hoskins, *Provincial England*, pp. 102–6.

36. *History of Chantries*, pp. 84–9.

37. Lancs RO, DDSh 202.

38. *LTB* II, pp. 479–80.

39. The probate records of 32 Liverpool individuals survive from before 1600. A further 21 survive from 1601–1620 providing additional material for individuals who were active commercially during the Tudor period. All probate records are housed at the Lancashire Record Office (class WCW) and are identified by name, location and date of probate.

40. *LTB* I, pp. 15, 177–8.

41. E. W. Cox, 'An Attempt to Recover the Plans of the Castle of Liverpool from Authentic Records', *THSLC* 42 (1890), pp. 195–254; R. Gladstone, 'A Report on Liverpool Castle 2nd October 1559', *THSLC* 59 (1907), pp. 162–4; F. C. Larkin, 'Excavations on the Site of Liverpool Castle', *THSLC* 79 (1927), pp. 175–97.

42. R. Stewart Brown, 'The Tower of Liverpool with some notes on the Clayton Family of Crooke, Fulwood, Adlington and Liverpool', *THSLC* 61 (1909), pp. 41–82.

43. *LTB* I, p. 293; H. Peet, 'St Nicholas's Church, Liverpool: Its Architectural History', *jviii* 65 (1913), pp. 73–118.

44. H. Peet, 'St Nicholas's Church, Liverpool: Its Architectural History', *THSLC* 65 (1913), p. 18.

45. J. Elton, 'The Chapel of St Mary del Key, Liverpool', *THSLC* 54 (1902), pp. 78, 101–2.

46. *LTB* I, p. 293.

47. NA, Duchy of Lancaster Records: Colleges and Chantries DL 14 Bundles 5/18, 5/19; Lancs RO, Molyneux of Sefton Papers DDM 12/30; *LTB* I, p. 402.

48. H. A. Ormerod, *The Liverpool Free School* (Liverpool, 1951), pp. 5–7.

49. S. Nicholson, *The Changing Face of Liverpool 1207–1727* (Merseyside Archaeological Society, 1981), pp. 10, 15.

50. R. Stewart Brown, *Birkenhead Priory and the Mersey Ferry* (Liverpool, 1925).

51. Muir, *History of Liverpool*, pp. 69, 85.

52. *LTB* I, pp. 10, 94, 169, 206, 340, 538.

53. *LTB* I, pp. 176, 270.

Chapter 2.   Merchants and traders

1. Hollinshead, thesis, p. 41.

2. Lumby, *Norris Deeds*; R. D. Radcliffe (ed.), 'Schedule of Deeds and Documents, the Property of Colonel Thomas Richard Crosse, Preserved in the Muniment Room at Shaw Hill, Chorley', *THSLC* 42 (1892).

3. Hollinshead, thesis.

4. Liv RO, More Deeds and Papers 920MOO 237;

E. Garton, *Tudor Nantwich* (Chester, 1983), pp. 11, 77–8; Hollinshead, thesis.

5. *Lancashire and Cheshire Wills and Inventories at Chester,* J. P. Earwaker (ed.), Chetham Society new series 3 (1884).

6. *Visitation of Chester 1580 by Richard Glover and William Flower,* Harleian Society Publications 18 (1882), pp. 265–6; *LTB* II, p. 172; Liv RO 920MOO 237.

7. *LTB* II, p. 154; see Chapter 8.

8. NA, Duchy of Lancaster Pleadings and Examinations DL1 vol. XIV A2, vol. XXXVI M5, vol. XLI A11; *LTB* II, p. 97.

9. See Chapter 5.

10. Liv RO, 920MOO 249; Lancs RO, DDSh 190.

11. J. I. Kermode, 'The Merchants of Three Northern Towns' in D. H. Clough (ed.), *Profession, Vocation and Culture in Later Medieval England* (Liverpool, 1982), p. 17; F. F. Foster, 'Politics and Community in Elizabethan London' in F. C. Jaher (ed.), *The Rich, the Wellborn and the Powerful* (Urbana, Chicago, 1973), p. 132; D. O'Hara. *Courtship and Constraint: Rethinking the Making of Marriage in Tudor England* (Manchester, 2000), pp. 1–2.

12. *Visitation of the County Palatine of Lancaster in 1567 by William Flower, Norroy King of Arms,* F. R. Raines (ed.), Chetham Society 81 (1870), pp. 98, 107; Lancs RO, DDSh 202; Childwall Registers; R. Stewart Brown and F. C. Beazley, 'The Crosse Family of Wigan, Chorley and Liverpool', *THSLC* 73 (1921), p. 60; HMC, Mss. of Captain Stewart of Alltyrodyn, 10th report (London, 1885), p. 60;

see Chapter 6.

13. *LTB* I, p. 253; *LTB* II, p. 44.

14. R. Hoyle, *Tudor Taxation Records: A Guide For Users* (London, 1994), pp. 15–30; J. F. Pound, 'The Social and Trade Structure of Norwich 1525–1575' *Past and Present* 34 (1966), p. 50, A. Dyer, *Decline and Growth in English Towns 1400–1640* (Basingstoke, 1991), pp. 66–71.

15. Dyer, p. 53.

16. BL, Harleian Manuscripts 2219, ff. 14v, 21.

17. D. M. Palliser, 'York under the Tudors: The Trading Life of the Northern Capital' in A. Everitt (ed.), *Perspectives in Urban History* (London, 1973), p. 40; D. M. Woodward, *The Trade of Elizabethan Chester* (Hull, 1970), pp. 73–87.

18. Woodward, p. 52; Garton, *Tudor Nantwich,* pp. 58–60; W. G. Hoskins, 'The Elizabethan Merchants of Exeter' in S. T. Bindoff (ed.), *Elizabethan Government and Society* (London, 1961), p. 172; J. F. Pound, 'Government and Society in Tudor and Stuart Norwich 1525–1675', University of Leicester Ph.D. (1974), pp. 140–1.

19. D. Portman, *Exeter Houses 1400–1700* (Exeter, 1966), p. 39.

20. T. Willan, *Elizabethan Manchester,* Chetham Society, third series 27 (1980), p. 30, pp. 154–5.

21. Hollinshead, thesis, pp. 843–4; P. J. Corfield and D. Keene (eds), *Work in Towns 850–1850* (Leicester, 1990), pp. 3–7.

22. See Chapter 4.

23. *LTB* II, p. 531.

Chapter 3.   Making a living

1. K. Wrightson, *English Society 1580–1680* (London, 1982), p. 12; Dyer, *Worcester in the Sixteenth Century,* pp. 81–4; D. M. Woodward, 'The Chester Leather Industry, 1558–1625', *THSLC* 119 (1967), p. 66; N. Goose, 'English Pre-Industrial Urban Economies', *Urban History Yearbook* 9 (1982), pp. 24–30.

2. A. K. Longfield, *Anglo-Irish Trade in the 16th Century* (London, 1929), pp. 58–69; Woodward, *Trade of Elizabethan Chester,* pp. 8, 36; Woodward, 'Chester Leather Industry', pp. 70–2.

3. L. A. Clarkson, 'The Organization of the English Leather Industry in the Late 16th and 17th Centuries', *Econ. HR* 13 (1960–1), pp. 246–7.

4. Hollinshead, thesis, pp. 814–16.

5. NA, Proceedings of the Court of Star Chamber STAC 5, B106/16.

6. Clarkson, 'Organization of English Leather', pp. 246–7.

7. Hollinshead, thesis, pp. 814–16.

8. Hollinshead, thesis, pp. 814–16.

9. Dyer, *Worcester in the Sixteenth Century,* pp. 122–3.

10. Collated from the town books, port books, probate records and Liverpool deeds and leases. Not until the 1590s is there sufficient surviving evidence to produce statistics.

11. *LTB* II, pp. 300, 463.

12. *LTB* II, pp. 5, 25, 163, 264, 395.

13. Hollinshead, thesis, pp. 817–18.

14. NA, Exchequer Queen's Remembrancer: Port Books E190/1323, /9, /12, 1324/4; Woodward, *Trade of Elizabethan Chester,* p. 42; T. S. Willan, *The Inland Trade* (Manchester, 1976), p. 6.

15. Hollinshead, thesis, pp. 817–18.

16. R. J. A. Shelley, 'Wigan and Liverpool Pewterers', *THSLC* 97 (1946), pp. 1–9.

17. Hollinshead, thesis, pp. 817–18.

18. T. S. Bell, 'Ancient Chester Goldsmiths and their

Works', *TLCAS* 32 (1914), pp. 180–5; *LTB* II, pp. 630–8.

19. W. Harrison, 'Ancient Forests, Chases and Deer Parks in Lancashire', *TLCAS* 19 (1901), pp. 24–33; Liv RO *Churchwardens' Accounts of Childwall Parish 1571–1674*, R. Stewart Brown (ed.), pp. 6, 51; *Churchwardens' Accounts of Prescot, Lancashire, 1523–1607*, F. A. Bailey (ed.), RSLC 104 (1953), pp. 51, 55, 110, 120.

20. Hollinshead, thesis, pp. 820–1; *LTB* I, p. 172.

21. Hollinshead, thesis, pp. 820–1.

22. *LTB* II, p. 229.

23. *Churchwardens' Accounts of Childwall*, p. 23.

24. *LTB* II, pp. 22, 231, 302, 459.

25. *LTB* I, p. 294.

26. *LTB* II, p. 268.

27. *Chester Freemen Rolls 1392–1700*, J. H. E. Bennett (ed.), RSLC 51 (1906), pp. 34–87; *Churchwardens' Accounts of Prescot*, pp. 95, 104, 125, 137; *LTB* II, p. 549.

28. *Churchwardens' Accounts of Childwall*, p. 56.

29. N. Lowe, *The Lancashire Textile Industry in the Sixteenth Century*, Chetham Society, third series 20 (1972).

30. Lowe, pp. 3–4.

31. Hollinshead, thesis, p. 841.

32. Hollinshead, thesis, pp. 840–1.

33. Woodward, *Trade of Elizabethan Chester*, pp. 8–25.

34. *LTB* I, pp. 9, 64; *LTB* II, pp. 52, 160, 264, 303, 423, 457, 475, 490.

35. *LTB* II, p. 26, p. 407.

36. Woodward, *Trade of Elizabethan Chester*, p. 15.

37. *LTB* I, p. 112.

38. Hollinshead, thesis, p. 842.

39. *LTB* II, pp. 423, 429, 456, 472.

40. S. Rappaport, *Worlds Within Worlds: Structures of Life in Sixteenth-century London* (Cambridge, 1989), p. 30.

41. Goose, 'English Pre-Industrial Urban Economies', p. 24.

42. J. Touzeau, *The Rise and Progress of Liverpool, 1551–1835* (Liverpool, 1910), pp. 13–15.

43. NA DL1 vol. 62 G2, vol. 147 M2; Liv RO 920MOO 945.

44. Liv RO 920MOO 242; Hollinshead, thesis, p. 826.

45. Archives of the University of Liverpool, Norris Deeds 17/53.

46. Hollinshead, thesis, p. 826.

47. *LTB* I, pp. 60, 189; *LTB* II, pp. 225, 531.

48. *LTB* I, p. 189; *LTB* II, pp. 126, 512.

49. Hollinshead, thesis, p. 827.

50. Lancs RO, WCW Thomas Bavand 1588.

51. *LTB* I, p. 993.

52. *LTB* I, pp. 183, 272; *LTB* II, pp. 22, 279, 993.

53. *LTB* I, pp. 246, 388; *LTB* II, pp. 169, 302, 344, 993.

54. *LTB* II, pp. 220, 689.

55. *LTB* I, pp. 155, 184, 304; *LTB* II, pp. 220, 584, 689.

56. Hollinshead, thesis, pp. 828–9.

57. HMC, Salisbury Mss, vol. IV (London, 1883), p. 250; HMC Mss of the Towns of Weymouth and Melcombe Regis, 5th report (London, 1876), p. 578.

58. Hollinshead, thesis, pp. 828–9.

59. Lancs RO, DDM 39/78; *LTB* I, pp. 283, 359; Stewart Brown, *Mersey Ferry*, pp. 146–55.

60. Hollinshead, thesis, p. 830.

61. *LTB* II, pp. 17, 672.

62. *LTB* II, pp. 62, 214, 230, 250, 373, 506, 536, 569, 672.

63. W. J. King, 'The Regulation of Alehouses in Stuart Lancashire: an Example of Discretionary Administration of the Law', *THSLC* 129 (1980), p. 32.

64. *Proceedings of Lancashire JPs at the Sheriff's Table During Assizes Week 1578–1694*, B. W. Quintrell (ed.), RSLC 121 (1981), p. 68.

65. *LTB* II, pp. 237, 354; P. Clark, *The English Alehouse: A Social History 1200–1830* (London, 1983), pp. 66, 79.

66. King, 'Regulation of alehouses', pp. 40–1; J. Laughton, 'The Alewives of Later Medieval Chester' in R. A. Archer (ed.), *Crown, Government and People in the Fifteenth Century* (Stroud, 1995), pp. 193–200.

67. *History of Chantries*, pp. 82–9; P. Carter, 'Economic Problems of Provincial Urban Clergy during the Reformation' in P. Collinson and J. Craig (eds), *The Reformation in English Towns 1500–1640* (Basingstoke, 1998), pp. 147–58.

68. *LTB* I, p. 124.

69. *LTB* II, pp. 60, 158, 486, 548.

70. *LTB* II, pp. 577, 675, 703, 730, 750–1.

71. NA, Duchy of Lancaster, Miscellaneous Books DL42/23; *LTB* II, p. 468.

72. *History of Chantries*, p. 85; Ormerod, *Liverpool Free School*, pp. 5–7.

73. NA, DL42/23; *LTB* I, p. 49.

74. *LTB* I, pp. 255, 300–1, 374.

75. Ormerod, *Liverpool Free School*, pp. 19–21; E. R. Johns, 'Some Aspects of Education in West Derby Hundred of Lancashire in the 17th Century', University of Manchester M.Ed. (1973), p. 214.

76. *LTB* II, pp. 779, 794; Ormerod, *Liverpool Free School*, p. 21.

77. *LTB* II, p. 269.

78. M. Spufford, 'The Schooling of the Peasantry

of Cambridgeshire 1575–1700' in J.Thirsk (ed.), *Land, Church and People* (Reading, 1970), p.129.

79. *Chester Freemen Rolls*, pp.34–87; *LTB* II, pp.560, 715, 762.

80. *LTB* II, pp.232, 629.

81. Liv RO, 920MOO 267.

82. *LTB* II, pp.238, 328, 420, 532, 566, 666, 696, 719, 787.

83. *LTB* II, p.204.

84. *LTB* II, pp.637, 776.

85. D.G.Hey, *An English Rural Community: Myddle under the Tudors and Stuarts* (Leicester, 1974), pp.169–70; A.Everitt, 'Farm Labourers' in J.Thirsk (ed.), *The Agrarian History of England and Wales, Vol.IV, 1500–1600* (Cambridge, 1967), p.398.

86. Hollinshead, thesis, p.851; C.Dyer, 'Small Towns', p.516.

87. J.Thirsk, 'The Farming Regions of England' in Thirsk, *Agrarian History*, pp.2–4, 81.

88. R.Stewart Brown, 'The Townfield of Liverpool', *THSLC* 68 (1916), pp.33–9; *LTB* I, p.156; *LTB*

II, pp.231, 553. Divisions of the town field had various names including selions, lands, fields, butts, acres and shoots.

89. *LTB* I, pp.30, 142–4, 149, 257, 264; *LTB* II, pp.53, 661.

90. *LTB* II, pp.151, 154, 660.

91. NA DL1 vol.207 T1; Duchy of Lancaster Special Commissions DL44/671; R.Griffiths, *The History of the Royal and Ancient Park of Toxteth, Liverpool* (Liverpool, 1907), p.19.

92. NA DL1 vol.172 D4; Duchy of Lancaster Depositions DL4 42/38; DL44/671; Records of the Court of Requests: Proceedings REQ2 200/38; Lancs RO, DDM 50/3, 50/8; H.O.Aspinall, *The Aspinwall and Aspinall Families of Lancashire* (Exeter, 1923), pp.9–11.

93. Henry E.Huntington Library, California, Ellesmere Mss. E393; L.Hall, 'The Ancient Chapel of Toxteth Park and Toxteth School', *THSLC* 87 (1936), p.24.

Chapter 4.   Domestic trade

1. *LTB* I, pp.172, 182; *LTB* II, pp.64, 483.

2. *LTB* I, pp.89, 239, 277–8, 350; *LTB* II, pp.352, 550, 648.

3. Willan, *Inland Trade*, p.56.

4. NA DL1 vol.19 G1, vol.89 H13; *LTB* I, p.346.

5. *LTB* II, p.560.

6. *LTB* I, pp.148, 200, 276, 305.

7. *LTB* II, pp.222, 307, 409, 558–9.

8. J.E.Hollinshead, 'An Unexceptional Commodity: Coal in South-West Lancashire in the Sixteenth Century', *THSLC* 145 (1995), pp.1–19.

9. *LTB* I, p.246; *LTB* II, pp.168, 344.

10. G.H.Tupling, 'The Origins of Markets and Fairs in Medieval Lancashire', *TLCAS* 49 (1933), pp.75–94.

11. *LTB* I, p.74; *LTB* II, pp.691, 1007–10.

12. J.A.Chartres, *Internal Trade in England, 1500–1700* (London, 1977), pp.7–12; Chartres, *Agricultural Markets and Trade*, pp.45–50; Willan, *Inland Trade*, p.2.

13. H.B.Rodgers, 'The Market Area of Preston in the 16th and 17th Centuries', *Geographical Studies* Vol.VI No.1 (1956), pp.46–55; Willan, *Elizabethan Manchester*, pp.77–97.

14. *LTB* II, pp.172, 335, 396, 553, 722, 764.

15. Lancs RO, WCW Ralph Edgecar 1578, Peter Ireland 1580, John Nailer 1584, George Ackers 1588, John Smith 1590, Thomas Hitchmough 1591, John Gore 1594, James Melling 1603.

16. Lancs RO, WCW George Darlington Roby

1561, Percival Crosse Huyton 1582, Thomas Gorsuch Huyton 1596.

17. *LTB* II, p.307.

18. NA E190/1324/21, 1325/1, 1325/9, 1325/21, 1326/8; *LTB* I, p.156; *LTB* II, p.428.

19. W.H.Chippindall (ed.), *A 16th Century Survey and Year's Accounts of the Estate of Hornby Castle Lancashire*, Chetham Society, new series 102 (1939), pp.115–19; J.Harland (ed.), *House and Farm Accounts of the Shuttleworths of Gawthorpe Hall, 1582–1621*, Chetham Society 35 (1856), pp.18, 80–1.

20. NA DL1 vol.14 B3; *LTB* I, p.170, p.354.

21. NA DL1 vol.19 G1; E190 1323/4, 1323/9, 1324/4, 1324/9, 1324/21, 1324/22, 1326/8, 1326/19, 1327/2, 1328/2; Lancs RO, DDSh 199; *LTB* I, p.354; Willan, *Elizabethan Manchester*, pp.51–6.

22. *LTB* I, p.292.

23. NA E190/1325/23, 1327/16; Garton, *Tudor Nantwich*, pp.77–9.

24. NA DL1 Vol.19 E24, E190/1323/4, 1323/12, 1324/4, 1324/6, 1325/1, 1325/9, 1325/21, 1326/8, 1326/9; *LTB* I, p.138, p.204, p.338; *LTB* II, pp.147–78.

25. Willan, *Inland Trade*, p.41; NA DL1 vol.20 M14, vol.89 H13; Lancs RO, DDSh 203; *LTB* I, pp.129, 172, 184, 186.

26. *LTB* I, pp.41, 53, 166, 320.

27. *LTB* II, pp.98, 181–2.

28. NA State Papers Elizabeth I, Domestic,

SP12/11/27; HMC, Salisbury Mss. XI/466; *LTB* I, p. 280.

29. T. O'Neill, *Merchants and Mariners in Medieval Ireland* (Dublin, 1987), pp. 107–12.

30. NA Exchequer Queen's Remembrancer: Port Books, E190. Prior to 1565 Liverpool shipping had been recorded as part of the customs area administered from Chester.

31. D. Burwash, *English Merchant Shipping 1460–1540* (1947; repr. Newton Abbot, 1969), p. 42.

32. NA E190/1323/4, 1323/9; *LTB* I, p. 280.

33. NA E190/1325/1, 1325/9, 1325/23, 1327/16, 1327/22.

34. D. Loades, *The Tudor Navy: An Administrative, Political and Military History* (Aldershot, 1992), p. 282.

35. NA E190/1325/17.

36. D. M. Woodward, 'Ships, Masters and Shipowners of the Wirral 1550–1650', *The Mariner's Mirror* 63 (1977), p. 235.

37. M. Stammers, 'Port Operations at Liverpool in the 16th and 17th Centuries'. I am grateful for use of this unpublished paper.

38. Stammers.

39. Woodward, p. 235.

40. O'Neill, *Merchants and Mariners*, p. 117.

41. NA DL1 vol. 143 M16; *LTB* II, p. 241.

42. NA SP12/150/12; APC VII/107.

43. NA SP12/193/16; *Calendar of State Papers Relating to Ireland*, H. C. Hamilton (ed.), (London, 1877), p. 62; O'Neill, *Merchants and Mariners*, pp. 119–22.

44. Lancs RO, WCW Richard Bird of Liverpool, 1595.

45. NA High Court of Admiralty HCA 1/36 ff. 245–98, 363–91; G. D. Owen, *Elizabethan Wales* (Cardiff, 1962), p. 137; Parkinson, *Rise of the Port of Liverpool*, p. 28.

46. NA Exchequer Queen's Remembrancer: Special Commissions, E178/499; *LTB* II, p. 97; J. R. Dickinson, *The Lordship of Man under the Stanleys: Government and Economy in the Isle of Man, 1580–1704*, Chetham Society 3rd series 41 (1993), p. 245.

47. NA E178/499.

Chapter 5. Overseas trade

1. Woodward, 'Ships, Masters and Shipowners', p. 233.

2. NA E190/1324/6, 1324/19, 1324/22, 1325/1, 1325/9, 1326/26, 1327/2.

3. NA E178/499.

4. NA State Papers Domestic: Addenda SP15/13/13; *LTB* II, pp. 107–108; P. H. Fox, 'Cumberland Ports and Shipping in the Reign of Elizabeth', *Transactions of the Cumberland and Westmorland Antiquarian and Archaeological Society*, new series 21 (1921), pp. 77–9.

5. NA E190/1325/21, 1326/26, 1327/2, 1328/2, 1328/7.

6. NA E190/1325/21; *LTB* I, p. 44, p. 179; *Pleadings and Depositions in the Duchy Court of Lancaster*, H. Fishwick (ed.), RSLC 35 (1897), p. 50.

7. NA E178/499; E190/1324/9, 1324/19, 1423/22; *LTB* I, pp. 138, 184; *LTB* II, pp. 585, 687.

8. NA E190/1327/16, 1325/23; Woodward, *Trade of Elizabethan Chester*, p. 36.

9. NA E190/1323/12, 1324/21, 1324/22; *A History of the Isle of Man*, W. Blundell (ed.), Manx Society 25 (1876), pp. 71, 83; Dickinson, *The Lordship of Man under the Stanleys*, pp. 246–70.

10. *Welsh Port Books 1550–1603*, E. A. Lewis (ed.), Cymrodorian Record Society 12 (1927), pp. xxv, xxxvii; Owen, *Elizabethan Wales*, pp. 94, 129.

11. NA E190/1325/21, 1328/2, 1328/7; *Welsh Port Books*, pp. 245, 280.

12. *LTB* I, p. 225, *LTB* II, pp. 423, 792.

13. *LTB* II, p. 710.

14. NA E190/1323/12, 1324/6, 1325/1, 1325/9, 1325/23, 1327/16, 1327/22.

15. *History of Chantries*, p. 83; *John Leland's Itinerary*, pp. 40–1; Woodward, *Trade of Elizabethan Chester*, p. 5.

16. NA E190/1324/21, 1324/22; A Cosgrove (ed.), *A New History of Ireland, Vol. II, Medieval Ireland 1169–1534* (Oxford, 1987), p. 487; O'Neill, *Merchants and Mariners*, pp. 30–2.

17. Longfield, *Anglo-Irish Trade*, pp. 41–70, 79, 88, 107, 222; Lowe, *Lancashire Textile Industry*, pp. 13–14; R. Gillespie, 'Small Towns in Early Modern Ireland' in Clark (ed.), *Small Towns in Early Modern Europe*, pp. 148–65.

18. R. Britnell, *Ireland 1050–1530: Economy and Society* (Oxford, 2004), pp. 509–13.

19. NA E190/1323/4–7; Longfield, *Anglo-Irish Trade*, pp. 132–60.

20. Woodward, *Trade of Elizabethan Chester*, p. 17; Hollinshead, 'An Unexceptional Commodity: Coal in South-West Lancashire', pp. 1–19.

21. NA E190/1323–1328/7; J. Hatcher, *The History of the British Coal Industry, Vol. I, Before 1700: Towards the Age of Coal* (Oxford, 1993), pp. 121, 476, 505.

22. N. P. Canny, *The Elizabethan Conquest of Ireland:*

A Pattern Established 1565–76 (Hassocks, 1576), pp. 2–6; Woodward, *Trade of Elizabethan Chester*, p. 25; A. Sheehan, 'Irish Towns in a Period of Change, 1558–1625' in C. Brady and R. Gillespie (eds), *Natives and Newcomers: Essays in the Making of Irish Colonial Society 1534–1641* (Dublin, 1986), pp. 95–8.

23. NA E190/1323/9; Canny, *Elizabethan Conquest of Ireland*, pp. 4–5.

24. *APC* VIII/392; *LTB* II, p. 750.

25. NA E190/1323/12, 1325/2, 1325/9; *Pleadings and Depositions*, pp. 35, 119.

26. *APC* VII/264; *LTB* I, p. 292, Canny, *Elizabethan Conquest of Ireland*, pp. 36–9, 61, 69, 78–87; C. Falls, *Elizabeth's Irish Wars* (London, 1950), pp. 88, 105.

27. NA E190/1324/6; State Papers Ireland SP63/47/32; BL, Harl. Mss. 2219 f. 50v.; *APC* VIII/113, VIII/185, VIII/202; *LTB* II, pp. 119–21, pp. 147–8.

28. BL, Harl. Mss. 1926/13 f. 31; PRO, SP63/183/98, 183/151, 188/25, 194/46; *APC* XVIV/326, XXV/281, XXV/315, XXVI/164; Falls, *Irish Wars*, pp. 175–211.

29. NA SP12/250/27, 251/61, SP63/183/98, 183/151, 188/25, 194/46; *APC* XVIV/326, XXV/281, XXV/315, XXVI/164; Falls, *Irish Wars*, pp. 175–11; J.J.N. McGurk, 'Chester: The Chief Military Port for the Irish Service in the 1590s' in J.E. Hollinshead and F. Pogson (eds), *Studies in Northern History* (Liverpool, 1997), pp. 37–50.

30. NA SP63/202/60, 202/83, 203/36, 205/41; *APC* XXVIII/610, XXIX/167, 490, 577, XXXI/23, 318; HMC Salisbury Mss. IX/86, 97, 133, X/12, XIV/136; Falls, *Irish Wars*, pp. 253–63.

31. NA SP63/207/59; HMC, Salisbury Mss. XI/466.

32. NA E190/1324/6, 1324/9, 1325/17, SP12/251/61, SP63/76/28, 76/70, 79/19, 79/21; *APC* XII/215; Cheshire Record Office, Mayor of Chester's Military Papers M/MP/3/32; B. Pearce, 'Elizabethan Food Policy and the Armed Forces' *Econ HR* 12 (1942), pp. 44–5.

33. NA E190/1327/30, 1328/2, 1328/7, SP63/183/98; Liv RO, Liverpool Deeds 920LIV 5/1.

34. NA SP63/187/51, 188/25, 196/25, 196/26; *APC* VIII/279, XXV/478; *LTB* I, p. 338; Falls, *Irish Wars*, pp. 59, 94.

35. P. Ramsey, *Tudor Economic Problems* (London, 1963), pp. 47–54; R. Davis, *English Overseas Trade 1500–1700* (London, 1973), p. 17.

36. T.S. Willan, *Studies in Elizabethan Foreign Trade* (Manchester, 1959), pp. 67, 87–9.

37. *The Spanish Company*, J.P. Croft (ed.), London Record Society 9 (1973), p. vii.

38. *Chester Customs Accounts 1301–1566*, K.P. Wilson (ed.), RSLC 111 (1969), pp. 31–3; J.I. Kermode, 'The Trade of Late Medieval Chester, 1500–1550' in R. Britnell and J. Hatcher (eds), *Progress and Problems in Medieval England: Essays in Honour of Edward Miller* (Cambridge, 1996), pp. 286–7.

39. Information about the local records of northern Spanish towns has been kindly supplied by S. Huxley Barkham of Onate, 1987; *Pleadings and Depositions in the Duchy Courts of Lancaster*, H. Fishwick (ed.), RSLC 40 (1899), pp. 135–6.

40. NA DL1 vol. 14 B3; Lancs RO, DDSh 196; *Chester Customs Accounts*, p. 79; J.P. Croft, 'English Trade with Peninsular Spain 1558–1625', University of Oxford D.Phil. (1969), pp. 392–425; J.E. Hollinshead, 'Chester, Liverpool and the Basque Region in the Sixteenth Century', *The Mariner's Mirror* 85 No. 4 (1999), pp. 387–95.

41. NA E190/1323/4.

42. Croft, thesis, p. 23; G.D. Ramsay, *The City of London in International Politics at the Accession of Elizabeth Tudor* (Manchester, 1975), pp. 136–8.

43. *LTB* I, p. 284, pp. 302–3.

44. NA E190/1324/4, 1324/9.

45. NA E190/1323/4, 1324/4, 1324/6, 1324/9, 1324/21, 1324/22, 1325/1, 1325/9; Croft, thesis, pp. 110–11.

46. NA SP12/44/56.

47. *Spanish Company*, pp. xiii–xix; Woodward, *Trade of Elizabethan Chester*, p. 78.

48. Croft, thesis, pp. 36–8; J.E. Gelabert, 'Intercambio y tolerancia: las villas marineras de la fachoda Atlantica y el conflicto Anglo-Espanol (1559–1604)', *Revista de Historia Naval* 5 (1987), pp. 57–68.

49. *Mss. of Towns of Weymouth and Melcombe Regis*, p. 578.

50. NA E190/1325/23, 1326/28; Croft, thesis, p. 84.

51. NA E190/1326/8, 1326/19, 1326/25, 1326/26, 1327/16, 1327/22, 1327/30; *LTB* II, p. 687.

52. NA SP12/252/58, 253/33.

53. NA E190/1328/2, 1328/7.

54. NA E190/1323/9, 1323/12; *LTB* I, pp. 127, 180, 188.

55. *LTB* I, pp. 221–4.

56. NA SP63/10/26, 10/27; *APC*, vol. VII, pp. 271, 305.

57. NA E190/1323/4, 1323/9, 1323/12, 1324/4, 1324/6; Croft, thesis, p. 161; J. Bost, *Saint-Jean-de-Luz* (Ekaina, 1992); M.M. Barkham, 'French Basque 'Newfoundland' Entrepreneurs and the Import of Codfish and Whale Oil to Northern

Spain *c.*1580–*c.*1620', *Newfoundland Studies* 10 (1994), pp. 1–4.

58. NA DL1, vol. 45 A24, A25; *LTB* I, p. 331; *LTB* II, p. 82.

59. NA E190/1325/17; Woodward, *Trade of Elizabethan Chester*, p. 42.

60. NA E190/1323/4, 1323/9; High Court of Admiralty: Oyer and Terminer Records, HCA 1/36/156; *LTB* I, pp. 202, 227.

61. T. K. Rabb, *Enterprise and Empire: Merchant and Gentry Investment in the Expansion of England 1575–1630* (Cambridge, 1967), pp. 26–7.

62. P. E. H. Hair, 'The First Liverpool Men in West Africa', *THSLC* 137 (1988), pp. 149–51.

63. D. B. Quinn, *New American World: A Documentary History of North America to 1612, Vol. III: English Plans for North America, The Roanoke Voyages and New England Ventures* (London, 1979), p. 239; D. N. Durant, *Ralegh's Lost Colony* (London, 1981), pp. 7–8.

64. NA DL1 vol. 101 M5; Lancs RO, DDM 52/22, 52/23; *Voyages and Colonizing Enterprises of Sir Humphrey Gilbert*, D. B. Quinn (ed.), Hakluyt Society, 2nd series 83 (1968), pp. 83–4, p. 333; D. B. Quinn, *England and the Discovery of America 1481–1620* (London, 1974), pp. 228–30; Quinn,

New American World, pp. 124, 156, 233–5, 345; D. B. Quinn and A. N. Ryan, *England's Sea Empire* (London, 1983), pp. 41–2.

65. G. Molineux, *Memoir of the Molineux Family* (private publication, 1882), p. 142; W. G. Gosling, *The Life of Sir Humphrey Gilbert* (London, 1911; repr. Connecticut, 1970).

66. *English Privateering Voyages to the West Indies 1588–1595*, K. R. Andrews (ed.), Hakluyt Society, 2nd series 140 (1959), pp. 253–4.

67. R. C. Jarvis, 'The Head Port of Chester, and Liverpool, its Creek and Member', *THSLC* 102 (1950), pp. 72–5.

68. J. A. Picton, *Chester and Liverpool in their Ancient Commercial Relations* (Liverpool, 1886), pp. 6–17; Jarvis, 'Head Port of Chester', pp. 72–5.

69. Woodward, 'Ships, Masters and Shipowners', p. 234; E. Rideout, 'The Chester Companies and the Old Quay', *THSLC* 79 (1928), pp. 141–74.

70. Woodward, 'Ships, Masters and Shipowners', pp. 233–4; *Letters and Papers Foreign and Domestic of the Reign of Henry VIII*, J. S. Brewer (ed.), vol. VI pp. 148, 366; vol. XXII, p. 292.

71. Parkinson, *Rise of the Port of Liverpool*, p. 29.

72. *Salisbury Mss*, Cheshire Sheaf XI (1914), p. 59.

Chapter 6.   Urban identity and status

1. W. T. MacCaffrey, *Exeter 1540–1640* (Harvard, 1975), pp. 137–49; Hoskins, 'Elizabethan Merchants of Exeter', p. 165.

2. *LTB* I, p. lxxvii.

3. *LTB* I, p. lxxi; *LTB* II, pp. 345–7.

4. *LTB* II, pp. 388, 416.

5. See Appendix 2.

6. *LTB* II, p. 692.

7. See Appendix 2.

8. T. Baines, *History of the Commerce and Town of Liverpool*, p. 82; see J. I. Kermode *et al.*, 'Small Beginnings'.

9. Rappaport, *Worlds Within Worlds*, p. 30.

10. *LTB* I, pp. 446–53; *LTB* II, pp. 830–41; E. M. Hance and T. N. Morton (eds), 'The Burgess Rolls of Liverpool during the 16th Century', *THSLC* 35 (1883), pp. 147–9.

11. *LTB* I, pp. 30, 60; *LTB* II, p. 454.

12. *LTB* I, pp. 420–9.

13. A. M. Johnson, 'Some Aspects of the Political, Constitutional, Social and Economic History of the City of Chester 1550–1662', University of Oxford D.Phil. thesis, 1970, pp. 93–4.

14. *LTB* I, pp. 117–18.

15. *LTB* I, pp. 249, 264; *LTB* II, pp. 7, 659.

16. *LTB* II, pp. 10, 169.

17. *LTB* II, pp. 240–1.

18. W. L. Woodfill, *Musicians in English Society from Elizabeth to Charles I* (New York, 1953), p. 33.

19. M. Higham, 'Musicians and Malefactors: Pipers and Harpers in Medieval Lancashire', *The Lancashire Local Historian* 10 (1995), p. 52.

20. *LTB* I, pp. 78–79, 110, 150, 197, 252, 350; *LTB* II, pp. 24–5, 77–8, 166, 269, 461.

21. *LTB* II, pp. 230, 262, 338, 399, 427, 461, 470, 478, 493, 511, 518, 541, 558, 561, 572, 585, 601, 681–2, 781, 788.

22. I. A. Archer, 'Politics and Government 1540–1700' in Clark (ed.), *Cambridge Urban History* II, p. 238.

23. J. E. Hollinshead, 'The Gentry of South-West Lancashire in the Later Sixteenth Century', *Northern History* 25 (1990), pp. 82–102.

24. J. J. Bagley, *The Earls of Derby 1485–1985* (London, 1985), pp. 18–23; B. Coward, *The Stanleys, Lords Stanley and Earls of Derby 1385–1672: The Origins, Wealth and Power of a Landowning Family*, Chetham Society 3rd series 30 (1983), pp. 2–9, 112.

25. Coward, *The Stanleys*, pp. 3–13; B. Coward, 'The Lieutenancy in Lancashire and Cheshire in the

16th and Early 17th Centuries', *THSLC* 119 (1968), p. 47.

26. Hollinshead, thesis, pp. 95–103; Stewart Brown, 'Tower of Liverpool', pp. 12–14; F. R. Raines (ed.), *Stanley Papers: The Derby Household Books*, Chetham Society 31 (1853), pp. 23–7.

27. *LTB* I, p. 312.

28. *LTB* II, pp. 156, 242.

29. *LTB* II, pp. 242–6.

30. *LTB* I, p. 138; *LTB* II, pp. 34–5, 185, 272, 387, 405.

31. *LTB* I, pp. 164–6.

32. A. L. Beier, 'The Social Problems of an Elizabethan County Town: Warwick 1580–90', in P. Clark (ed.), *The County Towns in Pre-Industrial England* (Leicester, 1981), pp. 47–51.

33. T. Baines, *History of the Commerce and Town of Liverpool*, p. 200; LRO, DDM 39/61, 62, 66, 67.

34. *LTB* I, p. 181; *APC* XXV/488; PRO, Duchy of Lancaster Inquisitions Post Mortem DL7 IX/2; LRO, DDM 39/80.

35. *LTB* I, p. 32, p. 41, p. 86; Muir, *History of Liverpool*, p. 72; LRO, DDM 39/76; PRO, DD1 vol. 7 M11, vol. 10 M1.

36. NA DL44/9, 44/419; LRO DDM 3/12.

37. NA DL1 vol. 72 M1, vol. 107 M2; LRO, DDM 39/107; LivRO, 920MOO 945.

38. NA DL14 Bundle 5/18; LRO, DDM 12/30, 39/71, 39/72; *Pleadings and Depositions*, p. 38.

39. *LTB* I, p. 125.

40. See, for example, M. J. Power (ed.), *Liverpool Town Books 1644–1671*, RSLC 136 (1998).

41. Liv RO 920MOO 100, 247, 256, 266, 745, 749; *Inquisitions Post Mortem, Stuart Period, Part I*, RSLC 3 (1879), pp. 13–14.

42. Liv RO 920MOO 229, 276, 279, 280.

43. NA DL7 11/22, 11/66, 13/15, 15/20, 16/28, 17/34, 18/9, 20/59, 40/57; Lancs RO, Blundell of Little Crosby Papers DDBl 23/12–14, Blundell of Ince Blundell Papers DDIn 64/82; *LTB* I, p. 92; *LTB* II, p. 632.

44. NA DL7 10/20; *Inquisitions Post Mortem, Stuart Period, Part II*, RSLC 16 (1887), p. 135; Stewart Brown and Beazley, 'Crosse family', pp. 169–78.

45. *Visitation of William Flower*, p. 107; R. Stewart Brown, 'Moore of Bank Hall', *THSLC* 63 (1911),

pp. 108–12.

46. *LTB* I, pp. 446–453; *LTB* II, pp. 830–8.

47. *LTB* I, pp. 234, 390; *LTB* II, p. 117.

48. M. A. R. Graves, *The Tudor Parliaments* (London, 1985), pp. 73, 124; M. A. R. Graves, *Elizabethan Parliaments 1559–1601* (London, 1987), pp. 27–8; M. A. Kishlansky, *Parliamentary Selection: Social and Political Control in Early Modern England* (Cambridge, 1986), pp. 12–24, 32–8.

49. See Appendix 3.

50. P. W. Hasler, *The House of Commons 1558–1603* (London, 1981), vol. I pp. 188–91; R. Somerville, 'The Palatine Court in Lancashire' in A. Harding (ed.), *Law Making and Law Makers in British History* (London, 1980), pp. 54–63.

51. Johnson, thesis, p. 68.

52. *LTB* I, p. 52a.

53. *LTB* I, p. 108; Hasler, *House of Commons* III, p. 364.

54. It could be construed that individuals from the local Molyneux family were a more likely choice for the earl of Derby than the Duchy Chancellor and that the town had, in fact, not received any instruction from the Chancellor.

55. *LTB* I, pp. 216–18; Hasler, *House of Commons* III, pp. 364–5.

56. *LTB* I, pp. 218–19.

57. *LTB* I, pp. 322, 337.

58. *LTB* I, p. 567.

59. T. E. Hartley, *Proceedings in the Parliaments of Elizabeth I, 1558–1581* (Leicester, 1981), p. 252; G. R. Elton, *The Parliament of England 1559–1581* (Cambridge, 1986), pp. 105–6.

60. Hasler, *House of Commons* III, p. 365, Hartley, *Proceedings in Parliament*, pp. 366, 384, 402; Elton, *Parliament in England*, p. 269.

61. Hartley, *Proceedings in Parliament*, pp. 386–7, 390, 409–10.

62. *LTB* II, p. 43.

63. *LTB* II, pp. 44–5; Hasler, *House of Commons* III, p. 365.

64. W. D. Pink and A. B. Beavan, *The Parliamentary Representation of Lancashire 1258–1885* (London, 1889), pp. 183–4.

65. *LTB* II, pp. 449–50.

Chapter 7.   Social contact

1. J. Barry and C. Brook (eds), *The Middling Sort of People: Culture, Society and Politics in England, 1550–1800* (London, 1994), pp. 18–20.

2. *LTB* II, p. 64; S. D. Amussen, *An Ordered Society: Gender and Class in Early Modern England* (Oxford,

1988), pp. 138–44.

3. *LTB* II, pp. 529–30.

4. Hollinshead, thesis, pp. 325–6.

5. Liv RO 920MOO 276, 280.

6. J. P. Rylands, 'Communications', *THSLC* 33

(1880–1), pp. 257–64.

7. BL, Harl. Mss. 1926/13 f. 31; *LTB* II, p. 562, p. 606.

8. K. Wrightson, 'The Social Order of Early Modern England: Three Approaches' in L. Bonfield, R. Smith and K. Wrightson (eds), *The World We Have Gained* (Oxford, 1986), pp. 177–91.

9. *LTB* I, p. 405.

10. P. Slack, 'Mortality Crises and Epidemic Diseases in England 1485–1610', C. Webster (ed.), *Health, Medicine and Mortality in the Sixteenth Century* (Cambridge, 1979), p. 9.

11. *LTB* I, pp. 16–17.

12. *LTB* I, pp. 104–5, 108.

13. *LTB* II, p. 276.

14. Liv RO 920MOO 289.

15. R. B. Outhwaite, 'Dearth, the English Crown and the Crisis of the 1590s', P. Clark (ed.), *The European Crisis of the 1590s* (London, 1985), pp. 28–34; W. G. Hoskins, 'Harvest Fluctuations and English Economic History 1480–1619', *Agricultural History Review* 12 (1964), p. 29.

16. *LTB* II, p. 275.

17. NA SP63/187/51, 194/36.

18. Hollinshead, thesis, p. 657.

19. *LTB* I, p. 144; *LTB* II, pp. 269, 458, 535, 703, 724.

20. *LTB* II, pp. 741, 757, 774.

21. *LTB* II, p. 220.

22. A. Cowan, *Urban Europe 1500–1700* (London, 1998), p. 151.

23. Bequests are found in 7 of the 30 Liverpool wills available for the Tudor period. See W. K. Jordan, *The Social Institutions of Lancashire*, Chetham Society 3rd series 11 (1962), pp. 21–3.

24. See registers of Childwall, Farnworth, Hale, Huyton, Prescot and Walton.

25. M. Levine, 'The Place of Women in Tudor Government', D. J. Guth and J. W. McKenna (eds), *Tudor Rule and Revolution* (Cambridge, 1982), pp. 109–23; D. Postles, 'An English Small Town in the Later Middle Ages: Loughborough', *Urban History Yearbook* 20/1 (1980), p. 27.

26. Liv RO 920MOO 256; quoted in *THSLC* 39 (1888), pp. 165–6.

27. For comparison, see B. Todd, 'Freebench and Free Enterprise: Widows and Their Property in Two Berkshire Villages', J. Chartres and D. Hey, *English Rural Society 1500–1800* (Cambridge, 1990).

28. *LTB* I, pp. 436–40.

29. J. Goody, 'Inheritance, Property and Women: Some Comparative Considerations', J. Goody, J. Thirsk and E. P. Thompson (eds), *Family and Inheritance: Rural Society in Western Europe 1200–*

1800 (Cambridge, 1976), pp. 10–36; V. Brodsky, 'Widows in Late Elizabethan London: Remarriage, Economic Opportunity and Family Orientations', Bonfield *et al.*, *The World We Have Gained*, pp. 123–46.

30. *LTB* I, p. 359; *LTB* II, p. 237.

31. *LTB* II, p. 25.

32. Chester, for instance had 24 gilds in the early Tudor period. See Johnson, thesis, p. 244.

33. *LTB* I, p. 52.

34. *LTB* I, p. 149, p. 271; *LTB* II, pp. 308, 340, 354.

35. *LTB* I, p. 349; *LTB* II, pp. 308, 340, 354.

36. *LTB* I, pp. 273–4.

37. *LTB* I, pp. 4, 246.

38. *LTB* I, pp. 75, 299; *LTB* II, pp. 354, 875–81.

39. *LTB* I, p. 326; *LTB* II, p. 603.

40. *LTB* I, p. 74; *LTB* II, pp. 2, 11, 491, 525–6, 851–74.

41. *LTB* I, p. 252.

42. NA DL1 vol. 25 M9.

43. *Pleadings and Depositions*, vol. 32/146.

44. *LTB* II, p. 530, p. 539; Amussen, *An Ordered Society*, pp. 122–3.

45. NA DL1 vol. 14 A2, vol. 19 G1.

46. *LTB* I, p. 289; *LTB* II, pp. 44, pp. 123–4.

47. *LTB* II, pp. 146–7, 179.

48. NA SP63/83/34; *APC* 13/64.

49. NA SP63/188/25; *LTB* II, p. 703.

50. *APC* 24/180, 25/9; *Churchwardens' Accounts of Prescot*, pp. 122, 126, 128, *Churchwardens' Accounts of Childwall*, pp. 43, 56; *Proceedings of Lancashire J.P.s*, p. 70.

51. A. L. Beier, 'Vagrants and the Social Order in Elizabethan England', *Past and Present* 64 (1974), pp. 3–27.

52. *LTB* II, pp. 16, 96.

53. *LTB* II, pp. 96, 210, 353, 423.

54. *LTB* II, pp. 460, 476, 490, 522, 622, 642, 716.

55. *LTB* I, pp. 12, 92, 143, 241; *LTB* II, pp. 2, 34, 372, 426, 522, 577, 740, 776–7, 781.

56. A. B. Appleby, *Famine in Tudor and Stuart England* (Liverpool, 1978), p. 1.

57. These proportions represent 12 of the 23 available Liverpool probate records and 37 of the 66 available Walton records.

58. J. F. Pound, *Poverty and Vagrancy in Tudor England* (London, 1971), pp. 58–68.

59. *LTB* II, p. 753; Pound, *Poverty and Vagrancy*, pp. 39–47.

60. *LTB* II, p. 43, Pound, *Poverty and Vagrancy*, pp. 47–53; Borthwick Institute of Historical Research, York, Visitation Act Books, R.VI.A. 7 f. 52v.

61. *LTB* II, pp. 9, 60, 95, 353.

62. Pound, *Poverty and Vagrancy*, pp. 53–7.

63. *LTB* II, pp. 751–2, 760, 771, 785.

64. P. Slack, 'Great and Good Towns 1540–1700' in Clark (ed), *Cambridge Urban History II*, p. 365; Pound, *Poverty and Vagrancy*, pp. 58–64; J. W. F. Hill, *Tudor and Stuart Lincoln* (Cambridge, 1956), pp. 89–90; Johnson, thesis, pp. 191–6.

65. Pound, thesis, p. 219; A. L. Beier, 'The Social Problems of an Elizabethan County Town: Warwick 1580–90', Clark, *County Towns*, pp. 46, 54.

8. Learning and godliness

1. See Collinson and Craig (eds), *The Reformation in English Towns 1500–1640*; C. Haigh, *English Reformations: Religion, Politics and Society under the Tudors* (Oxford, 1993); J. J. Scarisbrick, *The Reformation and the English People* (Oxford, 1984).

2. L. Stone, 'The Education Revolution in England, 1560–1640', *Past and Present* 28 (1964), pp. 42–4.

3. C. R. Lewis, *The History of Farnworth School* (Widnes, 1905), pp. 10–14.

4. Ormerod, *Liverpool Free School*, pp. 5–7; *History of Chantries*, p. 85; *Pleadings and Depositions*, p. 32, p. 156; *LTB* I, p. 49; T. Baines, *History of the Commerce and the Town of Liverpool*, pp. 206–7.

5. Ormerod, *Liverpool Free School*, pp. 20–3.

6. Liv RO 920MOO 258, 262, 267, 270.

7. NA DL42/23 f. 270; *LTB* I, p. 255.

8. *LTB* I, p. 374.

9. *LTB* I, pp. 300–1; *LTB* II, pp. 24, 556; Ormerod, *Liverpool Free School*, p. 19.

10. *Registers of Farnworth*.

11. *LTB* II, p. 779; Ormerod, *Liverpool Free School*, pp. 20–1.

12. *LTB* II, p. 794.

13. See for comparison M. Spufford, 'The Schooling of the Peasantry in Cambridgeshire 1575–1700', in Thirsk, *Land, Church and People*, p. 129.

14. Liv RO, 920MOO 937a.

15. R. W. Jeffrey, 'Brasenose Quatercentenary Monographs: The History of the College 1547–1603', *Oxford Historical Society* 53 (1909), p. 47.

16. Stone, 'Education Revolution', p. 71.

17. Liv RO 920MOO 937a, 937b.

18. Liv RO 920MOO 937a, 937b.

19. *LTB* I, pp. 246, 270.

20. *LTB* II, p. 397.

21. *LTB* II, pp. 937, 977.

22. G. D. Ramsay, 'The Recruitment and Fortunes of Some London Freemen in the Mid 16th Century', *Econ. HR* 31 (1978), pp. 526–40; F. W. Steer (ed.), *Scriveners' Company Common Paper 1357–1628*, London Record Society 4 (1968); E. Arber (ed.), *Transcript of the Registers of the Company of Stationers of London 1554–1640* (London, 1875); B. Marsh (ed.), *Records of the Carpenters' Company: Court Books 1533–1594* (Oxford, 1916).

23. W. M. Rising and P. Millican (eds), *Index of Indentures of Norwich Apprentices*, Norfolk Record Society 29 (1959); E. Ralph and N. W. Hardwick (eds), *Calendar of the Bristol Apprentice Book 1532–42, 1542–52*, Bristol Record Society 14 (1948), 33 (1980); Chester and Cheshire RO, Chester City Mayors' Records: Apprenticeship Books, M/Ap/B/1.

24. D. Cressy, *Literacy and the Social Order: Reading and Writing in Tudor and Stuart England* (Cambridge, 1980), pp. 11, 17, 176.

25. R. Stewart Brown, 'The Chester Stationers, Printers and Booksellers to about 1800', *THSLC* 83 (1931), pp. 102–27; J. J. Bagley, 'Mathew Markland, a Wigan Mercer', *TLCAS* 68 (1958), pp. 46–59.

26. A total of 113 men have been identified as merchants during the period 1550–1600. Signatures and marks have been collected from as many sources as possible, notably the town books, the port books, the Moore Deeds and Papers, and probate records.

27. *LTB* II, pp. 178, 440; *Derby Household Accounts*, pp. 32, 51, 56; E. K. Chambers, *The Elizabethan Stage*, vol. II (Oxford, 1923), pp. 118–27.

28. Johnson, thesis, pp. 3–14; C. M. Barron, 'London 1300–1540' in Palliser (ed.), *Cambridge Urban History*, vol. 1, p. 433.

29. F. N. Moreton (ed.), 'Selection from the Ancient Papers of the More Family', *THSLC* 40 (1888), pp. 180–2.

30. Moreton, 'Selection ', pp. 180–2; F. C. Beazley, 'A Legacy to St Mary del Key, 1509', *THSLC* 82 (1930), pp. 81–7; *History of Chantries*, pp. 82–9.

31. *History of Chantries*, pp. 82–9.

32. F. A. Bailey, 'Some Memoranda by William More Esquire Concerning Liverpool and Walton 1510–12', *THSLC* 100 (1948), pp. 33–44. In 1657 when Liverpool petitioned, unsuccessfully, for parochial status it was claimed that 'time out of mind' the town had had control of its chapel with nomination of its clergy and chapelwardens. See M. Power (ed.), *Liverpool Town Books 1649–1671*, RSLC 136 (1999), pp. 44, 58, 92.

33. *LTB* I, p. 51.

34. *LTB* I, pp. 249, 257, 292, 364; *LTB* II, pp. 309, 321, 495, 654.

35. J. E. Bailey and H. Fishwick (eds), *Inventories of Church Goods in the Churches and Chapels of Lancashire 1552*, Chetham Society 113 (1888), pp. 80–101; *History of Chantries*, pp. 82–9.

36. C. Haigh, *Reformation and Resistance in Tudor Lancashire* (London, 1975), pp. 6–10.

37. NA SP12/235, REQ2 200/38; Borthwick Institute of Historical Research, York, R.VI.A7 f. 47v.; Chester and Cheshire RO, Institution Act Books and Ordination Registers EDA 1/1 f. 49v, Visitation Call Books EDV 2/5 f. 4v.

38. Ibid.

39. NA DL42/23.

40. *Pleadings and Depositions*, p. 15, p. 32; Scarisbrick, *Reformation and the English People*, p. 44.

41. Chester and Cheshire RO, EDV 1/3 f. 33v; Lancs RO, DDBl 23/10–13; *LTB* I, p. 124; *LTB* II, p. 72; *History of Chantries*, p. 89.

42. *LTB* II, pp. 60, 158, 486, 548.

43. *LTB* II, pp. 242–5.

44. *LTB* II, pp. 577, 675, 703, 730.

45. *LTB* II, pp. 750–1, 766.

46. R. O'Day, 'The Reformation of the Ministry 1558–1642' in R. O'Day and F. Heal (eds), *Continuity and Change: Personnel and Administration of the Church in England 1500–1642* (Leicester, 1976), pp. 56–72.

47. NA DL42/23; *LTB* II, p. 468.

48. M. L. Zell, 'Economic Problems of the Parochial Clergy in the 16th Century' in R. O'Day and F. Heal (eds), *Princes and Paupers in the English Church 1500–1600* (Leicester, 1981), p. 32.

49. T. Baines, *History of the Commerce and Town of Liverpool*, pp. 205–7.

50. *LTB* I, p. 51.

51. See M. Byford, 'The Birth of a Protestant Town: the Process of Reformation in Tudor Colchester, 1530–80' in Collinson and Craig (eds), *Reformation in English Towns*, pp. 23–47; B. Coulton, 'The Establishment of Protestantism in a Provincial Town: A Study of Shrewsbury in the Sixteenth Century', *Sixteenth Century Journal* 27/2 (1990), pp. 307–35; M. Mullett, 'The Urban Reformation in North-West England, *North West Catholic History* 31 (2004).

52. *LTB* I, p. 196; *LTB* II, pp. 73–75, 461.

53. *LTB* II, pp. 570, 636.

54. *LTB* II, pp. 596, 608, 656; *Derby Household Books*, pp. 28–90; R. Halley, *Lancashire Nonconformity* (Manchester, 1869), p. 169.

55. R. C. Richardson, *Puritanism in North-West England* (Manchester, 1972), p. 66.

56. Haigh, *Reformation and Resistance*, J. Bossy, *The English Catholic Community 1570–1850* (London, 1975); W. R. Trimble, *The Catholic Laity in Elizabethan England* (Cambridge Massachusetts, 1964).

57. A. Pritchard, *Catholic Loyalism in Elizabethan England* (London, 1979); J. A. Hilton, 'Catholicism in Elizabethan Northumberland', *Northern History* 13 (1977), pp. 44–6.

58. J. C. H. Aveling, *Northern Catholics: The Catholic Recusants of the North Riding of Yorkshire 1558–1790* (London, 1966), p. 117.

59. Bossy, *English Catholic Community*, p. 93.

60. NA SP12/74/22.

61. NA SP63/10/26; Liv RO 920MOO 1750; *LTB* I, p. 130.

62. *LTB* II, p. 187.

63. Haigh, *Reformation and Resistance*, pp. 278–279; G. Anstruther, *The Seminary Priests* (Durham, 1968), pp. 157, 383.

64. *APC*, VII/5, VII/399, VIII/28.

65. *APC*, VIII/276, VIII/277.

66. *APC*, XII/77, XII/270, XIII/284.

67. Borthwick Institute of Historical Research, York, R.VI.A12 f. 71; F. R. Raines (ed.), *State Civil and Ecclesiastical of the County of Lancaster*, Chetham Society 29 (1853), p. 7.

68. Bossy, *English Catholic Community*, p. 136.

69. *APC*, XXII/549; *LTB* II, p. 753.

70. C. Z. Wiener, 'The Beleaguered Isle: A Study of Elizabethan and Jacobean Anti-Catholicism', *Past and Present* 51 (1971), p. 46.

71. NA SP12/235/4.

72. *LTB* II, p. 631.

73. NA SP12/235/4; M. M. C. Calthrop (ed.), *Recusant Roll No. 1, 1592–3*, Catholic Record Society 18 (1916); H. Bowker (ed.), *Recusant Roll No. 2, 1593–4*, Catholic Record Society 57 (1965); H. Bowker (ed.), *Recusant Rolls Nos 3 and 4, 1595–6*, Catholic Record Society 61 (1970).

74. *Recusant Rolls Nos 3 and 4*; Borthwick Institute of Historical Research, York, R.VI.A12 f. 71.

75. Wrightson, *English Society*, p. 165; R. B. Manning, *Religion and Society in Elizabethan Sussex* (Leicester, 1969), pp. xii–xiii.

76. R. G. Dottie, 'John Crosse of Liverpool and Recusancy in Early Seventeenth-Century Lancashire', *Recusant History* 20 (1990), pp. 31–47; P. H. W. Booth, 'From Medieval Park to Puritan Republic' in A. G. Crosby (ed.), *Lancashire Local Studies* (Preston, 1993), pp. 66–80.

Chapter 9.   Conclusion

1. A. Dyer, *Decline and Growth in English Towns 1400–1600* (Basingstoke, 1991), pp. 62–3; M. Kowaleski, 'Port Towns in England and Wales 1300–1540', Palliser (ed.), *Cambridge Urban History, Vol. 1*, pp. 469–93.
2. Haigh, *Reformation and Resistance*, p. 104.
3. Picton, *Chester and Liverpool*, pp. 5–17; Woodward, *Trade of Elizabethan Chester*, pp. 2–3, 61, 127; Jarvis, 'Head Port of Chester', pp. 69–79; C. Lewis and A.T. Thacker (eds), *The Victoria History of the County of Chester, vol. V, part 1: The City of Chester* (Woodbridge, 2003), pp. 53–67.
4. Lancs RO, DDK 1402/28.
5. See A. Shepard and P. Withington (eds), *Communities in Early Modern England* (Manchester, 2000).
6. S. Hindle, 'A Sense of Place? Becoming and Belonging in a Rural Parish, 1550–1650' in Shepard and Withington (eds), *Communities in Early Modern England*, pp. 96–7.

Index